EUROPEAN COMMUNITY FUNDING FOR BUSINESS DEVELOPMENT

EUROPEAN COMMUNITY FUNDING FOR BUSINESS DEVELOPMENT

A Complete Guide to Sources, Grants and Application Procedures

1991

Mishka Bienkowski
Rhona Walker
Kevin Allen
Rona Michie

KOGAN
PAGE

First published in 1991

Kogan Page Limited
120 Pentonville Road
London N1 9JN

© European Policies Research Centre Limited (EPRC) 1991

British Library Cataloguing in Publication Data

A CIP record for this book is available from the British Library.

ISBN 0-7494-0396-9

Typeset by DP Photosetting, Aylesbury, Bucks
Printed and bound in Great Britain by

CONTENTS

Contents

Contents

LIST OF FIGURES

LIST OF TABLES

ACKNOWLEDGEMENT

The primary purpose of this book is to provide a guide to the financial incentive programmes funded by the European Commission and other European Community institutions. Individual programme information has been drawn from the online AIMS database, a continually updated information service on financial assistance schemes. The information is structured and presented in such a way as to enable business managers and their advisers to identify quickly assistance which could be of relevance to their particular activities and requirements. A brief overview on the organisation and structure of the information is included in the Introduction.

In the ongoing maintenance and development of the information contained in the AIMS online service (and subsequently reproduced in this hardcopy publication) we have been greatly encouraged by the help we have received from a variety of sources. In particular, we are grateful to the departments and agencies who administer the various programmes, particularly at this very difficult time of ever-increasing workloads. Not only have they sent us an abundance of written material from which we prepared our draft descriptions but, more importantly, they have given their time in meetings, conversations and through regular correspondence, enabling us to pick up on changes, fill information gaps and avoid misinterpretation. In dealing with our many questions, these officials have applied courtesy, patience and efficiency. The majority have also read through our final drafts and provided invaluable comments and suggestions on the presentation of the detailed texts.

We are also grateful for the encouragement and positive comments received from the practitioners themselves, ie those who have direct experience applying for assistance under the individual programmes.

Finally, we would like to thank our colleagues in European Policies Research Centre (EPRC), without whose help this book would never be possible. In particular, we would like to extend a warm welcome to Rona Michie who has joined our 'European desk' and is responsible for updating our coverage of EC incentive programmes.

A book such as this is bound to have its shortcomings, we would therefore welcome any comments which may help us to improve future editions and the ongoing coverage of the online service. Responsibility for any shortcomings and errors of fact or judgement rests entirely with us.

Mishka Bienkowski
Rhona Walker
Kevin Allen
Rona Michie

February 1991

ALPHABETIC INDEX OF EC PROGRAMMES

INTRODUCTION

As the pendulum swings towards 1992, more and more businesses are turning their attention to Europe, not only to confront the new challenges brought about by the Single European Market, but also to take advantage of the many opportunities which are being created by the new European order. This book considers the financial incentive programmes operated by the European Community funding authorities (ie those funded from the General Budget of the European Communities) in addition to the activities of the European Coal and Steel Community (ECSC), European Investment Bank (EIB) and European Atomic Energy Community (EURATOM).

The book is structured into three principal parts, each of which is concerned with a key area of current EC policy: Investment and Infrastructure Financing; Employment and Training; and Research and Technological Development (RTD). Within each part, a separate overview explains the policy background and main operational features of the Commission's mechanisms for funding support. This is followed by a detailed description of the individual programmes currently in operation. Generally speaking, the administration of EC programmes is consistent throughout the different Member States. Where this is not the case, the programme is described in terms of its operation in the UK. Where required, further guidance should be sought from the relevant public authority in the Member State concerned. In a few cases, programmes operate only within specific Member States or regions, although UK organisations may tender for and participate in individual projects in these areas. In these cases, the description relates to the operation of the programme in the area concerned.

Together with its companion volume, 'Government Funding for United Kingdom Business', this guide is both a sequel to, and an offspring of EPRC's previous biennial publication 'Government Support for British Business'. Taken together, the two volumes provide a comprehensive overview of all business incentive programmes available from both UK and European Community sources. The new two-volume format has a number of advantages, aside from allowing complete coverage of the ever-increasing range and complexity of incentive programmes. Separate treatment of EC programmes has enabled the addition of considerable background information to each area of support in a bid to help readers understand the complex administration of the various programmes. This should help to remove some of the mystique surrounding EC money and encourage more UK companies to take advantage of the opportunities on offer from Europe. With respect to 'Government Funding for United Kingdom Business', separate treatment has permitted coverage to be extended to include incentive programmes for the primary sectors – agriculture, forestry and fishing.

As with its predecessor, this book benefits directly from its association with the AIMS online grants information service. AIMS overcomes the problem of changeabiltiy by providing continuously updated information on financial assistance programmes, together with a separate news update file to record changes in the incentives field. Accompanying search software tackles the complexity of the field by facilitating the identification of assistance schemes relevant to the specific characteristics of an individual business/concern. In commercial operation since 1983, AIMS is now widely acknowledged as the most authoritative source of up-to-date information on financial incentives available in the UK and is used extensively by many of the intermediary organisations which firms would commonly turn to for advice (ie accountancy practices, consultants, local authorities, development agencies, trade associations, etc.).

By drawing directly on the information contained in the daily-updated AIMS database, the text of 'European Community Funding for Business Development' is more up-to-date than would be the case if the information was taken in a 'snapshot' format and compiled over several months. For those who want to keep up-to-date on changes in the incentives field following publication of the book, the AIMS News file is available through a fortnightly hard copy Newsletter distributed by EPRC Ltd (see insert). This should be of particular interest to those interested in following the Commission's RTD Programmes, which are characterised by very short application deadlines. Details of calls for proposals under the various RTD programmes are generally in the AIMS News file within three or four days of their publication in the Official Journal.

The presentation of the information on individual EC programmes is structured in such a way as to enable business managers and their advisors to identify easily the aspects which concern them most. This structure is designed to answer a logical series of questions:

- What is it? – is it a shared cost contract, soft loan, co-ordination action, mobility grant, etc?
- Who can participate? – is my location, type of organisation, size of firm, etc. such that I am eligible?
- What is it worth? – what is the form and value of the support, eg the percentage contribution, loan premium, etc, and what expenditure is it paid on?
- What is the catch? – what other conditions must I fulfil in order to qualify?
- How do I get it? – what is the application procedure and where can I get more information?

The information for each programme is presented in fourteen sections as follows:

1. Summary:
Specifies the form of the incentive (ie grant, shared cost contract, soft loan, etc), the objectives of the programme and main eligibility restrictions, together with the way in which it is administered (ie direct or via a national public sector intermediary). In the case of RTD programmes the current status of the programme is described in terms of budget provision and previous and anticipated calls for proposals, where relevant.

In most instances, this section will allow the reader to recognise quickly whether the programme is of any interest.

2. Awarding Body:
Gives the name of the funding institution, and where relevant, the body which administers the programme within the UK.

3. Location Restrictions:
This is the first in a series of 'eligibility filters'. Others follow in sections 4 to 8 below. Location restrictions indicate whether the programme is available only in specified areas - such as coal and steel closure areas, regions designated under the European Regional Development Fund, etc - or whether it is available throughout the European Community. Where appropriate, specific location restrictions, as defined for the UK, are provided in detail.

4. Sectoral Restrictions:
Details industrial sectors supported under the programme, or conversely, any sectors which are excluded and, where relevant, the type of organisations (eg public, private, nationalised industries, research institutes, etc) eligible to participate.

5. Size Restrictions:
Lists any size restrictions or priorities, specified in terms of firm size or project size, applied under the programme.

6. Programme Duration:
Specifies the duration of the programme and the budget allocation, where this may restrict the availability of funds.

7. Submission of Applications/Proposals:
Covers any deadlines for the submission of applications under multiannual programmes and, where appropriate, provides details of when the next call for proposals is expected.

8. Other Restrictions:
Covers a variety of additional eligibility conditions, usually specific to the particular programme being covered.

9. Eligible Expenditure:
Specifies items or elements of expenditure which qualify for support.

10. Rate of Award:
The rate of award is generally expressed as a proportion of eligible costs. Any differences in rates, determined on the basis of priority size groups, areas or industries would also be noted here. In the case of loan schemes, this section gives an indication of interest rates and concessions, repayment holidays and any additional premia required.

11. Payment Procedure:
Explains whether grants are paid in line with expenditure, on project completion or with delays, and, for loan schemes, the repayment systems adopted.

12. Points to Note:
Covers other important aspects such as broader objectives of the programme, its relationship with other EC and national initiatives and, if known, expected continuation beyond its terminal date.

13. Application Procedure:
Indicates the method of application and gives details of any other aspects of the application procedure.

14. Further Information:
Gives contact addresses and telephone numbers where further information can be obtained. Where appropriate, the relevant addresses in the UK and at the European Commission are provided.

An overview of how the different programmes fit into general EC policy objectives and how the budget allocations are channelled into business activity, whether directly by application or indirectly through national authorities, is provided in the introductory chapter to each of the three main parts of the book. As already noted, these deal in turn with Investment and Infrastructure, Employment and Training and Research and Development. Readers can also go directly to a known programme by referring to the alphabetic index of EC programmes at the front of the book or to the general index at the back which includes acronyms as well as full programme names. In addition, to assist readers in tracking down programmes which, though widely referred to, are not currently active or are under proposal, Part 4 of the book lists these, with brief summary descriptions of each programme and details of its current status.

PART ONE

INVESTMENT AND INFRASTRUCTURE FINANCING

1

1.0 OVERVIEW

European Community financing for productive investment and infrastructure projects is channelled primarily through the national or regional authority responsible for economic development in the Member State concerned. To a large extent, the areas designated as eligible for investment aid under each Member State's own regional policy (eg the Assisted Areas in the UK) coincide with those targeted for European money. With the exception of certain large infrastructure investments which are required to display signs indicating European funding participation, most European grant-aid for investment projects cannot be distinguished from that awarded under a Member State's own national aid programmes. For many firms, therefore, familiarity with the opportunities available under the relevant national aid programmes (eg Regional Selective Assistance and Regional Enterprise Grants in the UK) completes the picture with respect to general direct investment aid, although additional European lending facilities may provide funding on attractive terms for certain projects. These include loan facilities operated by the European Coal and Steel Community (ECSC) and the European Investment Bank (EIB).

Consideration of European Community industrial policy and funding mechanisms from a broader perspective is essential from a strategic standpoint if new business opportunities in Europe are to be exploited. Not only has there been convergence between Member States' and EC regional policy measures, with the latter exerting more and more control over the former, but an understanding of current EC policy and longer-term objectives is central to any assessment of opportunities and threats arising from the implementation of the Single European Market and the aftermath of 1992. For the construction industry and businesses associated with it, the considerable sums of money allocated to infrastructure financing under current EC regional policy measures represent a direct business opportunity. For firms considering new investments in Europe, EC policy not only influences any grant-aid for which they might be eligible, but will also influence the relative growth and prosperity of different regions in the years to come. Knowledge of EC policy objectives and funding decisions is, therefore, essential to any assessment of business opportunities arising in the Single Market.

This section on Investment and Infrastructure Financing is concerned primarily with the European Community's instruments for promoting economic development, ie the so-called 'Structural Funds'. Two of these Funds – the European Regional Development Fund (ERDF) and European Agricultural Guidance and Guarantee Fund: Guidance Section (EAGGF) – focus firmly on support for productive investment and infrastructure projects. Other Community instruments, also covered in this section, work closely with the Funds to similar ends. These include the ECSC and EIB, both of which operate primarily through the provision of loan financing facilities. The third Structural Fund – the European Social Fund (ESF) – is concerned primarily with employment and training measures and is discussed more fully in Part Two.

The Structural Funds

Current EC policy objectives were established with the passing of the Single European Act in 1987. Not only did the Act provide the legislative framework necessary for the Single European Market, but it also led to the reform of the three Structural Funds in line with five priority objectives which aimed to counter the risks of regional imbalances resulting from market liberalisation, and to reinforce the need to speed adjustment in the structurally-weak regions and countries.

The five Structural Fund Objectives are:

1. Promoting the development and structural adjustment of the regions whose development is lagging;
2. Converting the regions, frontier regions or parts of regions (including employment areas and urban communities) seriously affected by industrial decline;
3. Combatting long-term unemployment (European Social Fund);
4. Facilitating the occupational integration of young people (European Social Fund);
5. With a view to the reform of the Common Agricultural Policy (CAP):
   (a) speeding up the adjustment of agricultural structures;
   (b) promoting the development of rural areas.

Measures funded under Objectives 1, 2 and 5(b) are restricted to particular regions of the Community. Objective 1 regions (structurally backward) are targeted to receive 80 percent of the total Structural Fund budget. Regions designated under Objective 1 for the period 1989-93 are: Northern Ireland, Ireland, southern Italy, southern Spain, Portugal, Greece, the French overseas departments and Corsica. Figure 1 shows the regions designated under Objective 1.

Objective 2 (industrial decline) and 5(b) (rural) regions are designated for a three year period. Those agreed for the UK under Objective 2 for the period 1989-91 correspond roughly with the current UK Assisted Areas map which determines eligibility for UK regional assistance. Figure 2 reproduces the areas designated under Objective 2 for the whole Community.

Objective 5(b) regions are rural areas, disadvantaged because of their dependence on agricultural production for which they are not ideally suited, and/or because of their peripherality, lack of infrastructure and business environment required to attract new economic development. Objective 5(b) regions in the UK cover the Highlands and Borders regions of Scotland, rural Wales and parts of Devon and Cornwall. Figure 3 reproduces the map of areas eligible under Objective 5(b) for the whole Community.

Taken as a group, the Structural Funds were allocated a total budget of approximately 11.5 billion ECU in 1990, accounting for roughly 23 percent of the total Community budget and making them second in importance only to the Common Agricultural Policy (CAP). The largest of the three funds is the European Regional Development Fund (ERDF), accounting for roughly

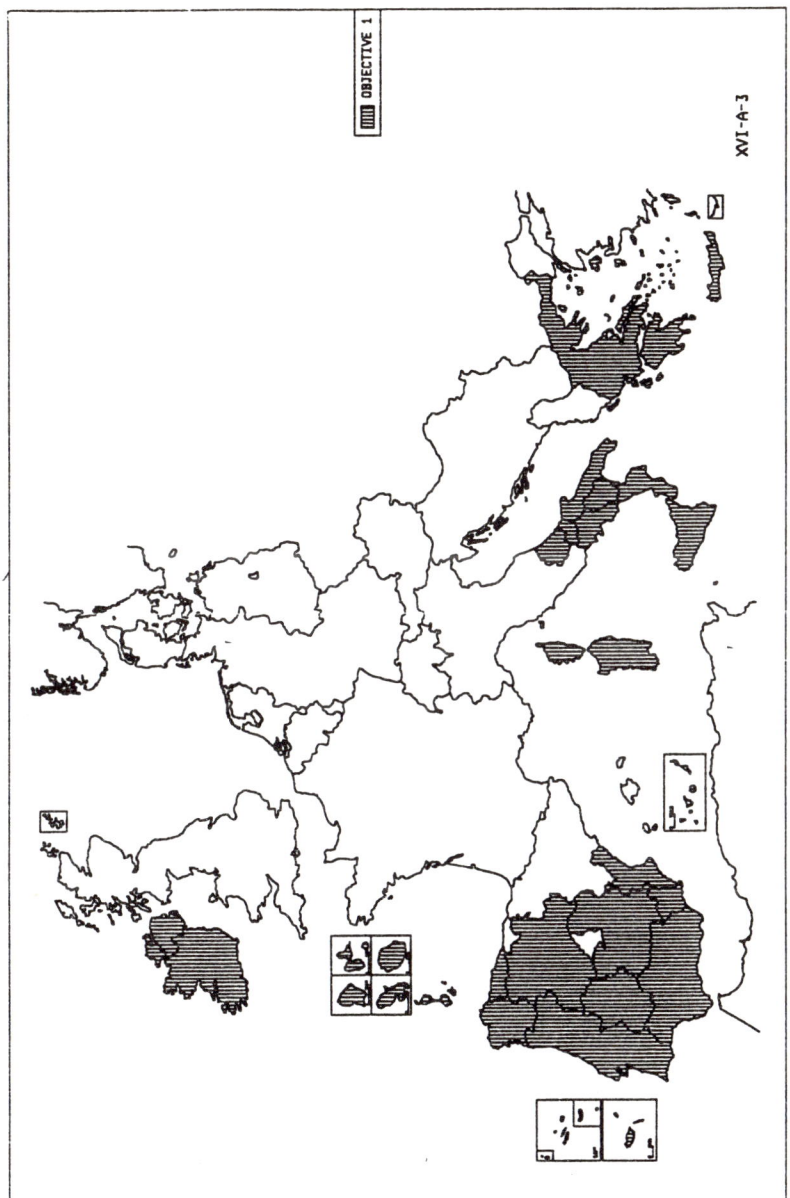

Figure 1: Objective 1 Designated Areas
Source: Commission of the European Communities (DG xvi)

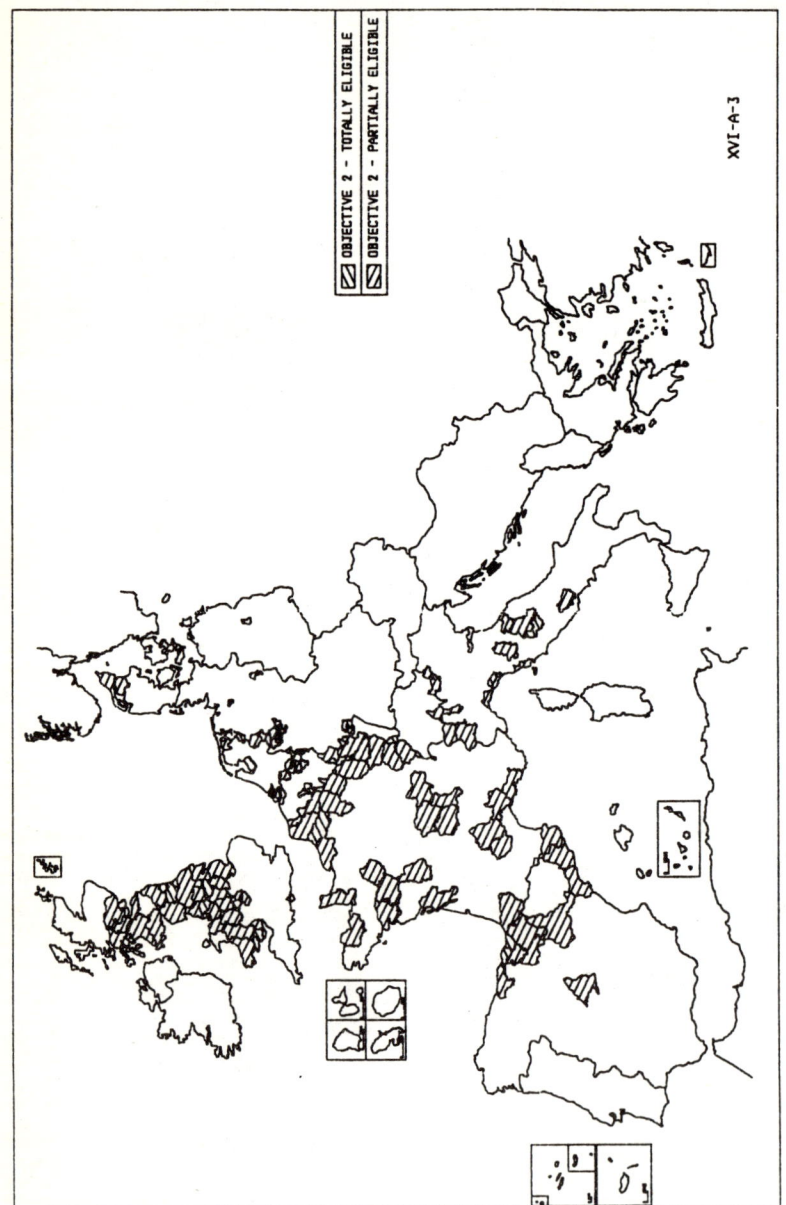

Figure 2: Objective 2 Designated Areas
Source: Commission of the European Communities (DG xvi)

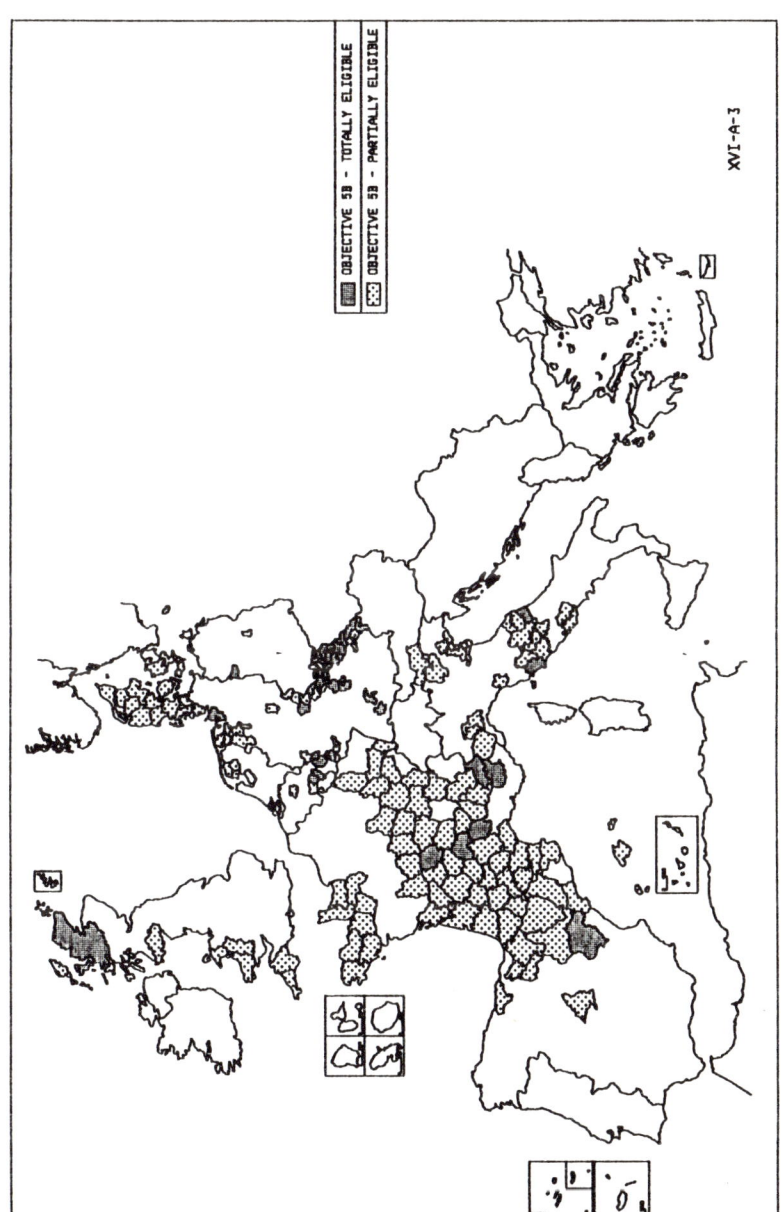

Figure 3: Objective 5(b) Designated Areas
Source: Commission of the European Communities

half of the total Structural Fund budget. It is the Community's principal instrument for promoting regional economic development through the funding of infrastructure and productive investment, with infrastructure accounting for most of ERDF expenditure (93 percent in 1988). Over 75 percent of the ERDF budget allocation is assigned to Objective 1 regions. Of the remainder, roughly 16 percent is intended for Objective 2 regions, 3 percent for Objective 5(b) regions and 5 percent to fund transitional measures and innovative operations without any specific regional restriction.

Following agreement on the Single European Act, new reforming legislation governing the operation of the Structural Funds was introduced in 1989 in order to target them more effectively on the central Community objective of promoting the economic and social cohesion of the regions. Objective 1 regions will, as a result of the reforms, receive double their 1987 commitment appropriations by 1993 (in real terms). One central aspect of the reforming legislation was that it strengthened a process already underway of shifting fund support away from individual project financing on to a 'programme' financing basis (ie the funding of a consistent series of multiannual measures designed to tackle specific objectives associated with the particular problems of an individual region). A second feature of the reforming legislation was that it required coordination in the activities of the three funds, both with each other, and with the activities of the other Community financing instruments – ECSC and EIB. To a certain extent, this type of coordination was already underway through the so-called 'Integrated Development Operations' (IDOs) which had been approved prior to the introduction of the reforming legislation. Each IDO consisted of a set of measures involving a partnership between a number of regional and local organisations working together to overcome the problems associated with a particular region's development. IDOs could include infrastructure provision as well as specific support schemes to promote small business development, tourism, etc. The first IDOs to be agreed were in Naples (launched in 1980) and Belfast (launched in 1985). In the UK, further IDOs were subsequently agreed for Birmingham and Strathclyde with budgets of £203 million and £395 million, respectively. Later IDOs agreed in the UK are in Bradford; Yorkshire and Humberside; and Dyfed/Gwynedd/Powys.

The early IDOs represented only one aspect of the type of measures funded by the ERDF – individual project financing was still predominant. However, the reforming legislation has channelled almost all ERDF funding into an IDO-type concept through agreement on so-called 'Community Support Frameworks' (CSFs). CSFs comprise a series of multiannual measures, agreed between the Commission and the Member State concerned, which are designed to tackle the problems of specific regions. Each CSF consists of a number of specified operational programmes dealing with particular aspects of the problem region (eg communications, training, tourism, transportation, etc) and involves, where appropriate, one or more Structural Funds, with additional financing available through the other Community financial instruments.

CSFs have been agreed for Objective 1 regions until 1993. Table 1 lists Objective 1 CSFs in terms of the individual operational programmes agreed within each CSF and the indicative budget allocation.

TABLE 1
COMMUNITY SUPPORT FRAMEWORKS IN OBJECTIVE 1 REGIONS

COUNTRY	PRIORITY AREAS	EC CONTRIBUTION (MECU)
GREECE	1. Infrastructure	1630.6
	2. Agriculture & rural development	339.4
	3. Improvement of competitiveness of firms	472.8
	4. Tourism	85
	5. Human resource development	503.5
	6. 13 Regional multifund operational programmes	1454
IRELAND	1. Agriculture, fisheries, forestry, tourism, rural development	1018.4
	2. Industry & services	1032.1
	3. Reducing the effects of peripherality (transport)	719
	4. Human resource development	1027.5
ITALY	1. Improved communications (transport and telecommunications)	793
	2. Industry, crafts, services	1319
	3. Tourism	786
	4. Agriculture and rural development	735
	5. Infrastructure	2647
	6. Human resource development	396
	7. Fisheries	11
PORTUGAL	1. Infrastructure	1116
	2. Productive investment support	1185
	3. Human resource development	1719
	4. Agriculture and rural development	558.5
	5. Industrial conversion and restructuring	296
	6. Regional/local development	1161
SPAIN	1. Improved communications (transport and telecommunications)	3218.8
	2. Industry, crafts sector & business services	699.2
	3. Tourism	182
	4. Agriculture and rural development	1441.9
	5. Infrastructure	1652.8
	6. Human resource development	891.2
UK: NORTHERN IRELAND	1. Social & physical environment (image enhancing)	34
	2. Reducing the effects of peripherality (transport)	155
	3. Industrial development	161.5
	4. Agriculture & tourism	188.2
	5. Human resource development	106.4

There are a great many more CSFs in Objective 2 regions, each responsible for a smaller regional area. In the UK, nine CSFs have been agreed, one for each of the main UK regions as follows:

Table 2
Objective 2 Community Support Frameworks in the UK

Region	Budget Allocation (million ECU)*
North East	156
East	214
Midlands	193
North West	268
West Cumbria	10
North Wales	32
South Wales	107
West Scotland	246
East Scotland	63
Total	1289

* As at 30 January 1991, 1 ECU = £0.7018.

A further set of CSFs relate to Objective 5(b) regions. Although funding for these can come from any of the three Structural Funds, the fact that their problems are associated with rural development and the need to reform agricultural structures make them the central concern of the European Agricultural Guidance and Guarantee Fund: Guidance Section (EAGGF), with the other two Funds – ERDF and ESF – involved in infrastructure provision and training measures, respectively.

Structural Fund support within the context of CSFs can range from a maximum of 75 percent (Objective 1 regions) to 50 percent (Objective 2 regions) of the Member State's own public expenditure on a particular measure. All projects/operations must attract financial backing from a national public sector authority to be eligible for any European grant-aid. As a result, local authorities and Government departments play a very central role in the award of European funding. Although European funding is meant to be additional to each Member State's intended expenditure on its regions, much criticism has been levied in recent years at the fact that Member States simply substitute European money for money already committed in national expenditure plans. Even though this may be the case, the Commission's influence over spending continues to increase as Member States are compelled to formulate their own expenditure plans in line with Commission priorities in order to maximise returns from Europe. It is also worth noting that the Commission's long-term plans, particularly its commitment to accelerating the development of the poorer and newest Member States (Greece, Spain, Portugal and, more recently, the former German Democratic Republic) and the amount of funding being concentrated on these areas, will no doubt have a much more significant impact on the development of these regions than would otherwise be the case.

Apart from the CSFs agreed with each of the Member States, the Commission has introduced, within the ERDF budget, a number of special Europe-wide 'Community Programmes' which are designed to tackle specific aspects of structural change. These include RECHAR for coal producing areas, RENAVAL for shipbuilding areas and RESIDER for steel producing areas. Where appropriate, funding under these Community programmes is amalgamated with other measures agreed under the relevant CSF. The funding allocated under these programmes is, however, additional to that which would normally be allocated. Some areas, previously ineligible under Objective 2, have, as a result of meeting eligibility criteria for RECHAR, RENAVAL or RESIDER, been redesignated under Objective 2 (for details of the areas eligible under these specific measures, see the relevant programme descriptions). A number of other Community programmes deal with other aspects which impede the development of specific regions. These include: STAR, to improve telecommunications; VALOREN, to exploit local energy potential; STRIDE, to promote R & D; and ENVIREG, to address environmental problems affecting the Mediterranean coastal regions.

Knowledge of operational programmes agreed under CSFs and under these special ERDF Community programmes is of direct relevance to any assessment of market opportunities being created in Europe. At the most immediate level, both types of measure result in the concentration of substantial expenditure on the provision of major infrastructure installations. Specific operational programmes defined within the CSFs indicate both the type, location and funding of any intended infrastructure investments and are open to tender from any firm based within the European Community. At a more indirect level, the concentration of European funding on certain regions of the Community is bound to accelerate the development of these regions, create new markets and generally improve the business environment within these regions.

Firms undertaking mobile investment projects should consider not only the current business environment that these regions offer, but their potential for development, with considerable backing from Europe, over the years to come. For firms prepared to take the risk and ride on the back of this anticipated development, a more immediate compensation for the current underdevelopment of these regions is the relatively high ceiling on capital grant aid available for setting up an investment within them. Table 3 below lists the Commission rulings on grant aid ceilings available through the national regional aid packages within each of the Community countries.

As can be seen from Table 3, highest grant-aid ceilings apply in the most severely disadvantaged regions of Portugal, Spain, Italy, Ireland and Greece. These are also covered by Objective 1 of the European Regional Development Fund and are, therefore, destined to receive a considerable injection of European funding over the next three to five years, and probably beyond. For the poorest of these regions – those in Portugal – a special ERDF Community programme, PEDIP (Programme for the Development of Portuguese Industry), has been created as an additional measure of support. As already mentioned, most ERDF expenditure will be used to modernise the poor infrastructure which is seen to be the principal cause of their current underdevelopment. It stands to reason that implementation of an efficient infrastructure will greatly improve the business environment which these

Table 3
Commission Ceilings on Member State Regional Aid Packages

Country	Incentive	Commission Ceiling(1)
Belgium	interest subsidy/capital grant	20% after tax
Denmark	regional development grant	25% before tax
France	regional policy grant	25% before tax
Germany	investment grant	23% before tax
Greece	investment grant	75% after tax
Ireland	new industry programme	75% after tax
Italy	capital grant	75% after tax
Luxembourg	capital grant	25% before tax
Netherlands	investment premium	25% before tax
Portugal	SIBR regional incentive system	75% after tax
Spain	regional investment grant	75% after tax
UK:		
Great Britain	regional selective assistance	30% after tax
Northern Ireland	industrial development assistance	75% after tax

(1) It should be noted that maximum ceilings apply only to the most disadvantaged regions with lower rates applying to less severely disadvantaged designated areas. Moreover, actual awards granted to individual projects would generally be considerably less than stated ceilings although other top-up subsidies may be added in to enhance the overall value of a given aid package.

Source: Yuill, D. et al (eds), European Regional Incentives, 10th Edition, Bowker-Saur, London, 1990.

regions can offer, while current incentive packages do much to enhance their attractiveness as locations for new investment in Europe.

Aside from the ERDF, the other EC Structural Fund which focuses particularly on investment and infrastructure financing is the European Agricultural Guidance and Guarantee Fund: Guidance Section (EAGGF), which promotes economic development activity within the poorer agricultural regions of the Community. The Guarantee Section of the EAGGF accounts for over 50 percent of the total Community budget and is used to fund the wide range of income support measures available under the Common Agricultural Policy. The Guidance Section of the EAGGF, accounting for roughly 18 percent of the total Structural Fund budget (or just over 4 percent of the total Community budget) is used to fund measures to promote the marketability of agricultural products by offering grants for marketing and processing investments in agriculture, forestry, aquaculture and fishery products. It is worth noting that EAGGF support has been extended to forestry products only since the introduction of the recent reforms. Within the UK, however, no specific implementation of any forestry support measures can be introduced until enabling legislation has been passed and there is currently no intention of introducing any new programmes to support this sector.

Other Community Financing Instruments

As already mentioned, other Community financing instruments which are closely co-ordinated with the investment and infrastructure activities of the Structural Funds are the EIB and ECSC. Although the former offers loan financing on commercial terms, it is able to pass on the benefits of being rated as 'AAA' in raising finance for onlending in the international markets. Where ECSC loans are available, they generally offer the most attractive lending terms for individual investment projects. Projects meeting certain employment creation conditions can qualify for substantial interest rebates. For loans up to £500,000, the Department of Trade and Industry also operates an Exchange Risk Guarantee Scheme which covers against exchange risk loss for non-sterling loans. In addition to these general, so-called 'Conversion Loans', the ECSC also operates two loan schemes designed to promote the consumption of European Community steel or coal.

Other Community Support Measures

Apart from the instruments used to assist the development of specific regions and sectors, the Community has relatively little involvement in promoting general investment financing. The only exceptions currently are: EURATOM loans offered by the European Atomic Energy Community for the building of nuclear power stations; and a new programme – International Investment Partners – designed to promote financial linkages between European firms and firms located outside the European Community.

Conclusion

The Structural Funds, and in particular, the ERDF, are the principal sources of European funding for investment and infrastructure projects. Firms engaged in medium to long-term strategy planning to identify good locations from which to serve the European market place should examine closely the operations and activities of the Structural Funds in the context of wider EC policy objectives, to assess the relative merits, both current and anticipated, of different regions of the Community. More immediate market opportunities are available to firms engaged in the supply of infrastructure. Most agreements to undertake infrastructure investments are now specified within the relevant CSF agreed for an individual region and it is therefore relatively easy to identify potential opportunities.

Whether the interest in European funding is directly in respect of infrastructure-related contracts or in a European production base, it is important to note that the central coordinator in the approval and distribution of European funds is the relevant national public sector body (ie generally the local or regional authority for infrastructure projects; and the central – or regional – Government department responsible for promoting economic development for productive investment projects). At the very least, the award of European money is conditional on the award of a proportionate sum from the relevant national public sector authority. Establishing good linkages with the relevant public sector authority in the country concerned is therefore vital for any firm wishing to tap fully the opportunities that may be available.

1.1 PROBLEM AREA DEVELOPMENT

ECSC: CONVERSION LOANS

1. Summary:
Loans at favourable market rates are available under Article 56 of the Treaty establishing the European Coal and Steel Community (ECSC) for approved investment projects which are associated with the creation of alternative employment opportunities for workers made redundant by the restructuring of the coal and steel industries. The proposed investment for which the loan is sought must permit the expansion or the creation of new economic activities leading to the creation of additional jobs, or the maintenance of existing jobs which are under threat. Under new operational guidelines published for the granting of ECSC Conversion Loans, certain changes have taken place in eligibility criteria. Areas eligible for ECSC assistance are currently being revised in line with Objective 2 regions under the European Regional Development Fund (ERDF) (regions in industrial decline). A new list of eligible areas was expected to be finalised by the end of 1990.

Conversion loans may be granted either in the form of direct loans or in the form of sub-loans administered by intermediary financial institutions to which the ECSC has granted a global loan. Subject to the availability of budgetary resources, an interest rebate related to the number of new jobs created by the investment may also be awarded (see 10).

2. Awarding Body:
European Coal and Steel Community.

Loans less than 7.5 MECU are granted under a global facility negotiated via an intermediary national or regional financial institution. In the UK, global loans are available through the following: Bank of Scotland plc; National Westminster Bank plc; Barclays Bank plc; Midland Bank plc; Clydesdale Bank plc; Royal Bank of Scotland plc; TSB Scotland plc; Welsh Development Agency; 3i plc (Investors in Industry), and Scottish Enterprise.

3. Location Restrictions:
Under the new guidelines, eligible areas are being revised in line with areas eligible under Objective 2 of the ERDF (areas in industrial decline). It was anticipated that a new list of eligible ECSC employment areas would be published by the end of 1990. Loans granted under the old guidelines were available in designated ECSC employment areas (areas particularly affected by the restructuring of ECSC industries).

Loans may also be granted for projects outside ECSC employment areas; the interest rebate is then calculated on the basis of the number of former ECSC workers effectively re-employed.

4. Sectoral Restrictions:
Conversion loans are granted to undertakings and to public bodies for economically sound investment projects in any industrial or service sector

which create new jobs or permanently maintain existing jobs which are under threat.

Sectoral restrictions may apply in certain cases. These vary from time to time in accordance with EC policies. Workers in the coal and steel industries who have been, or are to be, made redundant and who would like to set up on their own account are also eligible.

In industries whose activities relate to the coal and steel industries, investment projects are eligible only if they substantially modify the activity of the undertaking concerned by providing an entirely new employment-creating activity.

The establishment of industrial estates with advance factories and the redevelopment of industrial sites, particularly those formerly occupied by ECSC industries, may also be eligible for a conversion loan, provided that such investment is closely linked to the creation of new activities and employment opportunities.

5. Size Restrictions:

The maximum sub-loan (ie onlent through an intermediary financial institution) is 7.5 MECU (approximately £5 million). For larger loans, application is made direct to the ECSC.

Exchange risk cover is provided under the UK Government's Exchange Risk Guarantee Scheme but cover is limited to sub-loans of up to £500,000.

6. Programme Duration:

There is no specified terminal date for this loan facility.

7. Submission of Applications/Proposals:

Application must relate to an investment which has not yet started or is under way and can be completed within not more than three years of its start date (or, exceptionally, within five years).

Sub-loan applications submitted by financial intermediaries are normally approved by the Commission within one month. Where an application requires referral for sectoral or other reasons, approval may take up to four months. Approval of direct loan applications normally takes up to six months from receipt of the application at the Commission. Applications should therefore be submitted as early as possible.

8. Other Restrictions:

The social objective of the ECSC loan facility is to facilitate the re-employment of workers made redundant by the ECSC industries. An assessment is made of the employment situation in the area in which the investment projects are located, and in particular the ECSC jobs which have been lost or are likely to be lost, the vocational training opportunities available in that area and the projects' potential for the creation of new jobs suitable for the productive re-employment of former ECSC workers.

The interest rebate, granted on the basis of the number of jobs actually created or maintained, may be reduced if the durability of the jobs is considered to be inadequate.

The recipients of ECSC conversion loans must notify the new jobs resulting from the project being financed to the relevant employment offices and the undertakings which are liable to shed workers (via recognised trade unions where appropriate).

Appraisal of the economic aspects of the project will take account of the contribution of the investment to the development of the region, its financial viability, its level of technology, market prospects and the situation in the sector concerned. In addition, an assessment is made of the financial situation of the borrower and that of its parent companies, and of the value of guarantees.

9. Eligible Expenditure:

Eligible expenditure generally relates to the capital expenditure on an approved project and may include intangible assets such as patents, licences, know-how, and research and development expenditure directly linked to the investment concerned. Working capital is not eligible.

10. Rate of Award:

Private sector loans are available for up to 50 percent of the fixed investment needed to implement the project. Funds are made available generally at a rate slightly below the DTI's published broadly commercial rate. Interest rates are fixed for the life of the loan (generally 5 or 8 years).

Loans can be in a mixture of foreign currencies. Loans up to £500,000 qualify for exchange risk cover under the Exchange Risk Guarantee Scheme. For projects located outside designated ECSC areas, or for larger loans, the funds not eligible for exchange risk cover may be borrowed from a sterling drawdown.

Subject to the availability of budgetary resources, an interest rebate of 3 percent may be awarded during the first five years of the loan. The maximum amount of loan eligible for rebate is 20,000 ECU (approx. £14,000) per job to be created, calculated on two-thirds of the total number of jobs created by the project.

For loans granted outside ECSC employment areas, the interest rebate is calculated on the basis of the number of former ECSC workers effectively re-employed.

For public sector loans, the Government provides exchange risk cover. Cover is restricted to loans in excess of £25 million equivalent except in cases where they are associated with grants from the European Community, eg. in the case of integrated operations.

11. Payment Procedure:

Interest rebates are refunded to the firm in ten half-yearly instalments.

12. Points to Note:

An environmental impact assessment of the proposed investment is made on the basis of the national and Community legislation in force.

The Commission receives annual reports from borrowers on the implementation of investments, jobs created, jobs filled and the number of former ECSC workers re-employed. Investment projects for which loans have been granted may be inspected by the Commission to check that they are being implemented in accordance with the contract. The interest rebate may be redetermined for projects in ECSC employment areas if the number of jobs created within two years of the disbursement of the loan is less than the number first specified in the contract. In other areas, the interest rebate may be redetermined if the specified number of jobs has not been created and filled with ex-ECSC workers.

Where the project concerned or the jobs to be created are clearly not of a nature suitable for ex-ECSC workers, the interest rebate provisions may be withdrawn.

ECSC loans may be combined with assistance from the Community's Structural Funds (the European Regional Development, Social and Agricultural Guidance and Guarantee Funds) as part of an agreed operational programme. Under an operational programme, the ECSC may fund: productive investments, infrastructure investment, technology transfer investments and participation in the capital of enterprises (particularly small and medium-sized firms) which introduce new technology or innovative procedures.

13. Application Procedure:

Application for a direct loan is sent to the ECSC through the Department of Trade and Industry.

Application for an indirect loan is made to an intermediary financial institution to which a global loan has been granted.

14. Further Information:

European Commission
DG XVI – Division C-3
Rue de la Loi 200
B-1049 Brussels
Tel: (010 32 2) 235 8468

European Commission
DG XVIII – Division B-2
Batiment Jean Monnet
L-2920 Luxembourg
Tel: (010 35 2) 43011

Department of Trade
and Industry
Minerals and Metals Division
Ashdown House
123 Victoria Street
London SW1B 6RB
Tel: (071) 215 5000
Telex: 8813148

Scottish Office Industry Department
Alhambra House
45 Waterloo Street
Tel: (041) 248 2855
Telex: 777883

Welsh Development Agency
Investment Division
Pearl House
Greyfriars Road
Cardiff CF1 3XX
Tel: (0222) 222666

Scottish Enterprise
Investment Division
120 Bothwell Street
Glasgow G2 7JP
Tel: (041) 248 2700

3i (Investors in Industry)
Bank of Scotland plc
Barclays Bank plc
Clydesdale Bank plc

Midland Bank plc
National Westminster Bank plc
Royal Bank of Scotland plc
TSB Scotland plc

EUROPEAN INVESTMENT BANK (EIB)

1. Summary:
The European Investment Bank (EIB) offers loan financing on flexible terms for private and public sector capital investment projects meeting its eligibility and lending criteria. Loans are related to asset life and may be offered for projects in infrastructure, transport, telecommunications, energy, industry and tourism.

EIB loans are at fixed or floating rates at close to the EIB's cost of borrowings; other interest rate formulae can be considered. The rates reflect market conditions and are unaffected by the type or location of the project, by the nationality or nature of the borrower or by the size of the loan.

2. Awarding Body:
The European Investment Bank (EIB).

3. Location Restrictions:
Available in any Member State of the European Community.

For private sector loans, industrial projects costing up to £14 million from small and medium-sized enterprises (companies with assets of less than about £50 million and fewer than 500 employees) may be eligible irrespective of location through an EIB intermediary (currently Barclays Bank plc, 3i plc and the Allied Irish Bank in the UK); public or private sector projects costing £14 million or more are financed in industry, energy or infrastructure if they help regional development (normally in the Assisted Areas, Northern Ireland, Wales, the Scottish Highlands, or a recognised textile, steel, shipbuilding or fisheries zone) improve communications (transport and telecommunications), enhance the competitiveness of industry (introduction of advanced technology), protect and improve the environment, or help energy security (production, transportation, saving).

In countries outside the Community, EIB financing falls under protocols and agreements negotiated between the EC and countries in the Mediterranean region, as well as under the Lome Convention with 70 African, Caribbean and Pacific countries. Loans under these agreements are made with the consent of the governments of the countries concerned. Projects of direct benefit to the EC may also be supported outside the Community.

In Eastern Europe, EIB loans are currently available in Poland, Hungary and the former German Democratic Republic (GDR). The Commission has proposed the extension of EIB loans into Czechoslovakia, Bulgaria and Romania.

4. Sectoral Restrictions:
None, finance is available to nationalised industries, local authorities, companies or any sound borrower for capital investment projects in industry, energy, infrastructure, tourism, transport and telecommunications. Priority for private sector loans is given to independent companies.

5. Size Restrictions:
The minimum directly negotiated loan is around £7 million (ie minimum project costs of about £14 million); there is no absolute maximum.

Certain location restrictions apply according to project and company size (see 3).

6. Programme Duration:
There is no specified terminal date for this facility.

7. Submission of Applications/Proposals:
Application can be made after project start but must be made before completion of the project.

8. Other Restrictions:
A corporate guarantee from a well-diversified parent company may be adequate support for an EIB facility; if not then security may be needed from an outside guarantor such as from a bank, a banking syndicate or other acceptable party. The EIB often acts as a source of funding within a financing agreement put together in close collaboration with other banks. The EIB may sometimes take as security a charge on specific assets or an assignment of revenues.

Loans to local authorities are secured by a charge on future revenues and/ or government guarantee.

9. Eligible Expenditure:
Loans usually cover between 25 and 30 percent (maximum 50 percent) of the cost of a project, including permanent working capital requirements and intangible assets.

Minimum project cost for direct loans is normally about £14 million; there is no absolute maximum. Finance below this level is handled by an EIB intermediary (see 12 for further details).

10. Rate of Award:
EIB loans are at fixed or floating rates at just above the EIB's cost of borrowings; other interest rate formulae can be considered (eg adjustable fixed rates). Interest rates reflect market conditions and are not influenced by the type or location of the project, by the nationality or nature of the borrower or by the size of the loan.

EIB loans are in pounds sterling or in other currencies according to the borrower's preference. Disbursements can be in a single currency or a mixture of currencies. Loan maturities are usually from 4 to 12 years for industry and up to 20 years for infrastructure and energy projects. The EIB does not usually charge any arrangement fees, commitment fees or other expenses.

11. Payment Procedure:
Borrowers can drawdown loans in one or a number of instalments with flexibility on their timing.

Repayment is normally by yearly or half-yearly instalments of principal and interest, after a capital repayment holiday to suit the needs of the project or borrower. There are early repayment possibilities for both floating and fixed-rate loans.

12. Points to Note:
The European Investment Bank is a banking institution whose share-

holders are the Member Countries of the European Community. It raises most of its funds by borrowing on capital markets where it has an 'AAA' credit rating. The EIB can structure a facility in a flexible way to suit the debt financing requirements.

The facility can take the form of a loan or a guarantee; it can be made available on a direct basis, through an intermediary or through a lessor.

The EIB has arranged loan facilities for Barclays Bank plc, 3i plc and the Allied Irish Bank to help promote the long term financing of capital investment made by small and medium-sized enterprises (ie businesses with fewer than 500 employees, fixed assets up to £50 million and investment projects of up to £14 million) in the industrial and service sectors. Loans available as a result of this arrangement are made on the standard commercial terms set at the time of application by the intermediary financial institution concerned.

13. Application Procedure:
Application is made direct to the EIB.

14. Further Information:

Jos Van Kaam	Guy Baird
European Investment Bank	European Investment Bank
100 Bvd. Konrad Adenauer	Liaison Office for the UK
L-2950 Luxembourg	68 Pall Mall
Tel: (010 35 2) 4379 5406	London SW1Y 5ES
Telex: 0402 3530 bnkeu lu	Tel: (071) 839 3351
Fax: (010 35 2) 43 77 04	Telex: 919159 bankeu g
	Fax: (071) 930 9929

EUROPEAN REGIONAL DEVELOPMENT FUND (ERDF)

1. Summary:
The European Regional Development Fund (ERDF) is the European Commission's principal funding instrument for correcting regional imbalances within the Community. Five Objectives were set out in the Single Act and these outline the following basic tasks of the ERDF: promoting the development and structural adjustment of underdeveloped regions (Objective 1); converting regions seriously affected by industrial decline (Objective 2); and participating in measures to promote the development of rural areas (Objective 5b). The ERDF can co-finance the following types of activity: productive investment linked to job-creation/maintenance; infrastructure investment; the development of indigenous potential (ie. local development initiatives and services for SMEs); operations planned in the context of regional development at Community level (eg. frontier regions); studies and assessment measures. Activities financed by the ERDF can be undertaken within the context of regional operational programmes, the part-financing of national regional aid schemes, through individual project financing (infras-

tructure and productive investment – see 5), the provision of global grants to intermediaries (primarily in relation to local development initiatives) and direct support for studies and assessment measures related to ERDF operations.

ERDF financing is disbursed primarily through existing national aid schemes or through public sector intermediaries. The proposed ERDF budget for 1991 is 6725 MECU. Up to four-fifths of this budget is to be applied to Objective 1 regions (see 3).

2. Awarding Body:
European Regional Development Fund (ERDF).

3. Location Restrictions:
Support is restricted to measures undertaken within a region or regions designated by the Commission under one of the three Objectives with which the ERDF is concerned (see 1):

- Objective 1 regions (structurally backward) are generally designated at NUTS level II (equivalent to regions in the UK), are targeted to receive 80 percent of the total budget of the three Structural Funds, and remain in force for a five-year period. Regions designated under Objective 1 for 1989-93 include: Northern Ireland, Ireland, southern Italy, southern Spain, Portugal, Greece, the French overseas departments and Corsica.
- Objective 2 (in industrial decline) and 5(b) (rural) regions are designated at NUTS level III (county or district in the UK) and are agreed for a three year period.

   In the UK, Objective 2 assistance for the period 1989-91 is restricted to the most seriously affected parts of the following Travel to Work Areas:
- In England: Alnwick & Amble, Morpeth & Ashington, Newcastle-upon-Tyne, South Tyneside, Sunderland, Bishop Auckland, Darlington, Durham, Hartlepool, Stockton-on-Tees, Middlesbrough, Doncaster, Goole & Selby (Selby portion excluded), Grimsby, Hull, Scunthorpe, Barnsley, Rotherham & Mexborough, Sheffield (excluding part in Derbyshire), Castleford & Pontefract, Wakefield & Dewsbury, Ashfield, parts of North-East Derbyshire district and Bolsover district in Alfreton and Ashfield TTWA; Gainsborough, Mansfield, Nottingham (urban programme area), Retford, Worksop, Chesterfield, Manchester, Oldham, Rochdale, Bolton & Bury, Wigan & St. Helens, Accrington & Rossendale, Blackburn, Burnley, Pendle, Liverpool, Widnes & Runcorn, Wirral & Chester, Birmingham, Coventry & Hinckley (Hinckley part excluded), Dudley & Sandwell (excluding part in Hereford), Wolverhampton, Walsall, Telford & Bridgenorth, Workington, Whitehaven;
- In Wales: Ebbw Vale & Abergavenny, Merthyr & Rhymney, Newport, Pontypool & Cwmbran, Aberdare, Pontypridd & Rhondda, Bridgend (excluding part in S. Glamorgan), Neath & Port Talbot, Swansea, Llanelli, Flint & Rhyl, Wrexham, Cardiff (part only);
- In Scotland: Dunfermline, Kirkcaldy, Dundee, Arbroath, Alloa, Falkirk, Bathgate, Stirling, Glasgow, Dumbarton, Greenock, Irvine, Kilmarnock, Girvan, Ayr, Cumnock & Sanquhar, Lanarkshire, Midlo-

thian Local Authority District (LAD) and part of East Lothian LAD (wards of East, Central, West and South Musselburgh, Tranent North, Tranent Ormiston, Carberry, West and East Prestonpans and Cockenzie).

Objective 5(b) assistance for the period 1989-91 is restricted to the following areas:

- In Scotland: Highlands and Islands Enterprise administrative area; Intermediate Areas of Dumfries and Galloway (excluding parts designated under Objective 2).
- In Wales: the counties of Dyfed, Powys and Gwynedd, excluding Llanelli, that part of the Conway and Colwyn TTWA in Gwynedd, and parts already designated under Objective 2.
- In England: Assisted Areas of Devon and Cornwall.

Separate provision has been made for ERDF financing to be available in the Inner London boroughs of: Hackney, Islington, Lambeth, Tower Hamlets, Southwark, Lewisham and Newham.

Member States are entitled to review periodically the list of eligible areas at the end of the agreed three-year period (five years in the case of Objective 1 regions).

4. Sectoral Restrictions:

Measures supported by the ERDF are jointly funded with an appropriate public authority, eg local authorities, regional authorities, national governments.

A significant proportion of applications submitted by each Member State should be in respect of investment in industry, craft industry and services, particularly through the part-financing of aid schemes. Infrastructure investment is eligible provided it is financed wholly or partly by a public authority, or organisation responsible for infrastructure investment in the same way as a public authority. Investment in public buildings that is not linked to productive investment (eg social welfare, administrative, education and health), leisure not linked to tourism promotion, and house building is generally not eligible, although in Objective 1 regions it may be considered where a need is demonstrated. Further restrictions to infrastructure investment also apply depending on the severity of the regional problem (ie whether designated Objective 1, 2 or 5(b)).

5. Size Restrictions:

For operational programmes submitted in respect of Objective 1 regions, the total cost must generally reach 100 MECU with annual average costs greater than 15 MECU. Direct assistance from the ERDF may be provided in respect of major projects provided the total project cost exceeds 15 MECU for infrastructure investments or 10 MECU for productive investments. Measures relating to the development of indigenous potential should be tailored to the requirements of small and medium-sized firms.

6. Programme Duration:

There is no specified terminal date for the activities of the ERDF. The scope of its operations are, however, reviewed periodically.

7. Submission of Applications/Proposals:

A Community Support Framework (CSF), drawn up on the basis of a regional development plan submitted by the national Government must be agreed before any applications for grant-aid can be considered. Thereafter, applications relating to expenditure incurred under an approved measure must generally be lodged with the Commission on or before the date the expenditure was incurred, except in the case of part-financing of projects and aid schemes, where applications must be submitted within six months of the date the expenditure was incurred.

Agreement has been reached on CSFs in Objective 1, 2 and 5(b) regions.

8. Other Restrictions:

The relevant public authority (designated by the Member State) is required to draw up a regional development plan of three to five years' duration in relation to one or several regions designated under a particular Objective (see 3). Regional development plans are subsequently approved within the context of a CSF which specifies the measures eligible for assistance from the ERDF, and in the case of integrated programmes, from all participating Structural Funds and Community financial instruments. Assistance covered by a CSF is provided predominantly in the form of operational programmes. Fund assistance must represent a genuine additional economic impact in the regions concerned and result in an equivalent increase in the total volume of official structural aid in the Member State concerned.

9. Eligible Expenditure:

Eligible expenditure for ERDF part-financing includes:
- (a) productive investment linked to the creation or maintenance of permanent jobs;
- (b) infrastructure investment – in Objective 1 regions, must increase economic potential, development or structural adjustment although where a need is demonstrated, certain non-economic facilities (eg. health and education) may also be supported;
  - in Objective 2 regions, must relate to the regeneration of the area concerned or provide the basis for the creation or development of economic activity;
  - in Objective 5(b) regions, must be linked directly to economic activity which creates jobs other than in agriculture;
- (c) indigenous potential – services for SMEs, technology transfer, improving access to the capital market (through guarantees and equity participation), direct investment aid (where no aid scheme exists), the provision of small-scale infrastructure;
- (d) operations planned in the context of regional development at Community level (eg. frontier regions);
- (e) preparatory, accompanying and assessment measures necessary for the implementation of the ERDF Regulation carried out by the Commission or outside experts;
- (f) productive investment and infrastructure investment aimed at environmental protection where such investment is linked to regional development.

10. Rate of Award:

The rate of award in respect of the various Objectives is subject to the following ceilings:

- in Objective 1 regions: a maximum of 75 percent of total costs, and as a general rule, at least 50 percent of public expenditure on qualifying activities (not applicable to revenue-bearing investment);
- in Objective 2 and 5(b) regions: a maximum of 50 percent of total costs, and as a general rule, at least 25 percent of public expenditure on qualifying activities.

Fund contributions to investments in firms may not exceed 50 percent of the total cost of the regions covered by Objective 1 and 30 percent of the total cost in other regions. Rates of award for individual measures forming part of operational programmes are differentiated in accordance with agreements concluded in the relevant CSF. In determining the rate of support, the revenue generating capability of the investment is taken into account.

11. Payment Procedure:

Payment is normally made over to the public authority concerned (national or local) as a partial reimbursement for its contribution to the project. With respect to studies, payments will be determined on a case-by-case basis.

12. Points to Note:

On the initiative of the Member State or the Commission, operational programmes which are the subject of an agreed CSF, may take the form of an 'integrated' operation where the programme involves financing by more than one Structural Fund or at least one Fund and one financial instrument other than a loan instrument. Structural Funds which may participate in an integrated operation include the ERDF, the European Social Fund and the European Agricultural Guidance and Guarantee Fund: Guidance Section (EAGGF). Financial instruments include the ECSC and EIB. The relevant Community Support Framework will take in all acting partners within a single agreement.

13. Application Procedure:

Applications and expenditure claims are submitted by the public authority concerned to the ERDF.

14. Further Information:

General Information:
Department of Trade and
    Industry
Investment, Development and
    Accountancy Services Division
Kingsgate House
68–72 Victoria Street
London SW1E 6SW
Tel: (071) 215 8517

In England:
(infrastructure projects)
Department of the Environment
Regional Policy B
2 Marsham Street
London SQ1P 3EB
Tel: (071) 276 3815/3813

In Scotland:
Scottish Office Industry Department
Regional Policy Branch 3
New St Andrew's House
Edinburgh EH1 3TA
Tel: (031) 556 8400 Ext.5086/5309/
5400

In Wales:
Welsh Office Industry
  Department
ERP2 (A)
New Crown Building
Cathays Park
Cardiff CF1 3NQ
Tel: (0222) 825111

In Northern Ireland:
Department of Economic
  Development
Netherleigh
Massey Avenue
Belfast BT4 2JP
Tel: (0232) 63244 Ext.297

ENVIREG (MEDITERRANEAN COASTAL AREAS)

1. Summary:

ENVIREG offers grants and loans for projects tackling the environmental problems of the European Community's less developed regions. In particular, ENVIREG aims to reduce pollution in coastal areas whose economies depend on tourism; provide land use planning in coastal areas to preserve natural beauty and protect and enhance biotopes; improve the control and management of toxic and hazardous industrial waste and strengthen know-how relating to the above.

Measures funded under ENVIREG are only available in designated Objective 1 regions and Mediterranean coastal regions covered by Objectives 2 and 5(b) (see 3).

ENVIREG has been allocated a budget of 500 MECU for the period 1990–93, and will be implemented through operational programmes submitted by Member States, run mainly at a local level.

2. Awarding Body:

ENVIREG is funded from the budgets of the European Community's Structural Funds, ie European Regional Development Fund (ERDF), European Social Fund (ESF) and European Agricultural Guidance and Guarantee Fund (EAGGF) in conjunction with Member State governments. Loans may also be available from the European Investment Bank (EIB).

3. Location Restrictions:

Assistance for pollution reduction, the promotion of land-use planning and related know-how will be available in Objective 1 coastal regions, and Mediterranean coastal regions covered by Objectives 2 and 5b. (The eligible area being a zone starting at the coastline and extending inland not more than

10 km, except in duly justified cases.) Assistance for the control of toxic and hazardous industrial waste and related know-how is restricted to Objective 1 regions. Northern Ireland is the only region in the UK currently designated under Objective 1.

4. Sectoral Restrictions:
The programme will be implemented mainly by local authorities in regions concerned.

5. Size Restrictions:
None.

6. Programme Duration:
ENVIREG is set to run from 1990 to 1993.

7. Submission of Applications/Proposals:
Member States wishing to receive assistance under ENVIREG had until 9 November 1990 to submit detailed proposals for operational programmes to the European Commission.

8. Other Restrictions:
Possible actions under ENVIREG include:
1. Pollution reduction in coastal areas whose economies depend on tourism. Priority will be given to Mediterranean regions experiencing rapid economic growth with serious environmental problems, and subject to sharp sectoral population fluctuations. Actions may include: the construction or modernisation of infrastructure and equipment for the treatment of waste water (priority will be given to urban areas with less than 10,000 residents); the construction of infrastructure and equipment for the collection, treatment, storage, recycling and disposal of solid waste in urban areas; studies, soil analyses, technical assistance, agricultural extension services and demonstration projects relating to the agricultural use of compost/sludge from urban sewage; and port installations for storing and treating ships' ballast/washing/bilge water. (Priority will be given to projects undertaken jointly by more than one local authority.)
2. Land use planning for coastal areas: studies leading to regional land-use plans for coastal areas; schemes protecting biotopes while providing for tourism development; and the protection of biotopes in relation to agriculture;
3. Control and management of toxic and hazardous industrial waste: the construction of infrastructure and productive investments relating to the collection, treatment, storage and recycling of hazardous or toxic industrial waste; and studies to identify industrial activities giving rise to pollution;
4. Strengthening of know-how in connection with actions 1 – 3 above: feasibility studies determining appropriate treatment processes; service centres assisting local authorities with plant and equipment; facilitating the transfer of know-how between regional experts; and training measures.

9. Eligible Expenditure:
Eligible expenditure will relate to the total cost of approved measures.

10. Rate of Award:
The rate of award will be specified in the Commission decision on an operational programme, and will depend on the quality of the programme and importance of the problems to be tackled.

11. Payment Procedure:
The Member State concerned will be responsible for claiming payments from the Commission in respect of expenditure incurred under an agreed programme.

12. Points to Note:
The ENVIREG guidelines, and invitation for Member States to submit operational programmes were published in OJ C115; 9.5.90.

13. Application Procedure:
The UK government is required to apply to the Commission to receive approval for its own national programmes of assistance under ENVIREG. The Department of the Environment is coordinating UK projects.

14. Further Information:
Mr E Landaburu
DG XVI (Regional Policy)
European Commission
Rue de la Loi 200
B-1049 Brussels
Tel: (010 32 2) 235 1111

INTERREG (DEVELOPMENT OF BORDER AREAS)

1. Summary:
INTERREG offers grants and loans to assist border areas of the European Community overcome development problems arising from their isolation within national economies, and within the Community as a whole. INTERREG promotes the creation and development of co-operation networks across internal borders, assists the adjustment of external border areas to their new role as border areas within the Single Market, and promotes co-operation with non-EC countries across external borders.

Three types of action are envisaged: the joint planning and implementation of cross-border programmes; measures improving information flows between public agencies, private organisations and voluntary bodies across borders and amongst border regions; and the setting-up of shared institutional and administrative initiatives to sustain and promote cooperation. Most of the INTERREG budget will be targeted at European Regional Development Fund Objective 1 regions, although Objective 2 and 5(b) regions along internal and external Community land borders are also eligible for assistance. Limited assistance may also be offered to other border areas. In the UK, Northern Ireland (excluding Belfast) is fully eligible. Kent may be eligible for limited support. INTERREG has been allocated a budget of 800 MECU for the period 1990-93 and will be implemented through operational programmes submitted by Member States.

2. Awarding Body:
INTERREG will be funded from the budgets of the European Regional Development Fund (ERDF), European Social Fund (ESF), and European Agricultural Guidance and Guarantee Fund (EAGGF), in conjunction with Member State governments. Loans may also be available from the European Investment Bank (EIB).

3. Location Restrictions:
Eligible areas include all Objective 1, 2 and 5(b) regions along internal and external Community land borders delineated at sub-regional level. In the UK, Northern Ireland qualifies as an Objective 1 region (although Belfast has been excluded). In exceptional cases, assistance may also be available for the creation or promotion of co-operation networks (excluding investment in infrastructure) which extend outwith eligible border areas.

Limited assistance may be offered to border areas not eligible under Objectives 1, 2 and 5(b); in the UK, Kent falls into this category.

As far as possible, infrastructure investments should be concentrated in administrative areas at a sub-regional level, immediately adjacent to borders. In depopulated regions, however, where economic development is curtailed by the lack of road infrastructure, assistance may be available beyond sub-regional areas.

4. Sectoral Restrictions:
The Commission will give priority to proposals made by Member State governments in co-operation with regional and local authorities in border areas, which also include the establishment/development of shared institutional or administrative structures intended to extend cross-border co-operation between public agencies, private organisations and voluntary bodies. Where possible, these shared institutional or administrative structures should have the competence to implement jointly determined projects.

5. Size Restrictions:
None.

6. Programme Duration:
INTERREG is set to run from 1990–93.

7. Submission of Applications/Proposals:
Member States wishing to receive assistance under INTERREG had until February 1991 to submit detailed proposals for operational programmes to the European Commission (or amendments to the previously agreed Community Support Frameworks which outline Structural Fund spending in eligible regions).

8. Other Restrictions:

To promote co-operation between internal border areas of the EC, the following measures may be eligible for assistance: development-plan related studies; support and promotion of small and medium-sized firms and craft industries; tourism development (including agritourism and management of natural parks); the provision of local water, gas and electricity supplies and local telecommunications; the development of renewable energy resources, hydraulic resources and infrastructures; pollution prevention and control; waste disposal or environmental conservation programmes; rural development programmes; measures improving agricultural productivity, products and processes, and facilitating cross-border trade; the establishment or development of trade and other advisory/planning organisations; the creation or modernisation of transport and communications infrastructures; promotion of co-operation in higher education; and training and employment measures.

Along external borders of the EC, the following measures are eligible: improving infrastructures; the provision of local water, gas and electricity supplies; pollution prevention and control; waste disposal; aids to investment and provision of supporting services and facilities; tourism promotion; agricultural and rural development measures; and training and employment measures.

Measures assisted under INTERREG should have their main development impact on the population of eligible border areas. Particular attention should be given to creating alternative employment opportunities in areas where job losses may arise due to changes in customs and other border-related activities.

9. Eligible Expenditure:

Eligible expenditure relates to the Member State's total public expenditure on eligible activities.

10. Rate of Award:

The rate of award will be specified within each operational programme, and will depend on the quality of the programme and importance of the problems to be tackled.

11. Payment Procedure:

The Member State concerned will be responsible for claiming payments from the Commission in respect of expenditure incurred under an agreed programme.

12. Points to Note:

The INTERREG guidelines, and invitation for Member States to submit operational programmes were published in OJ C215; 30.8.90.

13. Application Procedure:

Proposals relating to internal border areas in the Community must be submitted in the form of a single operational programme by the two or more Member States concerned.

14. Further Information:

Mr E Landaburu
DG XVI (Regional Policy)
European Commission
Rue de la Loi 200
B-1049 Brussels
Tel: (010 32 2) 235 1111

In Objective 5(b) Regions:
Mr G Legras
DG VI (Agriculture)
European Commission
Rue de la Loi 200
B-1049 Brussels
Tel: (010 32 2) 235 1111

In Northern Ireland:
Department of Finance and Personnel
Parliament Buildings
Stormont
Belfast BT4 3UW
Tel: (0232) 63210

PEDIP (PROGRAMME FOR THE DEVELOPMENT OF PORTUGUESE INDUSTRY)

1. Summary:

PEDIP is a European Commission programme of assistance promoting the industrial development of Portugal. The development strategy consists of four priority funding areas: (i) Improvement of the Basic Industrial Infrastructure; (ii) Improvement of Basic and Vocational Industrial Training; (iii) the Financing of Productive Investment; (iv) Improvement of Productivity. The PEDIP development programme has been allocated a budget of 500 MECU over the five-year period from 1988–92. This support is additional to that available from the Structural Funds.

Within area (iii) of PEDIP, financial incentives are available under the SIN-PEDIP programme to promote investment in four main areas: 1. High Technology Equipment; 2. Technology Acquisition and Development; 3. Quality Control and Environmental Protection and 4. Innovation and Modernisation. A further programme promoting quality control (SIQ-PEDIP) has also been introduced.

2. Awarding Body:

Commission of the European Communities. The support is channelled through the Portuguese Ministry for Industry.

3. Location Restrictions:

SIN-PEDIP programmes 1–3 and the SIQ-PEDIP are available throughout Portugal. SIN-PEDIP programme 4 is available only in Lisbon and Oporto, and the coastal strip between Braga and Lisbon.

4. Sectoral Restrictions:

The programme is open to organisations from any Member State.
All SIN-PEDIP programmes are available to the manufacturing and

extractive sectors. In addition, they are available to producers of computer software for industrial applications. Specifically excluded are sectors which have been formally designated as undergoing restructuring. This currently applies to the wool spinning and weaving sub-sector.

No industry restrictions apply to the SIQ-PEDIP programme. Eligible organisations are, however, specified for each eligible project type.

5. Size Restrictions:

For SIN-PEDIP programmes 1–3 and SIQ-PEDIP there are no restrictions on project or firm size. For SIN-PEDIP programme 4 there are no restrictions in terms of firm size; there is, however, a minimum project investment of ESC 10 million and an award ceiling of ESC 250 million (except in exceptional cases). As a result, small projects are excluded and very large projects tend to be discriminated against.

6. Programme Duration:

There are no specified terminal dates for these programmes; however, budget provisions have been made to 31 December 1992.

7. Submission of Applications/Proposals:

Application can be made at any time to the relevant Portuguese authority.

8. Other Restrictions:

The following financial incentives are available under PEDIP:

1. Investment in High Technology Equipment: a project-related capital grant for the following types of project: the acquisition of equipment which makes a significant contribution to productivity; and the acquisition of equipment which improves health and safety conditions at work, the quality of products and processes and environmental protection.

2. Investment in Technology Acquisition and Development: a capital grant for projects covering: research and development activities with industrial applications either within firms or in collaboration with research centres; development of new products and processes including the construction of prototypes and experimental installations; development of high technology products and processes; and manufacture of pre-production models for production tests and market research.

3. Investment in Quality Control and Environmental Protection: a project-related capital grant comprising two elements: an industrial policy component where the rate of award is set as a percentage of eligible expenditure; and an employment component which takes the form of an award per skilled job created. The following project types are eligible: the acquisition of laboratory equipment for quality control or for metrology of raw materials or of industrial processes; setting-up and development of quality control systems in industrial firms; the certification of products and the calibration of instrumentation abroad, where necessary; the acquisition of equipment to ensure the levels of health and safety at work required for product and process quality; and the acquisition of equipment for protection of the environment.

4. Investment in Innovation and Modernisation: a project-related capital grant comprising two elements as above for 3. The following project types are eligible: investments with a high technology potential which aim to introduce advanced technology; investments in modernisation and innovation which aim to make significant improvements to products and/or processes; investments in modernisation and rationalisation of processes or existing products with a view to improving productivity and quality.

5. SIQ-PEDIP Incentives for Quality Assurance: grants to improve the competitiveness of Portuguese products through the reinforcement of the national system of quality control and its three main functions: standardisation; metrology; and registration. The scheme also aims to improve awareness of industrial design and quality within manufacturing firms and to create the necessary environment for mutual recognition of standards and organisations, particularly in a European context.

9. Eligible Expenditure:
Eligible expenditure varies according to the specific programme and project undertaken.

10. Rate of Award:
The rate of award varies according to project type and the relevant assistance programme.

11. Payment Procedure:
The award decision should be taken within 90 days of application submission. Award payment is made on project completion and within 30 days of presentation of relevant invoices. However, provision is made for the payment of interest-free advances in line with project progress.

12. Points to Note:
Council Regulation (EEC) No 2053/88 instituting PEDIP was published in Official Journal L185; 15.7.88.

13. Application Procedure:
Application is made to the administering Portuguese authorities.

14. Further Information:
Instituto de Apoio as Pequenas e Medias Empresas e ao Investimento
R. Rodrigo da Fonseca, 73
1297 LISBON CODEX
Tel: (010 351 1) 52 64 19/56 22 11
Telex: 15657 IAPMEI P

Gabinete do Gestor do PEDIP
Rua Braancamp, 9 – 5F
1200 LISBON
Tel: (010 351 1) 53 52 97
Telex: 61649 PEDIP P

RECHAR (COAL-MINING AREAS)

1. Summary:
 The RECHAR programme aims to assist the restructuring of coal mining areas. Assistance is concentrated in areas eligible under Objectives 1, 2 and 5(b) of the Structural Funds, and includes measures to improve the physical environment (eg the cleaning up and reclamation of derelict industrial land), and support for new businesses. The objective is to regenerate local economies through support for small and medium-sized firms, the introduction of new technologies and alternative industries in mining areas. RECHAR has been allocated a budget of 300 MECU for the period 1990-94. and will be implemented through operational programmes submitted by Member States.

2. Awarding Body:
 RECHAR is funded by the European Regional Development Fund (ERDF) and European Social Fund (ESF), in conjunction with Member State governments. The European Coal and Steel Community (ECSC) also provides funding in the form of redeployment aids and interest subsidised loans, under Article 56 of the ECSC Treaty.

3. Location Restrictions:
 Available in coal mining areas located in areas eligible under Objectives 1, 2 or 5(b) of the Structural Funds which meet the following criteria:
 (1) strong dependency of the area's economy on coal mining activity;
 (2) significant job losses in the coal mining industry in the past and/or expected job losses which are likely to worsen the regional unemployment situation. The RECHAR initiative may also apply in areas not eligible under Objective 1, 2 or 5(b) provided they meet the above criteria and have an unemployment rate at or above the Community average, taking into account likely increases in unemployment as a consequence of expected job losses.
 Eligible UK regions include, in England: Nottinghamshire, Derbyshire, Staffordshire, Warwickshire, Greater Manchester, Lancashire, Merseyside, West Yorkshire, North Yorkshire, Northumberland, Durham and Tyne and Wear; in Wales: Mid and West Glamorgan, Powys, Gwent and Dyfed; in Scotland: Fife, Central, Lothian, Strathclyde and Dumfries.
 The UK Government has submitted eleven programme applications covering the following regions: Eastern Scotland; Western Scotland; County Durham; industrial South Wales; Lancashire coal fields; Mid-Yorkshire; South Yorkshire coal fields; East Midlands (Nottinghamshire and North Derbyshire coal fields); North Warwickshire; South Staffordshire; Tyne & Wear; and South-East Northumberland.

4. Sectoral Restrictions:
 Industry restrictions have not yet been specified.

5. Size Restrictions:
 None.

6. Programme Duration:
 RECHAR has been adopted to run over the period 1990-94.

7. Submission of Applications/Proposals:

Member States had to submit their proposals for eligible areas to the Commission by 27 February 1990; the Commission then determined and published a list of eligible areas (OJ C177; 18.7.90). Member States with eligible areas were required to submit detailed proposals for operational programmes within six months. The UK Government submitted eleven programme applications on 26 July 1990.

8. Other Restrictions:

Action under RECHAR may include:

1. Environmental improvement of areas seriously damaged by coal mining activity, including: coal tip reclamation, the cleaning-up and conversion of disused buildings, the modernisation of premises for SMEs, the creation of green areas, work on the problem of subsidence, and access roads;
2. The provision of advance factory units and workshop premises;
3. The provision of alternative economic activities, in particular the creation/development of SMEs including easier access for SMEs to risk capital, market research and the promotion of innovation;
4. The promotion of industrial heritage-based and other tourism activities;
5. The creation and development of economic conversion bodies and regional development teams;
6. Renovation and modernisation of social infrastructures in mining villages (where it also contributes to the economic regeneration of the area);
7. Interest rebates on ECSC loans for investments in SMEs and, under certain conditions, for investments aimed at strengthening the competitiveness of potentially viable coal production sites;
8. The provision of employment related training;
9. Redeployment aids available under Article 56 of the ECSC Treaty.

9. Eligible Expenditure:

Eligible expenditure relates to the Member State's total public expenditure on eligible activities.

10. Rate of Award:

The rate of award will be specified by the Commission when operational programmes are approved.

11. Payment Procedure:

The national government concerned will be responsible for claiming payments from the Commission in respect of expenditure incurred under an agreed programme.

12. Points to Note:

Member State governments and regional authorities should select the main priorities for action in their coal mining areas, taking into account the particular problems of the regions concerned and the main areas of development potential. RECHAR measures will be complementary to those receiving ERDF or ESF assistance under the Community Support Frameworks for the areas in question.

13. Application Procedure:

The UK Government is required to apply to the Commission to receive approval for its own national programmes of assistance under RECHAR and undertake their complete administration. For individual firms, in respect of whose projects the DTI may subsequently be reimbursed, application procedure is as set out under the relevant assistance scheme.

14. Further Information:

European Commission
DG XVI – RECHAR
Rue de la Loi 200
B-1049 Brussels
Tel: (010 32 2) 235 1111
Telex: 21877 COMEU B

Department of Trade and Industry
Kingsgate House
68–72 Victoria Street
London SW1E 6SW
Tel: (071) 215 8517

RENAVAL (SHIPBUILDING AREAS)

1. Summary:

The RENAVAL programme aims to assist the conversion of declining industrial regions adversely affected by the restructuring of the shipbuilding industry. The purpose of the programme is to contribute to the removal of obstacles to the development of new, job-creating economic activities through the implementation of consistent, multiannual measures aimed at improving the infrastructure and the physical and social environment in the areas concerned, as well as the establishment of new activities, the growth of small and medium-sized enterprises, the development of innovation, and investment in tourism activities. Under RENAVAL, the ERDF may contribute to schemes to aid industry and infrastructure projects. In the UK, RENAVAL will contribute to expenditure on infrastructure projects and Regional Enterprise and Consultancy Grants.

2. Awarding Body:

European Regional Development Fund through the Department of Trade and Industry, Department of the Environment and the Scottish Office.

3. Location Restrictions:

Available in regions of the European Community adversely affected by the restructuring of the shipbuilding industry. To be eligible for RENAVAL funding, the area must satisfy certain criteria relating to job losses in the shipbuilding industry, dependency on the shipbuilding industry for employment, and the extent to which the socio-economic situation in the region in which the area is located is characterised by particular employment difficulties.

Member States were required to submit to the European Commission

applications supporting the designation of areas eligible under RENAVAL as and when areas satisfied the criteria set out in Article 3 of the RENAVAL Regulation. In the UK, the following areas are eligible:
- Plymouth TTWA: Plymouth city, part of the district of South Hams, Caradon and West Devon;
- Fife: Kirkcaldy TTWA, Dunfermline TTWA (excluding West and East Kinross wards) and the Kincardine/Culross ward of Alloa TTWA;
- Strathclyde: Glasgow and Greenock TTWAs;
- Teesside: Tyne and Wear, Middlesbrough and Langbaurgh districts;
- Merseyside: Wirral and Sefton districts.

4. Sectoral Restrictions:
The purpose of RENAVAL is to support diversification from the shipbuilding sector into other activities. Activities in the shipbuilding sector are not, therefore, eligible for assistance. Public, local and regional authorities are eligible for assistance directly from the Structural Funds, whilst local and regional development corporations, other businesses, cooperatives or self-employed persons carrying on a productive activity may benefit indirectly through participation in measures and projects undertaken by those authorities.

5. Size Restrictions:
Support is available in respect of small and medium-sized enterprises. In the UK this will generally be those with less than 500 employees but in certain instances less than 25 employees. Local and public authorities are not so restricted.

6. Programme Duration:
RENAVAL is set to run from 16 August 1988 to 31 December 1993. Member States had until 30 April 1990 to submit applications supporting the designation of areas eligible under RENAVAL.

7. Submission of Applications/Proposals:
Member States are required to submit a programme of assistance within six months of the Commission's decision on the application for eligibility of a given area. The Member State administers any regional aid schemes approved under the programme and reclaims the ERDF contribution against its expenditure. Applications for infrastructure projects can be submitted at any time.

8. Other Restrictions:
In the UK, RENAVAL will be used to contribute to national aid schemes to industry, and infrastructure projects which satisfy the criteria set out in the RENAVAL Regulation (EEC) No 2506/88 (published in Official Journal No L33; 5.02.88).

9. Eligible Expenditure:
Eligible expenditure for ERDF purposes relates to the Member State's total public expenditure on eligible activities.

10. Rate of Award:
Assistance from the ERDF may not exceed 55 percent of the total public

expenditure taken into account in a programme. With respect to infrastructure projects, ERDF participation is restricted to 50 percent of public expenditure.

11. Payment Procedure:
The national government concerned is responsible for claiming payments from the ERDF in respect of expenditure already incurred under an agreed programme.

12. Points to Note:
None.

13. Application Procedure:
The UK Government is required to apply to the Commission to receive approval for its own national programmes of assistance under RENAVAL and to undertake their complete administration. For individual firms, in respect of whose projects the DTI may subsequently be reimbursed, application procedure is as set out under the relevant assistance schemes.

14. Further Information:

European Commission
DG XVI
Rue de la Loi 200
B-1049 Brussels
Belgium
Tel: (010 32 2) 235 11 11
Telex: 21877 Comeu B

Department of Trade and Industry
Kingsgate House
68–72 Victoria Street
London SW1E 6SW
Tel: (071) 215 8517

RESIDER (STEEL INDUSTRY AREAS)

1. Summary:
The RESIDER programme aims to assist the conversion of industrial regions affected by the restructuring of the steel industry. The purpose of RESIDER is to contribute to the removal of obstacles to the development of new, job-creating economic activities through the implementation of a series of consistent, multiannual measures aimed at improving the infrastructure and the physical and social environment in the areas concerned, as well as the establishment of new activities, the growth of small and medium-sized enterprises, the development of innovation, and investment in tourism activities.

In the UK, RESIDER contributes to expenditure on infrastructure projects, Regional Enterprise Grants and Consultancy Grants.

2. Awarding Body:
European Regional Development Fund (ERDF) through the Department of Trade and Industry and the Department of the Environment.

3. Location Restrictions:

Available in regions of the European Community adversely affected by the restructuring of the steel industry. To be eligible for RESIDER funding, the area must satisfy certain criteria relating to the number of jobs in the steel industry, dependency on the steel industry for employment, major job losses in the steel industry, and the extent to which the socio-economic situation in the region in which the area concerned is located is characterised by particular employment difficulties.

Member States were required to submit to the European Commission applications supporting the designation of areas eligible under RESIDER as and when areas satisfied the criteria set out in Article 4.1 of the RESIDER regulation.

In the UK, the county of South Yorkshire (including the Sheffield Travel to Work Area) and the Scunthorpe TTWA are the only areas which met the criteria of the RESIDER Regulation.

4. Sectoral Restrictions:

The purpose of RESIDER is to support diversification from the steel sector into other activities. Activities in the steel sector are not, therefore, eligible for assistance.

5. Size Restrictions:

Support is available in respect of small and medium-sized enterprises. In the UK this will generally be those with less than 500 employees but in certain instances less than 25 employees. Local and public authorities are not so restricted.

6. Programme Duration:

RESIDER is set to run from February 1988 to 31 December 1992. Member States had until 30 April 190 to submit applications supporting the designation of areas eligible under RESIDER.

7. Submission of Applications/Proposals:

Member States were required to submit a programme of assistance within six months of the Commission's decision on the application for eligibility of a given area.

The Member State administers any regional aid schemes approved under the programme and reclaims the ERDF contribution against its expenditure. Applications for infrastructure projects can be submitted at any time.

8. Other Restrictions:

In the UK, RESIDER will be used to contribute to national aid schemes to industry, and infrastructure projects which satisfy the criteria set out in the RESIDER regulation (EEC) No 328/88 (published in Official Journal No L33; 5.02.88).

The programme is used to extend Regional Enterprise Grants (REGs) for investment and innovation to eligible companies located in the Barnsley, Sheffield and Doncaster Intermediate Areas of South Yorkshire. REGs are normally only available in the Development Areas of Great Britain.

9. Eligible Expenditure:
Eligible expenditure for ERDF purposes relates to the Member State's total public expenditure on eligible activities.

10. Rate of Award:
Assistance from the ERDF may not exceed 55 percent of the total public expenditure taken into account in a programme. With respect to infrastructure projects, ERDF participation is restricted to 50 percent of public expenditure.

11. Payment Procedure:
The national government concerned is responsible for claiming payments from the ERDF in respect of expenditure already incurred under an agreed programme.

12. Points to Note:
None.

13. Application Procedures:
The UK Government is required to apply to the Commission to receive approval for its own national programmes of assistance under RESIDER and undertake their complete administration. For individual firms, in respect of whose projects the Department of Trade and Industry may subsequently be reimbursed, application procedure is as set out under the relevant assistance scheme.

14. Further Information:

European Commission
DG XVI
Rue de la Loi 200
B-1049 Brussels
Tel: (010 32 2) 235 1111
Telex: 21877 Comeu B

Department of Trade and Industry
Kingsgate House
68–72 Victoria Street
London SW1E 6SW
Tel: (071) 215 8517

STAR TELEMATIQUE

1. Summary:
The STAR programme, financed through the European Regional Development Fund (ERDF), aims to promote the development of certain less-favoured regions by improving access to advanced telecommunications services, fostering job creation and raising technological standards.

In the UK, Northern Ireland – the only region eligible for assistance under STAR – will receive a total of £8.5 million from the ERDF. Eighty-five percent of the funds will be used to instal an optical fibre network throughout the Province and optical fibre links with Great Britain and the Republic of Ireland; the remaining 15 percent will be spent on promotion and demand stimulation. The contract for laying the optical network and optical fibre links has gone to British Telecom.

2. Awarding Body:
The work is to be funded jointly by British Telecom (NI), the Department of Economic Development for Northern Ireland and the ERDF.

3. Location Restrictions:
In the UK, Northern Ireland is the only region eligible for assistance under the STAR programme.

4. Sectoral Restrictions:
Contracts for work under STAR will be undertaken by British Telecom.

5. Size Restrictions:
None.

6. Programme Duration:
Funding has been allocated for the period 1 November 1986 to 31 October 1991. The European Commission has proposed to extend the programme until 1993 to promote the use of the advanced telecommunications services which have been established, in particular encouraging the use of services linked to advanced communications systems within small and medium-sized firms. The follow-up phase will be called TELEMATIQUE.

7. Submission of Applications/Proposals:
The Northern Ireland Department of Economic Development is responsible for the implementation of the programme, for issuing contracts and for claiming assistance from the ERDF.

8. Other Restrictions:
Work under this programme is currently being undertaken through contracts awarded to British Telecom.

9. Eligible Expenditure:
Not relevant.

10. Rate of Award:
Northern Ireland will receive up to 55 percent of its expenditure on the installation of an optical fibre network and optical fibre links with Great Britain and the Republic of Ireland from the ERDF.

11. Payment Procedure:
Payment will be made over to the Northern Ireland Department of Economic Development to be passed on to British Telecom as appropriate.

12. Points to Note:
None.

13. Application Procedure:
Not relevant.

14. Further Information:

Mr W Carlisle
Department of Economic
   Development
The Arches Centre
11/13 Bloomfield Avenue
Belfast BT5 5HD
Tel: (0232) 732411

Fernando Toledano
European Commission
DG XIII
Rue de la Loi 200
B-1049 Brussels
Tel: (010 32 2) 236 0235

STRIDE (REGIONAL RESEARCH AND DEVELOPMENT)

1. Summary:

STRIDE supports the improvement of regional capabilities for research and technological development and innovation.

Three categories of measure have been specified for support under the programme: A. Strengthening the research facilities in Objective 1 regions; B. Promoting greater participation in EC and other international research programmes and networks; and C. Promotion of linkages between research centres and industry.

Most of the STRIDE budget will be targeted at designated Objective 1 regions (Northern Ireland in the UK), although Objective 2 regions may qualify for certain types of assistance under Measure C (see 8).

STRIDE has been allocated a budget of **400 MECU** for the period 1990–93, and will be implemented through operational programmes submitted by Member States.

2. Awarding Body:

STRIDE is funded from the budgets of the European Community's European Regional Development Fund (ERDF) and European Social Fund (ESF) in conjunction with Member State governments. Loans may also be issued to further the objectives of the programme through the European Investment Bank (EIB) and European Coal and Steel Community (ECSC).

3. Location Restrictions:

Assistance for measures A. and B. (see 8) will be available in regions eligible under Objective 1 of the Structural Funds (structurally underdeveloped regions). Northern Ireland is the only region in the UK currently designated as Objective 1. Assistance for measure C will be available in regions eligible under Objectives 1 and 2 (regions in industrial decline). For a full list of UK Objective 2 regions, see European Regional Development Fund (ERDF).

4. Sectoral Restrictions:

No industry restrictions have been specified.

5. Size Restrictions:

None.

6. Programme Duration:
The STRIDE budget has been agreed for the period 1990-1993. The Commission may consider extending the programme at a later date.

7. Submission of Applications/Proposals:
Member States wishing to receive assistance under STRIDE had until February 1991 to submit detailed proposals for operational programmes to the European Commission (or amendments to the previously agreed Community Support Frameworks which outline Structural Fund spending in eligible regions).

8. Other Restrictions:
Possible actions under STRIDE may include:
  A. The strengthening of research facilities in a small number of research fields and research centres in Objective 1 regions (priority will be given to precompetitive research capable of enhancing the region's requirements; investment in basic equipment; and investment in infrastructure relating to science parks, research centres and laboratories); and the transfer of R & TD resources to eligible regions;
  B. Promoting participation in EC and other international research programmes and networks, through: information dissemination; support for preparatory work; demonstration and pilot activities; and the development of twinning arrangements.
  C. The promotion of linkages beween research centres and industry, through: the setting up of consortia; establishing aid schemes supporting the purchase of equipment; approved research projects undertaken by small and medium-sized firms; and expert studies evaluating research plans (Objective 1 regions only); the creation and development of technology transfer and innovation services; the extension of inter-regional co-operation networks; vocational training; and short-term secondments.

9. Eligible Expenditure:
Eligible expenditure relates to the Member State's total public expenditure on eligible activities.

10. Rate of Award:
The rate of award will be specified within each operational programme, and will conform to the regulations governing Structural Fund assistance. Maximum rates available through the Structural Funds are as follows:
  - Objective 1 regions: a maximum of 75 percent of total costs and, as a general rule, at least 50 percent of public expenditure on qualifying activities (not applicable to revenue-bearing investment);
  - Objective 2 regions: a maximum of 50 percent of total costs and, as a general rule, at least 25 percent of public expenditure on qualifying activities.

11. Payment Procedure:
Member States are responsible for claiming payments from the Commission in respect of expenditure incurred under an agreed operational

programme. Funding may also take the form of a global grant disbursed to an intermediary in the Member State concerned.

12. Points to Note:

STRIDE will complement and co-ordinate with other Community activities supporting research and development, especially those within the regional Community Support Frameworks, the Framework Programme for R & TD, SPRINT and COMETT. The STRIDE guidelines and invitation to Member States to submit operational programmes were published in OJ C196; 4.8.90.

13. Application Procedures:

Each Member State must submit detailed proposals for operational programmes to the Commission.

14. Further Information:

Mr B Spiekermann
STRIDE Programme
DG XVI (Regional Policy)
European Commission
Rue de la Loi 200
B-1049 Brussels
Tel: (010 32 2) 236 1323
Fax: (010 32 2) 235 0149

In Northern Ireland:
Department of Economic
  Development
Netherleigh
Massey Avenue
Belfast BT4 3SB
Tel: (0232) 63244

VALOREN (ENERGY)

1. Summary:

The VALOREN programme, financed through the European Regional Development Fund, aims to promote the development of certain less-favoured regions of the European Community through the exploitation of local energy potential.

In the UK, Northern Ireland – the only eligible region -will receive up to £5.74 million. This funding will be used to offset part of the Department of Economic Development and other public bodies' expenditure on selective financial assistance offered to projects which are concerned with the exploitation of local energy resources or the efficient use of energy in small and medium-sized enterprises.

2. Awarding Body:

The programme is funded jointly by the Department of Economic Development for Northern Ireland or other public bodies, and the European Regional Development Fund (ERDF).

3. Location Restrictions:

Northern Ireland is the only eligible region in the UK.

4. Sectoral Restrictions:
None.

5. Size Restrictions:
To be partly financed under VALOREN, projects promoting the efficient use of energy must be undertaken by small and medium-sized enterprises or be related to infrastructure provision.

6. Programme Duration:
The VALOREN Regulation is in force until 31 October 1991.

7. Submission of Applications/Proposals:
Not relevant. The Member State concerned is responsible for the implementation of the programme and for claiming assistance from the ERDF.

8. Other Restrictions:
No specific assistance schemes are likely to be introduced under VALOREN. However, projects normally applying for selective assistance will be part-financed under this programme if they relate to one of the following areas:
- exploitation of local energy resources, covering investment projects and related feasibility studies relating to (a) alternative and renewable energies, namely solar and wind energy, biomas, energy-generating exploitation of urban and industrial waste, small-scale hydro-power and geothermal energy; (b) small deposits of peat and lignite;
- efficient use of energy in small and medium-sized undertakings, covering investment projects and feasibility studies relating to energy saving and oil substitution;
- promotion, at local and regional level, of improved use of energy potential covering surveys and studies, provision of advisory services and technical back-up for small and medium-sized enterprises, and information and publicity campaigns.

9. Eligible Expenditure:
Eligible expenditure covers the total expenditure on each project.

10. Rate of Award:
The Department of Economic Development for Northern Ireland will receive up to 55 percent of its expenditure on eligible projects.

11. Payment Procedure:
Payment will be made over to the Department of Economic Development as a partial reimbursement for its contribution to any projects, or for disbursal to other public bodies.

12. Points to Note:
None.

13. Application Procedure:
Further information on application procedure is available from the Department of Economic Development.

14. Further Information:

Mr W Carlisle	Mr. H Finlay
Department of Economic	European Commission
Development	DG XVI
The Arches Centre	Rue de la Loi 200
11/13 Broomfield Avenue	B-1049 Brussels
Belfast BT5 5HD	Tel: (010 32 2) 235 2282
Tel: (0232) 732411	

TRANSPORT INFRASTRUCTURE PROGRAMME

1. Summary:

The European Commission's action programme in the field of transport infrastructure aims to co-ordinate and promote infrastructure projects of Community interest, creating a modern and efficient EC transport network. Financial assistance is aimed at: the elimination of bottlenecks; the integration of landlocked or peripheral areas; the reduction of costs associated with transit traffic; the improvement of links on land/sea routes; and the provision of high-quality links between the major urban centres, including high-speed rail links with a view to the completion of an integrated transport market in 1992. The programme funds: feasibility studies or preparatory work for infrastructure projects; related schemes; and the development of part or the whole of a project.

Support for transport infrastructure projects will take the form of subsidies, or in exceptional cases, any other form of support felt to be appropriate. The programme's budget allocation for 1991 is 118 MECU.

2. Awarding Body:

Commission of the European Communities.

3. Location Restrictions:

Specific individual projects selected for support must be components of the following major projects:

1. Contribution to the high-speed rail network linking Paris-London-Brussels – Amsterdam-Cologne and connecting lines to other Member States; Seville-Madrid-Barcelona-Lyons-Turin/Milan-Venice and from there to Tarvisio and Trieste; Oporto-Lisbon-Madrid;
2. The Alpine transit route (Brenner route);
3. Contributions to the combined transport network of Community interest;
4. International trans-Pyrenean road link (Somport);
5. The road link with Ireland (A5/A55 North Wales coast road) and the improvement of the Dublin-Belfast cross-border railway line;
6. The Scanlink;
7. The strengthening of land communications in Greece.

4. Sectoral Restrictions:
None.

5. Size Restrictions:
Support is limited to projects of such a scale that they present particular difficulties for financing, and cannot be financed by national or regional authorities alone.

6. Programme Duration:
The programme is set to run until 31 December 1992 and, depending on progress, may be extended.

7. Submission of Applications/Proposals:
Funds awarded under the programme are allocated to central governments in Member States, who then place contracts with industry.

8. Other Restrictions:
Transport infrastucture projects are assessed on the basis of the following criteria:
- The benefit of the project to international Community traffic and broad programme objectives. Among the factors which must be included are: the importance of exchanges between the Community and third countries on the route involved in the project; and the extent of the projects contribution to the creation of a homogeneous and balanced network within the Community framework, geared to existing and future transport needs;
- The socio-economic return on the project;
- The project's consistency with other Community policies and national transport policies;
- Particular difficulties in raising finance;
- Inability of national or regional authorities to carry out the project alone.

9. Eligible Expenditure:
Eligible expenditure is decided on a case-by-case basis.

10. Rate of Award:
The rate of award is decided on a case-by-case basis but grant aid generally covers up to 25 percent of total project costs (or costs of that part of the project granted assistance), and up to 50 percent for preparatory studies for construction work.

Where a specific project forming part of one of the approved major projects (see 3) is already being granted non-repayable EC support, that project may only receive aid in the form of loans.

11. Payment Procedure:
Funds under the programme are disbursed to central governments within the relevant Member States, who then place contracts with industry. An advance payment of no more than 40 percent of the Community contribution may be provided to accelerate the execution of projects.

12. Points to Note:

Council Regulation (EEC) 3359/90 adopting the programme was published in OJ L326;24.11.90.

Projects may only receive support if all EC public procurement requirements are met. Where a project receiving support has not been carried out as planned, or where conditions imposed are not fulfilled, financial support may be reduced or cancelled.

13. Application Procedure:

Projects are submitted by the governments of Member States to the Commission for approval with an indication of anticipated total costs, a work schedule, information necessary for the evaluation of the Community interest of the project, and an environmental impact assessment.

14. Further Information:

European Commission
DG VII/C-2
Rue de la Loi 200
B-1049 Brussels
Tel: (010 32 2) 235 1111
Telex: 21877 COMEU B

PART ONE

INVESTMENT AND INFRASTRUCTURE FINANCING

1.2 SECTORAL SUPPORT

1.2 SECTORAL SUPPORT

ECSC: INDUSTRIAL LOANS PROMOTING COAL
CONSUMPTION

1. Summary:
Loans are available under Article 54(2) of the Treaty establishing the European Coal and Steel Community (ECSC) for investment projects which promote the consumption of European Community coal. Loans may be granted directly or indirectly through financial agents under a global ECSC loan (although at the present time no agents have been appointed).

2. Awarding Body:
European Coal and Steel Community (ECSC).

3. Location Restrictions:
Available in any Member State of the European Community.

4. Sectoral Restrictions:
Loans are available to businesses, public bodies or local authorities. Loans may be granted directly or indirectly through financial agents under a global ECSC loan, but at the present time no agents have been appointed.

5. Size Restrictions:
There is no limit on the size of direct loans. Unless prior agreement is reached with the Commission, the total investment value of projects for which an individual loan is sought under a global loan may not exceed 15 MECU.

6. Programme Duration:
There is no specified terminal date for the granting of these loans, although they are subject to the availability of funds.

7. Submission of Applications/Proposals:
Applications must normally relate to investment projects on which work has not been started, and which can be completed within three years.

8. Other Restrictions:
The following types of investment projects may qualify: installations and equipment relating to the combustion, transformation, handling and preparation of coal, and to the treatment and disposal of effluents, whose purpose is to promote the consumption of Community coal. The Commission will assess the economic aspects of the industrial project, principally in terms of the contribution the investment will make to the consumption of Community coal and of the technical and financial prospects for its implementation. The Commission will also assess the financial situation of the borrower and of any parent companies, and the value of the guarantees offered.

An analysis will be made of any significant effects on the environment from emissions and waste produced by the project. Projects must in any event meet the requirements of Community legislation on the environment.

It is a condition of an industrial loan that Community coal only is used for a period of five years from the date the project is completed.

9. Eligible Expenditure:

Eligible expenditure relates to the investment value of the project (excluding working capital requirements).

10. Rate of Award:

The maximum loan is set at 50 percent of the investment value of the project. Unless there is specific agreement by the ECSC to the contrary, this maximum will be reduced proportionately if any non-Community coal is used in the period of five years after the project is completed. The interest rate on the loan is set by the Commission in line with the cost of borrowed funds. A rebate of 3 percent per annum may be granted for a period of five years on the interest payable on the loans, except for projects relating to power stations and coking plants. The rebate is calculated on the total amount of the loan expressed in ECU. The amount of rebated loan is linked to the consumption of Community coal and may therefore, in some circumstances, be lower than the loan granted.

11. Payment Procedure:

An industrial loan is granted direct to the promoter of the project. The rebate is paid direct to the borrower in the relevant national currency on the date the interest falls due.

12. Points to Note:

In determining any interest rebate, the Commission takes account of any national aid granted to the project, and ensures in particular that the cumulative effect of national and Community aid does not distort competition in a way which is contrary to the public interest.

Borrowers must send the Commission periodical reports on the progress of investment projects and the consumption of Community coal. The Commission will make selective inspection visits to the projects to ensure that they are being carried out as planned.

Loans are also available from the ECSC towards the cost of converting gas or oil fired boiler systems to coal. Loans are usually made in foreign currencies and repayment is required in the same currencies; they are available directly or through 3i plc. However, no loans have been made by 3i plc under this facility for several years, since the abolition of exchange risk cover.

13. Application Procedure:

Loan applications should be directed to the European Commission.

14. Further Information:

Ms Judith Elles
European Commission
DG XVIII/Division B3
Batiment Wagner
L-2920 Luxembourg
Tel: (010 35 2) 4301 6368

ECSC: INDUSTRIAL LOANS PROMOTING STEEL CONSUMPTION

1. Summary:

Loans are available under Article 54(2) of the Treaty establishing the European Coal and Steel Community (ECSC) for investments aimed at promoting the consumption of European Community steel. Loans may be granted directly or indirectly through financial agents under a global ECSC loan (although at the present time no agents have been appointed).

2. Awarding Body:

European Coal and Steel Community (ECSC).

3. Location Restrictions:

Available in any Member State of the European Community.

4. Sectoral Restrictions:

Loans are available to properly constituted enterprises.

Eligible products covered by the term 'steel' are defined in the Annex to the decision (85/C121/03) and broadly include: raw materials for iron and steel production; pig iron and ferro-alloys; crude and semi-finished products or iron, ordinary steel or special steel, including products for re-use and re-rolling; hot finished products of iron, ordinary steel or special steel; and end products of iron, ordinary steel or special steel.

5. Size Restrictions:

There is no limit on the size of direct loans. Unless prior agreement is reached with the Commission, the total investment value of projects for which an individual loan is sought under a global loan facility may not exceed 15 MECU.

6. Programme Duration:

There is no specified terminal date for the granting of these loans, although they are subject to the availability of funds.

7. Submission of Applications/Proposals:

Applications should relate to investment projects on which work has not been started or is still in progress and which, as a rule, can be completed within three years.

8. Other Restrictions:

The following types of industrial projects may qualify for support: those aimed at introducing new applications for steel or at improving the competitiveness of steel in relation to any other products; projects by undertakings for which the cost of steel purchased, reflected in the price of the finished product, accounts for (a) at least 50 percent of the total cost of raw materials (including steel) or, if this provision cannot be applied for technical reasons, (b) at least 20 percent of the total cost of the constituents (including raw materials) of the finished product or, if this provision cannot be applied for technical reasons, (c) at least 5 percent of the selling price of the finished product. Only expenditure on installations directly connected with the continuous use of steel will be considered. Loans are also available for major infrastructure projects of European interest, but for these the continuous use of steel is waived.

The Commission assesses the economic aspects of the project, principally in terms of the contribution the investment will make to the consumption of Community steel and of the technical and financial prospects for its implementation, its viability, the market outlook for the products and the situation in the sector concerned. The Commission also assesses the financial situation of the borrower, of any parent companies and the value of any guarantees offered. An analysis may be made of any significant effects on the environment from emissions and waste produced by the project. Projects must in any event meet the requirements of Community legislation on the environment.

9. Eligible Expenditure:

Eligible expenditure in relation to industrial projects relates to the investment value of the project (excluding working capital requirements).

Eligible expenditure in relation to major infrastructure projects of European interest is limited to the total actual value of the steel used in the project, provided always that that total does not exceed 20 percent of fixed capital investments.

10. Rate of Award:

Loans may be for up to 50 percent of the investment value of projects aimed at increasing or maintaining the level of consumption of Community steel.

Loans of up to 20 percent are available for major infrastructure projects.

The loans are provided in a mixture of foreign currencies. Interest rates are at favourable market rates reflecting the rate paid by the ECSC itself on financial markets on which it has borrowed funds.

11. Payment Procedure:

Payment is arranged between the applicant and the Commission on a case-by-case basis.

12. Points to Note:

Borrowers must send the Commission periodical reports on the progress of investment projects and the consumption of Community steel. The Commission will make selective inspection visits to the projects to ensure they are being carried out as planned.

13. Application Procedures:

Loan applications should be sent to the European Commission.

14. Further Information:

Ms Judith Elles
European Commission
DG XVIII/Division B3
Batiment Wagner
L-2920 Luxembourg
Tel: (010 35 2) 4301 6368

EAGGF: PROCESSING AND MARKETING OF AGRICULTURAL PRODUCTS

1. Summary:

Under Regulation (EEC) 866/90 financial assistance is available from the European Agricultural Guidance and Guarantee Fund: Guidance Section (EAGGF) for capital investments designed to improve and rationalise the treatment, processing and marketing of agricultural products.

EAGGF financing takes place within the framework of Sectoral Plans drawn up by Member States. Eligible projects conforming most closely to the aims of the Regulation and to Sectoral Plan priorities are incorporated into Operational Programmes for consideration by the European Commission.

2. Awarding Body:

European Agricultural Guidance and Guarantee Fund: Guidance Section. Assistance is disbursed through the relevant Agriculture Ministry/Department: ie the Ministry of Agriculture, Fisheries and Food in England; the Scottish Office Agriculture and Fisheries Department, the Welsh Office Agriculture Department and the Department of Agriculture for Northern Ireland.

3. Location Restrictions:

Available in any Member State of the European Community. Higher rates of assistance are available in Objective 1 regions (structurally underdeveloped). In the UK, Northern Ireland is the only Objective 1 region.

4. Sectoral Restrictions:

Support is intended to benefit the primary producer, and as such, investments eligible for assistance must guarantee the producers of the basic agricultural product an adequate and lasting share in the resulting economic benefits.

5. Size Restrictions:

Total project costs must be between £70,000 and £6,000,000.

6. Programme Duration:

Member States are required to submit to the European Commission Sectoral Plans covering the agriculture sector for a period of up to five years. There are currently two UK Sectoral Plans: one covering crops, and one covering livestock and livestock products. Agriculture Departments will submit Operational Programmes for consideration by the Commission at six-monthly intervals, in June and December each year.

7. Submission of Applications/Proposals:

Grant applications can be submitted at any time.

The scheme is competitive; projects conforming most closely to the aims of the scheme will be shortlisted by Agriculture Ministries/Departments and submitted to the EC for approval.

Applications for individual projects must be received and acknowledged in writing before any work on a project is started. (Exceptions to this are: site purchase, obtaining planning permission; architect/consultancy work; obtaining quotations and ordering (but not taking delivery of) equipment.)

This will take approximately four weeks from the date of an application's despatch. The acknowledgement will indicate the earliest date when work may commence. For work starting between 1 January and 30 June in any year, application must be made at least four weeks in advance, and no later than 31 March. For work starting between 1 July and 31 December, application must be made at least four weeks in advance and no later than 30 September.

8. Other Restrictions:

Guidelines published by the European Commission in OJ L91; 6.4.90, outlined the following types of project as eligible for support: rationalising or developing the preparation and processing of agricultural products or recycling of by-products or manufacturing waste; improving marketing channels; applying new processing techniques, including the development of new products and by-products, or opening up new markets and innovative investments; and improving product quality. Priority may be given to projects improving market structures for agricultural products, particularly if they encourage the development of new outlets by facilitating the marketing of new products or of high quality products, including those grown organically.

The two UK Sectoral Plans, Crops and Livestock and Livestock Products cover the following agricultural commodities (including those produced by organic methods): (1) Crops: Cereals (including straw disposal; potatoes; horticultural produce (including ornamentals); oilseeds; field peas and beans; dried fodder; hops; (2) Livestock: Utilisation and recycling of waste and by-products; red meat; pigmeat; poultry; eggs; milk and milk products. Applicants should contact Agriculture Departments for a detailed summary of eligible projects within each of these sectors.

Applicants must be able to justify the need for grant aid, and each application must refer to a complete project or separate viable part of a project (phasing of projects into viable self-contained parts is acceptable). No more than 80 percent of project inputs may be the applicant's own produce, and at least 80 percent by volume of primary produce used as a result of the project must come from EC countries. Projects should not be solely concerned with hygiene upgrading.

9. Eligible Expenditure:

The following items or areas of expenditure are not eligible: land purchase costs; the purchase of buildings which have previously been used for the same purpose; working capital; items not coming into an applicant's beneficial ownership within four years after award of aid (including hire purchase and leasing arrangements); vehicles for external transportation (forklift trucks, or similar, used for internal transportation and handling are eligible); any second-hand equipment; harvesting equipment (items such as field rigs used to wrap and box vegetables and equipment primarily for processing and packing are eligible); own labour and equipment costs; costs related to the transfer and installation of existing plant and equipment into a new building or other place of work where the project will be realised; consumables; maintenance costs; and one-for-one replacement. The inclusion of any of these items would not normally render the whole project costs eligible for grant aid. Apart from land purchase costs, the value of these items must not make up more than 40 percent of total project costs, or the project will be ineligible.

10. Rate of Award:

Successful projects will normally be awarded a grant of up to 25 percent of eligible costs, up to a maximum grant of £900,000 (and up to 50 percent of eligible costs in Objective 1 regions – Northern Ireland in the UK). Projects must attract a UK grant of not less than 5 percent of eligible costs. Where this cannot be obtained from other sources, the appropriate Agriculture Ministry/Department will be prepared to consider providing a 'back-up' grant, but only if EAGGF assistance is awarded and the subsequent claim approved. Beneficiaries of EAGGF assistance must make a financial contribution of at least 25 percent of project costs in Objective 1 regions and 45 percent in other areas.

11. Payment Procedure:

EAGGF assistance is disbursed via the relevant Agriculture Ministry/Department. Grant is paid only after proven expenditure has been incurred and claimed.

12. Points to Note:

Regulation (EEC) 866/90 replaces Regulation (EEC) 355/77 (commonly referred to as FEOGA).

13. Application Procedure:

Applications are submitted on form MAP/1 (with one copy). Applicants should contact the relevant Ministry/Department (see 14) for advice and guidance with preparing an application.

14. Further Information:

England:
Ministry of Agriculture
    Fisheries and Food
Rural Structures and Grants Div.
Ergon-Nobel House, Room 324
17 Smith Square
London SW1P 3HX
Tel: (071) 238 6315/6317
Fax: (071) 238 6591

Wales:
Welsh Office Agriculture
    Department
Floor 2, Room 2003
Crown Buildings
Cathays Park
Cardiff CF1 3NQ
Tel: (0222) 825130
Fax: (0222) 823562

Scotland:
Scottish Office Agriculture and
    Fisheries Department
Pentland House
47 Robb's Loan
Edinburgh EII14 1TW
Tel: (031) 244 6388/9
Fax: (031) 244 6001

Northern Ireland:
Department of Agriculture for
    Northern Ireland
EC Division
Room 145
Dundonald House
Upper Newtownards Road
Belfast BT4 3SB
Tel: (0232) 650111 Ext. 799/277
Fax: (0232) 659856

EAGGF: PROCESSING AND MARKETING OF FISHERY AND AQUACULTURE PRODUCTS

1. Summary:

Under Regulation (EEC) 4042/89, financial assistance is available from the European Agricultural Guidance and Guarantee Fund: Guidance Section (EAGGF) for capital investments designed to improve the conditions under which fisheries and aquaculture products are processed and marketed. Investment needs have been identified in the following areas: the modernisation and increased efficiency of existing processing and marketing facilities; technical innovation; and improvements in hygiene standards needed to meet the requirements of new EC fish and shellfish hygiene legislation taking effect in 1993.

EAGGF financing takes place within the framework of Sectoral Plans drawn up by Member States. Eligible projects conforming most closely to the aims of the Regulation and to Sectoral Plan priorities are incorporated into Operational Programmes for consideration by the European Commission.

2. Awarding Body:

European Agricultural Guidance and Guarantee Fund: Guidance Section. Assistance is disbursed through the relevant Ministry/Agriculture Department – ie the Ministry of Agriculture, Fisheries and Food in England, the Scottish Office Agriculture and Fisheries Department, the Welsh Office Agriculture Department, and the Department of Agriculture for Northern Ireland.

3. Location Restrictions:

Available in any Member State of the European Community. Higher rates of assistance are available in Objective 1 regions (structurally underdeveloped). In the UK, Northern Ireland is the only Objective 1 region.

4. Sectoral Restrictions:

Priority may be given to investments undertaken by primary producers, producers' groups, associations and co-operatives.

5. Size Restrictions:

Total project costs must be between £25,000 and £6,000,000.

6. Programme Duration:

Regulation (EEC) 4042/89 came into force on 1 January 1990. Under this Regulation, each Member State is required to submit to the European Commission a Sectoral Plan covering the entire fisheries and aquaculture sector. The UK Sectoral Plan will run for three years, from 1991 to 1993. Agriculture Departments will submit Operational Programmes for consideration by the Commission at six-monthly intervals, in April and October each year.

7. Submission of Applications/Proposals:

Grant applications can be submitted at any time.

The scheme is competitive; projects conforming most closely to the aims of the scheme will be shortlisted by Agriculture Departments and submitted to the EC for approval.

Applications for individual projects must be received and acknowledged in writing before any work on a project is started. This will take at leat four weeks from the date of an application's despatch. Applications received between 16 August and 15 February will be eligible for the April Operational Programme. Work on these projects may have started (after acknowledgement) from 1 November. Applications received between 16 February and 16 August will be eligible for the October Operational Programme. Work on these projects may have started (after acknowledgement) from 1 May.

8. Other Restrictions:

Guidelines published by the European Commission in OJ L388; 30.12.89 outlined the following priority investment areas: the construction, modernisation and rationalisation of auction markets and halls for the first-hand sale of products landed by EC vessels; the storage, smoking and handling of fishery and aquaculture products; facilities for preparation for the first hand sale and filleting of fresh fish and the preparation of deep-frozen fish; the preparation of finished products from fish caught by and/or deep-frozen on board EC vessels; technically advanced production units, producing preserved and semi-preserved products; the development of new products and technologies based on the results of research, pilot and demonstration projects; improvement of the quality and hygiene of production and marketing processes; enhancement of the added value of production.

Priority will be given to projects which offer more in terms of investment and producer benefit than simply upgrading to meet legislative requirements.

The following investments are not eligible: investments at the retail level; product processing on board ship, fishery/aquaculture produce intended for purposes other than human consumption (except investments intended solely for the treatment, processing or marketing of fishery wastes), and vehicles used for the transport and distribution of fishery/aquaculture products; products not listed in Annex II of the Treaty of Rome, although consideration will be given in cases where the beneficiary has a direct contractual link with producers; projects in respect of which work commenced more the six months before the date on which the Commission receives the Operational Programme for which the project is to be be considered; and investments for the production of processed goods for which the existence of realistic potential outlets has not been demonstrated.

Applicants must be able to justify the need for grant aid, and each application must refer to a complete project or a separate viable part of a project (phasing of projects into viable self-contained parts is acceptable). At least 20 percent of the primary produce to be marketed/processed must come from fishermen other than the applicant, and at least 51 percent by volume of primary produce used as a result of the project must originate from landings by EC vessels.

9. Eligible Expenditure:

The following items or areas of expenditure are not eligible: land purchase costs; the purchase of buildings which have previously been used for the same purpose; working capital; items not coming into an applicant's beneficial ownership within four years after award of aid (including hire purchase and leasing arrangements); any second-hand equipment; own labour and equipment costs; costs related to the transfer and installation of existing plant and equipment into a new building or other place of work where the project will be realised; consumables; maintenance costs; and one-for-one replacement. The inclusion of some of these items would not render the whole project ineligible, but their cost would be deducted from the total project costs eligible for grant aid. Apart from land purchase costs, the value of these items must not make up more than 40 percent of the total project costs, or the project will be ineligible.

10. Rate of Award:

Successful projects will normally be awarded a grant of up to 30 percent of eligible costs, up to a maximum grant of £900,000 (and up to 50 percent of eligible costs in Objective 1 regions – Northern Ireland in the UK). Projects must attract a UK grant of not less than 5 percent of eligible costs. Where this cannot be obtained from other sources, the appropriate Agriculture Ministry/Department will be prepared to consider providing a 'back-up' grant, but only if EAGGF assistance is awarded and the subsequent claim approved.

Beneficiaries of EAGGF assistance must make a financial contribution of at least 25 percent of project costs in Objective I regions and 45 percent in other areas.

11. Payment Procedure:

EAGGF assistance is disbursed via the relevant Agriculture Ministry/Department. Grant is paid only after proven expenditure has been incurred and claimed.

12. Points to Note:

Regulation (EEC) No. 4042/89 came into force on 1 January 1990, replacing Regulation (EEC) 355/77 which also covered agricultural products.

13. Application Procedure:

Applications are submitted on form MAP/2 (with one copy). Applicants should contact the relevant Department for advice and guidance with preparing an application.

14. Further Information:

England:
Ministry of Agriculture
  Fisheries and Food
Rural Structures and Grants Div.
Ergon-Nobel House, Room 325b
17 Smith Square
London SW1P 3HX
Tel: (071) 238 6315/6316

Wales:
Welsh Office Agriculture
  Department
Floor 2
Crown Buildings
Cathays Park
Cardiff CF1 3NQ
Tel: (0222) 825130/825379

Scotland:
Scottish Office Agriculture and
  Fisheries Department
Pentland House
47 Robb's Loan
Edinburgh EH14 1TW
Tel: (031) 244 6388/7

Northern Ireland:
Department of Agriculture for
  Northern Ireland
EC Division
Room 145
Dundonald House
Upper Newtownards Road
Belfast BT4 35B
Tel:: (0232) 650111 Ext.799

PART ONE

INVESTMENT AND INFRASTRUCTURE FINANCING

1.3 OTHER SUPPORT

1.3 OTHER SUPPORT

EURATOM Loans

1. Summary:
Loans are available on terms reflecting market rates, for promoting the use of nuclear energy and thus reducing the Community's dependence on external energy supplies. Eligible projects are those relating to investment in nuclear power stations and industrial nuclear fuel cycle installations.

2. Awarding Body:
Commission of the European Communities.

3. Location Restrictions:
Available in any member state of the European Community.

4. Sectoral Restrictions:
Available to any individual, organisation or group of organisations investing in nuclear power stations or industrial nuclear fuel cycle installations.

5. Size Restrictions:
By a Council Decision of 23 April 1990 the ceiling for Euratom loans has been set at 4,000 MECU. There are no specified upper or lower limits to the size of project that can be aided.

6. Programme Duration:
There is no specified terminal date for the availability of Euratom loans.

7. Submission of Applications/Proposals:
Application can be made at any time directly to the Commission.

8. Other Restrictions on Eligibility:
The decision on whether to issue a loan is at the discretion of the Commission and decisions are made on a case-by-case basis.

9. Eligible Expenditure:
Eligible expenditure covers total project costs.

10. Rate of Award:
The rate of award is at the discretion of the Commission and is normally up to 20 percent of total project costs. The terms and interest rates reflect market conditions.

11. Payment Procedure:
The pattern of payment and repayment is decided on a case-by-case basis.

12. Points to Note:
None.

13. Application Procedure:
Application is made direct to the Commission of the European Communities.

14. Further Information:
European Commission
DG XVIII
Batiment Jean Monnet
L-2920 Luxembourg
Tel: (010 35 2) 43011

INTERNATIONAL INVESTMENT PARTNERS

1. Summary:
The European Commission's International Investment Partners (ECIIP) initiative is an experimental facility offering grants, interest-free loans and equity loans to promote joint ventures between firms located in EC Member States and firms located in Latin America, Asia and the Mediterranean. Financial support may be awarded for the following types of operation undertaken during the course of a joint investment project: the identification of potential projects and partners; operations prior to launching a joint venture; the financing of capital requirements; and the development of training and management expertise.

2. Awarding Body:
Commission of the European Communities, through approved financial intermediaries. In the UK, the Commonwealth Development Corporation (CDC), the Midland Bank, and Morgan Grenfell act as intermediaries for the scheme.

3. Location Restrictions:
The initiative is open to any national of an EC Member State or eligible country, whose domicile or registered office is located in that country. Firms from more than one EC Member State may apply jointly for support, providing that the third party in the joint venture comes from an eligible country. Eligible countries are:
- Latin America: Argentina, Bolivia, Brazil, Chile, Colombia, Ecuador, Mexico, Peru, Uruguay, Venezuela;
- Central America: Costa Rica, El Salvador, Guatemala, Honduras, Nicaragua, Panama;
- Asia: Bangladesh, Brunei, India, Indonesia, Malaysia, Pakistan, Phillipines, Singapore, Sri Lanka, Thailand;
- the Mediterranean: Algeria, Cyprus, Egypt, Israel, Jordan, Lebanon, Morocco, Malta, Syria, Tunisia, Turkey, Yugoslavia.

4. Sectoral Restrictions:
Individual firms with specific investment projects are eligible for interest-free loans to support the cost of finding suitable partners and for preliminary operations (eg feasibility studies, prototypes, etc). Subsequently, equity loans are available for the financing of capital requirements and to support staff and management training.

Grants for the identification of potential projects and partners (ie not in relation to any specific investment project) are restricted to financial institutions, Chambers of Commerce, professional associations and public agencies.

The participation of small and medium-sized firms is particularly encouraged.

5. Size Restrictions:

When co-financing a joint venture operation in respect of capital requirements and training and management expertise (through or with a financial institution), the European Commission's contribution will never exceed that of the financial institution in question.

6. Programme Duration:

There is no specified terminal date for this scheme.

7. Submission of Applications/Proposals:

Application is made to an approved financial intermediary, who assesses the proposal and, if successful, forwards it to the Commission. If the application is approved, a response will be received within 20 working days. For studies identifying potential partners and projects, support will be granted directly to the applicant.

8. Other Restrictions:

The following types of operations may receive support:

1. Identification of potential projects and partners (restricted to financial institutions, Chambers of Commerce, professional associations and public agencies, ie not for a firm's individual investment project); supports studies identifying countries and sectors suitable for involvement in joint ventures and the identification of local firms which would be suitable as joint venture partners. Grants are provided under an agreement which authorises both the EC and the sponsoring organisation to use the results of the studies undertaken;

2. Operations prior to launching a joint venture: interest-free loans are available to support: a search for partners for an individual investment project; marketing and feasibility studies; the setting up of pilot production units; and the manufacture of prototypes. The loan does not have to be repaid if the sponsor does not proceed with the project. (However, the Commission will be free to use the results of any study financed under the facility.) If a project resulting from an EC-funded study goes ahead, and the financial intermediary decides to fund the project itself, the loan must either be repaid to the EC, or the sponsoring firm may apply to the EC, via the financial intermediary, to convert it into a loan with equity features (ie an equity loan) or into an equity holding by the EC in the capital of the joint venture.

3. Financing of capital requirements: equity loans and equity holdings are available to support the setting-up of a new joint venture or the renovation and expansion of an existing one. The European sponsor must have, or take, an equity holding of at least 10 percent of the joint venture's capital;

4. Training and management expertise: equity loans are available to

support the setting up of new joint ventures or the renovation and expansion of existing ones through assistance with staff and management training, eg the training of local technicians and managers; the temporary appointment of consultants; secondments.

9. Eligible Expenditure:

Eligible expenditure depends on the type of project being undertaken (see 8).

10. Rate of Award:

The following rates of award apply:

1. Identification of potential projects and partners: grants covering up to 50 percent of costs, up to a grant ceiling of 100,000 ECU.
2. Operations prior to launching a joint venture: interest-free loans covering up to 50 percent of costs, up to a maximum loan of 250,000 ECU.
3. Financing of capital requirements: equity holdings or equity loans up to 20 percent of the joint venture's total capital, with a maximum loan of 500,000 ECU.
4. Training and management expertise: equity loans covering up to 50 percent of costs, up to a maximum loan of 250,000 ECU. When facilities 2, 3, and 4 are combined, the upper limit of financial support available is 500,000 ECU per investment project.

11. Payment Procedure:

When all terms and conditions surrounding the application have been satisfied, the EC and the financial intermediary concerned draw up a specific financial agreement. The financial intermediary then makes a back-to-back financial agreement with the applicant, after which the funds may be released. For studies identifying potential partners and projects, support will be granted directly to the applicant.

12. Points to Note:

Applications for assistance may be submitted by a firm in the EC, or a firm in an eligible country (see 3).

The willingness of a financial intermediary to support a project will depend, among other things, on its own investment portfolio at the time the application is made.

13. Application Procedure:

UK applicants should contact one of the EC-approved financial intermediaries who will then assess the proposal and send an application to the European Commission. If the application is approved, a reply will be received within 20 working days.

14. Further Information:

EC International Investment
 Partners
European Commission
DG I – External Relations
Rue de la Loi 200
B-1049 Brussels
Tel: (010 32 2) 235 4027
 – Mr P Defraigne (Director)
Tel: (010 32 2) 236 0549
 – Mr P Phillipe (Admin)

Mr Suratgar
Director
Morgan Grenfell
23 Great Winchester Street
London EC2P 2AX
Tel: (071) 588 4545
Fax: (071) 588 5598

Mr Brzozowsky
Business Development Adviser
Commonwealth Development
 Corporation (CDC)
1 Bessborough Gardens
London SW1V 2JQ
Tel: (071) 828 4488
Fax: (071) 828 6505

Mr Paul McCulloch
Asset Conversion Group
Midland Bank
110 Cannon Street
London EC4N 6AA
Tel: (071) 260 6317
Fax: (071) 260 4525

PART TWO

EMPLOYMENT AND TRAINING

2.0 OVERVIEW

Employment and training link the economic and social policies of the European Community, and accordingly, constitute an important aspect of Commission activities. The Commission's principal instrument for tackling employment and training-related problems is the European Social Fund – one of the three Structural Funds. Since it was established in 1957, the Social Fund has made financial assistance available to public authorities, private firms and voluntary bodies to support the cost of vocational training and job-creation schemes. As is the case with the other Structural Funds, projects must be wholly or partly financed from public funds in the beneficiary state. In other words, projects submitted by non-public sector organisations must attract support from a national public sector authority to qualify for support from the Social Fund. In the UK, public authorities most commonly associated with projects assisted by the Social Fund include local authorities, and the Training Agency (operating through Training and Enterprise Councils (TECs) in England and Wales and Local Enterprise Companies (LECs) in Scotland).

The European Social Fund contributes to the achievement of all five Objectives of the Single Act legislation (see page 4), but is primarily concerned with the achievement of Objectives 3 and 4. These apply across the whole Community and are aimed at combatting long-term unemployment and the occupational integration of young people. It is expected that projects falling within Objectives 3 and 4 will receive just over 12 percent of the total Structural Fund budget. When employment and training activities undertaken in Objective 1 regions are added to Objectives 3 and 4 activities, the total accounts for almost 20 percent of Structural Fund resources (representing almost half of the total European Social Fund budget).

A total of 7450 million ECU has been allocated from the Fund for the period 1989–93 for expenditure on Objectives 3 and 4. Of this, 4128 million ECU has been allocated to Community Support Frameworks (CSFs) covering the period 1990–92. These CSFs outline the key priorities for Fund activity over the three-year period.

The two principal types of activity supported by the Social Fund are: vocational training projects (accompanied where necessary by vocational guidance) and subsidies toward recruitment into newly created stable jobs and self-employment activities. Roughly 80 percent of Social Fund expenditure is devoted to training activities.

Up to 5 percent of the total Social Fund budget is set aside to support innovatory training and employment operations, studies and technical assistance, information exchange concerning technology transfer and guidance counselling for the long-term unemployed.

Implementing Regulation (EEC) 4255/88 specifies the types of activities eligible for Social Fund support as follows:

(a) the income of persons receiving vocational training;
(b) the costs of preparing, operating, managing and assessing training

operations including vocational guidance, costs of training teaching staff, and subsistence and travel costs of those covered by vocational training operations;

(c) the cost of granting recruitment subsidies for a maximum period of 12 months and costs associated with the creation of self-employed activities; the cost of recruitment subsidies of at least six months' duration per person associated with non-productive projects which fulfil a public need and have been relocated in Objective 1 regions;

(d) the cost of technical assistance and studies related to the implementation of the Social Fund Regulation; the cost of transnational exchange of information between undertakings related to the modernisation of production technology; the cost of guidance counselling for the reintegration of the long-term unemployed.

In Objective 1 regions eligible activities qualify for a Social Fund contribution of up to 75 percent of total expenditure and, as a general rule, at least 50 percent of the amount of public expenditure committed to a project. Elsewhere, the maximum Social Fund contribution is 50 percent of total costs and, as a general rule, at least 25 percent of the public expenditure committed to a project. The maximum level of recruitment subsidy permissible is determined annually at a rate equal to 30 percent of the average gross earnings of workers in the Member State concerned. Preparatory studies and technical assistance measures may attract up to 100 percent financing.

As with the other Structural Funds, recent reforms have shifted the operation of the Social Fund from a project-based to a programme-based approach, with operational programmes running for a three-year period within the content of agreed CSFs. In the UK, operational programmes are administered by a number of intermediary organisations. In Objective 2 regions (see page 23), applications will be channelled through a series of regional working groups and/or operational programme committees, set up to co-ordinate and administer measures funded by all of the Structural Funds. Applications covered by Objective 3 and Objective 4 operational programmes are co-ordinated by local authorities, TECs, LECs, voluntary organisations operating through the National Council for Voluntary Organisations, Industrial Common Ownership Movement, Women's Training Network, Industry Training Boards and the higher education sector.

The UK has been one of the chief beneficiaries of Social Fund assistance, receiving between 15 and 20 percent of the total Social Fund budget allocation in recent years. For the majority of firms in the UK, Social Fund support comes indirectly through jointly-funded Government programmes such as Employment Training and Youth Training, which address Objectives 3 (long-term unemployed) and Objectives 4 (youth unemployed), respectively. Further opportunities for setting up training programmes to address specific skill shortages within firms are being co-ordinated through the TECs and LECs, local authorities and other organisations mentioned earlier, under the auspices of the Business Growth Training Programme. Social Fund support plays an important role in funding training programmes in the UK, and under the new system of administration through agreed operational programmes, is accessible without the added complexity of making individual applications directly to Commission authorities.

The Social Fund is, therefore, the Community's central policy instrument for addressing employment-related problems which give rise to poor and unbalanced economic development. A number of other training programmes are designed to promote objectives such as integration into the Single Market, competitiveness of European industry, etc. These programmes differ from the Social Fund in that they are administered directly by the relevant Commission directorate and in most cases, application for support must be made direct to the Commission. The main programmes in this category are as follows.

COMETT (Education and Training for Technology) aims to improve the Community's technological base, by providing financial assistance for a wide range of transnational measures designed to strengthen and encourage co-operation between universities and industry in developing training programmes. Both initial and continuing training programmes, in advanced technology areas which will strengthen economic and social cohesion within the Community, are eligible. Application is made in response to calls for proposals published in the Official Journal.

ERASMUS promotes co-operation between higher education establishments in the Community, including staff and student exchanges, while the newer TEMPUS programme promotes similar ventures with Eastern Europe. LINGUA promotes training in the official languages of the Community, while the Young Worker Exchange Programme enables young people to experience working in another Member State. Finally, the Scientific and Executive Training Programmes support the cost of sending EC scientists and executives to Japan to benefit from Japanese expertise, and encourage the making of commercial contacts.

PART TWO

EMPLOYMENT AND TRAINING

2.1 EMPLOYMENT TRAINING

2.1 EMPLOYMENT TRAINING

COMETT II

1. Summary:

The second phase of the COMETT action programme in Education and Training for Technology provides grants for a range of transnational measures designed to strengthen and encourage co-operation between universities and industry in developing training programmes within the European framework. COMETT covers both initial and continuing training programmes, in particular advanced technology areas which, in the context of the completion of the Single European Market, will strengthen economic and social cohesion in the Community. In the course of COMETT II, measures will be implemented under the following broad headings (see 8 for further details): A. European Network; B. Transnational Exchanges; C. Joint projects for continuing training in advanced technology and for multi-media distance training; D. Complementary promotion and back-up measures.

COMETT II is set to run from 1 January 1990 to 31 December 1994, with a budget allocation of 200 MECU.

2. Awarding Body:

Commission of the European Communities.

3. Location Restrictions:

Available in any Member State of the European Community. EFTA countries may also participate in COMETT II. Universities and undertakings in EFTA countries may co-operate with each other on COMETT projects, provided that similar bodies from at least two Community Member States are also involved.

4. Sectoral Restrictions:

COMETT II is designed to stimulate co-operation between universities and industries. For the purposes of the programme, 'university' is used as a general term covering all types of post-secondary education and training establishments which offer, within the framework of initial and/or continuing training, qualifications or diplomas of that level. The term 'industries' covers all types of economic activity, including large and small and medium-sized businesses, whatever their legal status and manner of applying new technologies. It also covers independent economic organisations, in particular Chambers of Commerce and Industry and/or their equivalents, professional associations and organisations representing employers or employees.

Measures to be implemented under COMETT II are directed at trainees, including those who have completed their initial training, and at persons in active employment, including employers' and workers' representatives and the training officers concerned.

5. Size Restrictions:

There is no restriction on the size of measures to be implemented under the programme.

Within the overall budget allocation, Strand A activities (see 8) will be allocated up to 12 percent, Strand B up to 40 percent, Strand C up to 40 percent, and Strand D up to 8 percent.

6. Programme Duration:
COMETT II is set to run from 1 January 1990 to 31 December 1994.

7. Submission of Applications/Proposals:
Application is made within the deadlines specified in each of the Commission's invitations for proposals to be submitted, published in the Official Journal. The Commission has published an outline schedule of the planned calls for applications during COMETT II (subject to annual review). The provisional schedule for the next two years is as follows: in 1991, a restricted call may be issued under heading A to fill gaps in the regional patterns of UITPs, and also under headings B & C (for short courses). Under D there may be a further call for applications for preparatory visits. In 1992 an open call may be issued under headings A, B and C, no call is foreseen under D.

8. Other Restrictions:
The following measures will be implemented in the course of COMETT II:
  A. The development and reinforcement of university-industry training partnerships (UITPs) and the extension of the regional and sectoral European network, to further transnational co-operation, particularly through the identification and resolution of technology training needs; the development and exploitation of projects within the other strands of COMETT II; strengthening of co-operation and inter-regional transfer in the development of training for the needs of technology, their application and transfer; and the development of transnational sectoral networks.
  B. Transnational exchanges through the allocation of grants for students undergoing 3 to 12 months training in industry in another Member State; industrial placements from six months to two years to undertake an industrial development project following completion of initial training; personnel seconded from universities and industry to industry or a university respectively in another Member State to bring their skills to the industry or university in question for the improvement of the training activities and professional practices of the host organisations.
  C. Joint projects for continuing training, in particular in advanced technology and for multi-media distance training – ie briefly, training courses designed for rapid dissemination of the results of R & D in the field of new technologies and their application, and the transfer of technological innovation to new sectors; devising, developing and testing joint training projects; multilateral agreements for training aimed at establishing systems for distance learning utilising new training technologies and/or resulting in transferable training products; and operations (as above) initiated by employers' and workers' organisations.
  D. Complementary promotion and back-up measures covering support

for preparatory activities particularly for the less developed regions; structured exchanges of information and experience; setting up a data bank on COMETT projects, and electronic mail facilities between project partners; a programme of conferences, seminars, exhibitions, etc; analysis and monitoring of skills needed by industry and consequent training needs; identification of obstacles to transnational co-operation; and evaluation of COMETT II. Priority is given to training geared towards new skills, both in the growth technology industries and in more traditional sectors, and as regards technology transfer and administration.

9. Eligible Expenditure:

Eligible expenditure under each strand of the programme relates to the following:

A. European Network: support for activities with a European dimension and towards the functioning of the UITPs; additional expenditure by universities incurred in the preparation and implementation of joint training projects may qualify for a higher rate of award (see 10).

B. Transnational Exchanges: support for direct and indirect mobility costs, the costs of organising and monitoring activities implemented and, where necessary, of foreign language preparation for grant recipients.

C. The costs of joint projects for continuing training, especially in advanced technologies, and for multi-media distance training; additional expenditure by universities in the preparation and implementation of joint projects may qualify for a higher rate of award (see 10).

D. The costs of complementary promotion and back-up measures.

10. Rate of Award:

The rates of award under each strand of COMETT II are as follows:

A. European Networks: up to 50 percent of eligible expenditure, reducing progressively with a ceiling per UITP of 70,000 ECU, 60,000 ECU and 50,000 ECU respectively for the first three years (however, in certain exceptional cases, the contribution may exceed three years). Additional expenditure incurred by universities may, if necessary, be financed up to 100 percent.

B. Transnational Exchanges: up to 6,000 ECU for twelve months for students undergoing three to twelve months' training in another Member State; up to 25,000 ECU for 24 months for placements of new graduates of between six to 24 months; up to 15,000 ECU for three months for personnel seconded to other Member States. Shorter contracts will receive pro rata awards.

C. Joint projects: up to 50 percent of total expenditure, generally up to a maximum of 30,000 ECU for crash training courses, and 50,000 ECU per project for devising, developing and testing joint training projects and for multilateral agreements for training. Additional expenditure incurred by universities may, if necessary, be financed up to 100 percent.

D. Complementary promotion and back-up measures: up to 100 percent of the annual expenditure committed for these initiatives.

11. Payment Procedure:
Payment varies according to the nature of the project and is decided on a case-by-case basis.

12. Points to Note:
COMETT II aims to reinforce training, in particular in advanced technology, the development of highly skilled human resources and the competitiveness of European industry. It is centred on the changing skill requirements of industry and its personnel requirements which necessitate complementary action both in the Member States and at Community level. COMETT II will contribute to the utilisation and exploitation of the results, methods and tools of technology developed by EC policy for R & D, and is intended to facilitate innovation and technology transfer as well as the balanced economic and social development of the Community.

Council Decision (EEC) 27/89 adopting COMETT II was published in Official Journal No L13; 17.1.89.

13. Application Procedures:
All the information necessary for the submission of applications is given in the Guide for Applicants which can be requested by writing to the COMETT Technical Assistance Unit. The Guide contains application forms, a description of the Programme, conditions of eligibility, and criteria and principles governing the award of Community support.

14. Further Information:
European Commission
DG V
Task Force Human Resources
   Education, Training & Youth
Rue de la Loi 200
B-1049 Brussels
Tel: (010 32 2) 235 1111
Telex: 21877 COMEU B

The Guide for Applicants is
   available from:
COMETT Technical
   Assistance Unit
Avenue de Cortenberg 71
B-1040 Brussels
Tel: (010 32 2) 733 9755
Fax: (010 32 2) 734 5641

The UK contact is:
Miss E M A Moss
UK COMETT Liaison Office
Department of Education and Science
Room 6/7A
Elizabeth House
York Road
London SE1 7PH
Tel: (071) 934 9654/9385
Fax: (071) 934 9082

ERASMUS

1. Summary:

The ERASMUS programme (European Community Action Scheme for the Mobility of University Students) promotes and supports the mobility of university students and staff in the European Community, and greater co-operation between universities in the field of vocational training. The programme includes the following four types of action (see 8 for further details): establishment and operation of a European University Network; student grant scheme; measures to promote mobility through the academic recognition of diplomas and periods of study; complementary measures to promote student mobility in the Community.

The current phase of ERASMUS is set to run until 1994. A budget of 192 MECU has been allocated to cover the three years from 1990 to 1992.

2. Awarding Body:

Commission of the European Communities. Student grants are administered through the UK ERASMUS Student Grants Council.

3. Location Restrictions:

Available in any Member State of the European Community. EFTA countries and Liechtenstein may also participate in the programme but will not be eligible for EC funding.

4. Sectoral Restrictions:

ERASMUS is open to any post-secondary education and training establishment (and staff and students at such establishments) which offers, where appropriate within the framework of advanced training, qualifications or diplomas at that level. ERASMUS covers all subject areas taught at university level, including language and teacher training. Research and technological development activities are not covered.

5. Size Restrictions:

None.

6. Programme Duration:

The current phase of ERASMUS runs until 1994.

7. Submission of Applications/Proposals:

Applications may be submitted at any time, but must be made at least six months before any visit is due to take place.

8. Other Restrictions:

ERASMUS covers four Action Lines:

1. Establishment and operation of a European University Network, designed to stimulate Community-wide exchange of students and to allow students of one university to undertake a fully recognised period of study in at least one other Member State, as an integral part of their academic qualification. Universities receive support for each joint programme in which they participate. Support is also available for exchanges allowing teaching staff to carry out integrated teaching assignments in another Member State; joint curriculum development

projects; the organisation of short, intensive teaching programmes for students from several Member States; visits for teaching staff and unviersity administrators for the preparation of integrated study programmes; and for teaching staff to conduct a series of specialised lectures.

2. Student Grants scheme: supports students (up to doctorate level) who carry out a recognised part of their higher education in another Member State. Priority is given to student mobility organised within the European University Network.

3. Measures to promote mobility through the academic recognition of diplomas and periods of study: supports the pilot European Community Course Credit Transfer System (ECTS) and centres facilitating the exchange of information on the academic recognition of diplomas from other Member States (particularly where the information exchange is computerised).

4. Complementary measures: support for associations and consortia of universities, teaching of administrative staff and students; publications; other initiatives promoting inter-university co-operation in the field of vocational training; dissemination of information on ERASMUS; and an annual ERASMUS prize, for an outstanding contribution to the development of EC inter-university co-operation.

9. Eligible Expenditure:
Eligible expenditure relates to the costs of the action being undertaken.

10. Rate of Award:
The rate of award varies depending on the measure undertaken.

11. Payment Procedure:
Payment procedures vary with the type of action being undertaken; full details are available from the ERASMUS Bureau.

12. Points to Note:
Council Decision (EEC) 327/87 adopting the ERASMUS programme was published in OJ L166; 25.6.87. An invitation to tender was published in OJ C199; 8.8.90, concerning the undertaking of an evaluation study of ERASMUS.

13. Application Procedure:
Application is by form, available as part of the Programme Guidelines for Applicants from the ERASMUS Bureau.

14. Further Information:

Mrs A Trusso
ERASMUS Bureau
Rue d'Arlon 15
B-1040 Brussels
Tel: (010 32 2) 233 0111
Fax: (010 32 2) 233 0150
Telex: 63528

UK ERASMUS Student Grants
 Council
The University
Canterbury
Tel: (0227) 762712
Fax: (0227) 762711

LINGUA

1. Summary:

The LINGUA programme supports training within the European Community in the official languages of the Community. LINGUA aims to promote a quantitative and qualitative improvement in EC foreign language training and to ensure the necessary levels of foreign language expertise in the workforce, enabling EC enterprises to take full advantage of the Single Market. LINGUA provides grants in support of mobility schemes and innovative projects concerned with the initial and in-service training of foreign language teachers, language learning in vocational and higher education, and the setting up of strategies for language training in business and commerce.

Five main action areas have been identified: I. Measures to promote in-service training of foreign language teachers; II. Measures to promote the learning of foreign languages in universities, and develop the initial training of foreign-language teachers; III. Measures to promote the development of foreign language teaching in the business community; IV. Measures to promote educational exchanges for young people; V. Complementary measures.

This description focuses on Action III; brief details of the other action areas can be found in Section 12.

LINGUA is set to run from 1st January 1990 to 31 December 1994 with a budget allocation of 200 MECU. The bulk of the LINGUA budget is being allocated to Actions I, II and IV.

2. Awarding Body:

Commission of the European Community.

3. Location Restrictions:

Available in any Member State of the European Community. In most cases, projects require participants established in two different Member States, one participant must be established in the Member State in which the chosen language is spoken. Priority will be given to the less-used Community languages.

4. Sectoral Restrictions:

Applications will be considered from: education and research establishments; bodies actively involved in developing training materials and/or certification; professional associations; local, regional and national organisations such as Language Export Centres and Chambers of Commerce; and recognised economic development agencies including local authorities. Representatives from professional associations of small and medium-sized enterprises (SMEs) and 'trainers' in SMEs are eligible for study visits only.

5. Size Restrictions:

None, although the needs of small and medium-sized enterprises are particularly considered.

6. Programme Duration:

LINGUA is set to run from 1 January 1990 to 31 December 1994.

7. Submission of Applications/Proposals:

Applications should be submitted to the designated UK national authority responsible for the administration and implementation of LINGUA (see 14). Applications are accepted on a continuous basis, with annual deadlines of 1 April and 1 October. Applications for study visits (measure C) are likely to have to be submitted six months before the visit is due to take place.

8. Other Restrictions:

Languages covered are: Spanish, Danish, German, Greek, English, French, Irish, Italian, Letzeburgesch, Dutch and Portuguese, when taught as foreign languages.

Action III of the LINGUA programme is designed to promote the development of foreign language teaching and learning in the business community. It provides for a series of measures which cover the essential stages in the setting-up of appropriate language training strategies and the design of relevant training curricula and materials. There is also provision for a study visit scheme. It is not designed to provide financial support to individual firms for giving foreign language training to their workforces. The measures covered are as follows:

- A. Strategies for language training: the development and dissemination of linguistic audit techniques; the development of language training curricula and certification systems; pilot projects developing innovative teaching materials and self-teaching methods. Priority will be given to the following sectors over the years 1990 to 1992: the automobile repair industry; tourism, hotel and catering; road transport; and local government and administration departments directly involved in establishing and maintaining links with other EC Member States.
- B. Developing mobility and linguistic exchanges, for representatives of small and medium-sized firms and relevant professional and workers organisations, and for trainers working in the field of foreign language teaching in a business environment.

9. Eligible Expenditure:

Eligible expenditure varies according to the measures being undertaken.

10. Rate of Award:

No specific rates of award are specified under Action III.

11. Payment Procedure:

Payment procedure varies according to measures undertaken.

12. Points to Note:

Council Decision (EEC) 489/89 adopting LINGUA was published in OJ L239; 16.8.89.

LINGUA involves various Commission measures to support and complement the activities of Member States in the field of foreign language teaching and training. As well as Action III LINGUA covers the following main Action Areas:

- I. Measures to promote the in-service training of foreign language teachers and trainers: grants to enable foreign language teachers and trainers to take part in in-service training courses and activities;

assistance with the setting up of European Cooperation Programmes (ECPs) between in-service training establishments in different Member States. (There will be no funding for ECPs until August 1991.)
- II. Measures to promote the learning of foreign languages in universities and other higher education institutions, in particular, to support the initial training of future foreign language teachers; support for Inter-University Cooperation Programmes (ICPs) in the teaching of LINGUA programme languages, when taught as foreign languages; grants for individual foreign language students to spend periods of time studying in another Member State (generally within an ICP); and mobility grants for teachers and administrators. (This Action is managed jointly with the ERASMUS programme.)
- IV. Measures to promote educational exchanges for young people: grants for preparatory visits; and grants for young people involved in exchanges.
- V. Complementary measures: the necessary technical assistance at Community level to underpin LINGUA activities.

The Commission published a call for tenders for an organisation to provide assistance with the animation, coordination and technical administration of the programme (Official Journal No C207; 12.8.89); deadline 15 November 1989.

13. Application Procedure:
Applications should be submitted to the designated UK national authority responsible for the administration and implementation of LINGUA.

14. Further Information:
In England & Wales:
UK LINGUA Unit
Seymour Mews House
Seymour Mews
London W1H 9PE
Tel: (071) 224 1477
Fax: (071) 224 1906

LINGUA Bureau
European Commission
2/3 Place du Luxembourg
B-1040 Brussels
Tel: (010 32 2) 233 0111
Fax: (010 32 2) 233 0150

In Scotland:
The LINGUA Office
The Central Bureau
3 Bruntsfield Crescent
Edinburgh EH10 4HD
Tel: (031) 447 8024
Fax: (031) 452 8569

In Northern Ireland:
The LINGUA Office
Central Bureau
16 Malone Road
Belfast BT9 5BN
Tel: (0232) 664418/9
Fax: (0232) 661275

TEMPUS

1. Summary:

The TEMPUS programme (Trans-European Mobility Programme for University Studies) aims to enable higher education establishments and industry in EC countries and Central/Eastern Europe to co-operate in meeting the vocational training needs of Central and Eastern Europe. The programme will operate by: promoting staff and student exchanges and mobility; improving training in Central and Eastern European countries and encouraging co-operation with EC partners; providing industrial placements; and increasing opportunities for the teaching and learning of foreign languages in Central and Eastern European countries.

For the first year of operation, the programme was allocated a budget of 20 MECU, covering projects in Poland and Hungary only.

2. Awarding Body:

Commission of the European Communities.

3. Location Restrictions:

Available in any Member State of the European Community. In Central and Eastern Europe, eligible countries are those designated as eligible for economic aid under Regulation (EEC) 3906/89. Currently Hungary, Poland, Bulgaria, Czechoslovakia and Yugoslavia have been designated as eligible (OJ L257; 21.9.90). EFTA countries, the USA, Canada, Japan, Australia, New Zealand and Turkey may also participate in TEMPUS, but are not eligible to receive EC funding.

4. Sectoral Restrictions:

TEMPUS is open to all categories of higher education establishment and industry, including public and local authorities, private firms, chambers of commerce and industry, professional bodies, associations and employer or employee organisations.

Joint European Projects (JEPs) (see 8) must include at least one university (ie all types of post-secondary vocational training establishment) or enterprise (ie all types of economic activity) from a Central/Eastern European country and partners in at least two Community Member States.

5. Size Restrictions:

None.

6. Programme Duration:

TEMPUS has been adopted to run for five years from 1 July 1990, with an initial pilot phase of three years.

7. Submission of Applications/Proposals:

Applications are assessed as they are received, and decisions taken on a continuous basis. The final application deadline for projects due to start in the academic year 1991/92 was 15 March 1991. The deadline for the academic year 1992/93 is 30 November 1991.

8. Other Restrictions:

TEMPUS covers three Action Lines:

1. Joint European Projects (JEPs): linking universities and/or enterprises in Central/Eastern Europe with EC partners. Grants may be awarded for: co-operative education and training actions (eg development and organisation of mobility programmes, curriculum development, continuing education and retraining schemes, development of open and distance learning provision); structural development of higher education (eg creation of new or restructuring of existing higher education centres/establishments, upgrading of facilities, development of universities' capacities to co-operate with industry); and sector specific actions (eg development of education/training capacities at higher education level in selected priority areas).
2. Mobility Grants for Staff and Students: grants for staff (higher education teachers, administrative staff, and training staff from private enterprises) for training and teaching assignments, practical placements and short visits for specific activities, and grants for students for study periods and practical placements – all involving moving from Central/Eastern Europe to the EC or vice versa;
3. Complementary Activities: support for European associations in higher education; publications and information activities; surveys and studies; and youth exchanges.

TEMPUS will concentrate initially on the following priority subject areas: management and business administration; applied economics; applied sciences, technologies and engineering; modern European languages; agriculture and agro-business; environmental protection; social and economic sciences; medicine; and fine arts (Czechoslovakia only).

9. Eligible Expenditure:
Eligible expenditure relates to the total costs of the approved project.

10. Rate of Award:
The rate of award varies depending on the type of project undertaken.

11. Payment Procedure:
Payment procedure varies depending on the nature of the project, and is decided on a case-by-case basis.

12. Points to Note:
Council Decision (EEC) 233/90 adopting TEMPUS was published in OJ L131; 23.5.90. TEMPUS is intended to complement other EC education and training programmes such as ERASMUS, COMETT and LINGUA.

13. Application Procedure:
The TEMPUS Vademecum and application forms are available from the TEMPUS Office in Brussels.

All Joint European Project (JEP) applications should be sent to the EC TEMPUS Office in Brussels. Block applications for mobility awards, organised within the framework of a JEP, should be submitted as an integral part of the JEP application by the consortium of organisations concerned.

Individual applications for mobility grants from staff and students not participating in a JEP should be sent by EC applicants to the EC TEMPUS

Office, and by applicants from Central/Eastern European countries to the national TEMPUS office in those countries.

14. Further Information:
TEMPUS Office
Rue de Treves 45
B-1040 Brussels
Tel: (010 32 2) 238 7833
Fax: (010 32 2) 238 7733

EUROPEAN SOCIAL FUND

1. Summary:
The European Social Fund (ESF), one of the three Community Structural Funds, aims to improve employment opportunities within the Community by funding vocational training and employment creation measures contributing to the attainment of the five objectives agreed in the Single Act, namely: the development and structural adjustment of underdeveloped regions (Objective 1); converting regions seriously affected by industrial decline (Objective 2); combatting long-term unemployment (Objective 3); facilitating the occupational integration of young people (Objective 4); promoting the development of rural areas (Objective 5b). Priority use of ESF assistance is directed towards Objectives 3 and 4. With respect to Objectives 1, 2 and 5b, the ESF can act in concert with the European Regional Development Fund (ERDF) and the European Agricultural Guidance and Guarantee Fund: Guidance Section (EAGGF), as appropriate, to support approved employment and training measures.

The ESF will co-finance measures within the context of operational programmes undertaken by various intermediary organisations (see 13). The following types of activity are eligible for support: vocational training operations; subsidies in relation to recruitment to new permanent jobs and for the creation of self-employed activities. Up to 5 percent of the total ESF budget can be directed towards relevant innovatory training and employment operations, studies and technical assistance, information exchange in relation to technology transfer and guidance counselling for the long-term unemployed.

2. Awarding Body:
European Social Fund. Applications in the UK must be channelled through the relevant intermediary organisation/sector who are responsible for selecting projects for support and recommending them to the Employment Department for formal approval (see 13).

3. Location Restrictions:
Assistance granted in respect of Objectives 3 and 4 is available throughout the European Community. ESF assistance granted in respect of a plan which includes the European Regional Development Fund (ERDF) and/or

European Agricultural Guidance and Guarantee Fund (EAGGF) support under Objectives 1, 2 or 5(b) is restricted to regions designated under each of these, respectively (for a full list of qualifying regions see the European Regional Development Fund).

4. Sectoral Restrictions:
None.

5. Size Restrictions:
Applications by, or in respect of, individuals are not eligible for support.

6. Programme Duration:
There is no specified terminal date for the activities of the ESF.

Current Community Support Frameworks (CSFs), outlining how Social Fund Assistance will be implemented, cover the period 1990–93. Within these CSFs, operational programmes outline groups of individual projects or measures to be supported throughout the lifetime of the agreed CSF. The CSFs and operational programmes may be revised annually if there are changes in the labour market. Progress of individual projects will be reviewed yearly, and funding adjusted if necessary.

7. Submission of Applications/Proposals:
Individual projects will receive support within the context of agreed operational programmes which outline groups of projects or measures to be assisted throughout the period of a CSF. (CSFs outline the broad measures which will receive Social Fund assistance over a three to five year period.)

Individual projects are channelled through intermediate organisations, which submit selected projects to the Employment Department for formal approval.

8. Other Restrictions:
ESF assistance is implemented in the form of operational programmes, outlining a series of projects or measures to be supported.

Of the operational programmes approved in the UK, fifteen cover Objective 2 regions over the period 1990–91, three cover Objective 3 measures (for the long-term unemployed), and a further three cover Objective 4 measures (the occupational integration of young people) over the period 1990–92. Operational programmes in Objective 2 regions cover: Yorkshire/Humberside; the North-West, West Midlands, Cumbria and Eastern Scotland. The priorities for action are: small business development training and employment; tourism-related training and employment; research and development training; and training measures aimed at improving the regions' environment and image. Operational programmes taking the form of Integrated Development Operations (IDOs), combining assistance from several of the Community Structural Funds, cover: Western Scotland, North-West England, North-East England, West Midlands, Eastern England, Clwyd, and Industrial South Wales.

The Objective 3 and 4 operational programmes cover the following:

For the long-term unemployed (Objective 3):

(1) Training (327 MECU): to be carried out by local authorities, the higher education sector, industry training boards, the voluntary

sector, Training and Enterprise Councils (TECs) in England and Wales, and Local Enterprise Companies (LECs) in Scotland (mainly through the Employment Training scheme);

(2) Job creation measures (68 MECU): to be carried out by local authorities, by offering premiums for new permanent jobs. The creation of self-employment opportunities will be undertaken by the TECs and LECs (through the Enterprise Allowance scheme), and the local authorities promoting Local Enterprise Agency schemes.

(3) Special assistance for women, migrants, and handicapped people (118 MECU): providing good quality vocational training, job creation, and innovatory transnational projects, to be implemented by the TECs and LECs.

For the young unemployed:

(1) Vocational training (308 MECU): mainly through the Employment Training scheme.

(2) Higher skills training (96 MECU): to be provided by the TECs and LECs, the higher education sector, local authorities, industry training boards and the voluntary sector.

(3) Women, migrants and handicapped young people (64 MECU): the provision of good quality vocational training, the creation of stable jobs and innovatory projects, to be run mainly through the local authorities and the TECs and LECs.

9. Eligible Expenditure:

Eligible expenditure for ESF part-financing includes:

(a) the income of persons receiving vocational training;

(b) the costs of preparing, operating, managing and assessing training operations including vocational guidance, costs of training teaching staff and subsistence and travel costs of those covered by vocational training operations;

(c) the cost of granting recruitment subsidies for a maximum period of twelve months and costs associated with the creation of self-employed activities; the cost of recruitment subsidies of at least six months' duration per person associated with non-productive projects which fulfil a public need and are located in Objective 1 regions;

(d) the cost of technical assistance and studies related to the implementation of the ESF Regulation; the cost of transnational exchange of information between undertakings related to the modernisation of production technology; the cost of guidance counselling for the reintegration of the long-term unemployed.

10. Rate of Award:

The rate of award in respect of the various Objectives (see 1) is subject to the following ceilings:

– in Objective 1 regions (in the UK – Northern Ireland), a maximum of 75 percent of total costs, and as a general rule, at least 50 percent of public expenditure on qualifying activities;

– elsewhere, a maximum of 50 percent of total costs, and as a general rule, at least 25 percent of public expenditure on qualifying activities.

Rates of award for individual measures forming part of operational programmes are differentiated in accordance with agreements concluded in the relevant CSF. With respect to recruitment subsidies, the maximum eligible amount per person and per week is determined each year at a rate equal to 30 percent of the average gross earnings of individual workers in the relevant Member State.

11. Payment Procedure:
The Employment Department will make payments through the relevant intermediary organisation/sector.

12. Points to Note:
Measures covered by the agreed operational programmes include many of the existing employment and training schemes, such as Youth Training, Employment Training, Enterprise Allowance etc.

13. Application Procedures:
Individual organisations wishing to apply for Social Fund support should contact the appropriate coordinating body. In Objective 2 regions, applications will be coordinated by a series of regional working groups and/or operational programme committees. Applications for support under Objectives 3 and 4 (nationwide) should be made to the relevant organisation/sector: Training and Enterprise Councils (TECs) in England and Wales, and Local Enterprise Companies (LECs) in Scotland; the National Council for Voluntary Organisations (NCVO); local authorities; Industrial Common Ownership Movement; Women's Training Network; Industry Training Boards; or higher education sector.

Any organisation uncertain as to which co-ordinating body covers their interests should contact the Employment Department. The European Social Fund Unit of the Department has produced guidance notes on application procedures, available from the address below.

14. Further Information:

In Great Britain:
Employment Department
European Social Fund Section
Civil Service College
11 Belgrave Road
London SW1V 1RB
Tel: (071) 834 6644

In Northern Ireland:
Dept. of Economic Development
European Communities Branch
The Arches Centre
11–13 Bloomfield Avenue
Belfast BT5 5HD
Tel: (0232) 732411

Initial enquiries to find out which intermediary organisation should be contacted:
Tel: (071) 834 6644
Ext.1352 Scotland and the North of England
1340 North and South-West England
1337 Yorkshire, Humberside and East Anglia
1338 West and East Midlands, South-East England (south of the Thames)
1345 South-East England (north of the Thames)
1336 Wales

EXECUTIVE TRAINING IN JAPAN

1. Summary:
Grants are available from the European Commission to sponsor executives from export-oriented firms in Europe on an eighteen-month training course in Japan. The executives undertake a twelve-month full-time intensive course in business Japanese followed by a six-month attachment to one or perhaps two Japanese companies normally operating in a related field. There is also a parallel programme of seminars, conferences, visits to firms and professional contacts.

2. Awarding Body:
Commission of the European Communities. The scheme is administered in the UK by KPMG Peat Marwick McLintock.

3. Location Restrictions:
Applicants must be EC nationals. Sponsoring companies will normally be EC-based.

4. Sectoral Restrictions:
None, although the applicant's firm must either be doing business with Japan or be planning to do so. Bodies such as Chambers of Commerce which are responsible for promoting exports to Japan by small and medium-sized firms on a sectoral or regional basis may also submit applications.

5. Size Restrictions:
There is no restriction on the size of an applicant's firm; applications from small and medium-sized firms are particularly welcome. Only one individual per group of companies is eligible for full assistance; for subsequent placements, the firm must put forward 50 percent of the costs at the start of the scheme.

6. Programme Duration:
There is no specified terminal date for this scheme.

7. Submission of Applications/Proposals:
The programme is open to applications on an annual basis. Applications may be submitted at around the same time each year; the 1990 programme opened to applications in February and the closing date was 1 July 1990. Successful 1990 applicants will undertake their training programme from May 1991 to November 1992.

8. Other Restrictions:
Applicants should be of graduate calibre, aged 25 – 35, with a minimum of two years' business experience. They must have a linguistic ability of 'better than A-level standard', international exposure (ie show an ability to live in different environments), and demonstrate an interest in international business.

Applicants will normally be working in (or be intended to occupy) an export-related or international capacity. The programme aims to extend to as many areas as possible and therefore the candidates' business backgrounds will vary from marketing to technical and even scientific fields.

9. Eligible Expenditure:
The assistance is available towards a monthly living and rent allowance, language tuition costs and allowances towards installation and resettlement at the commencement and completion of the Programme. The cost of travel to and from Japan at the start and end of the secondment is not eligible and must be paid by the applicant's firm.

10. Rate of Award:
The level of assistance is decided on a case-by-case basis. Firms are expected to contribute to the participants' upkeep.

Firms sponsoring a second or subsequent participant must pay approximately 50 percent of the total costs, and 100 percent of total costs for every additional candidate.

11. Payment Procedure:
Successful applicants receive a monthly allowance, as well as one-off payments for installation and resettlement.

12. Points to Note:
None.

13. Application Procedure:
Application should be made by the sponsoring company, application forms are available from the address below. Applications are reviewed and, where necessary, supplementary information is elicited from both the applicants and their sponsoring firms. Nominations are then forwarded to the European Commission for shortlisting.

14. Further Information:
Ms A MacNamara
KPMG Peat Marwick McLintock
PO Box 486
London EC4V 3PD
Tel: (071) 236 8000 Ext.4224

SCIENTIFIC TRAINING IN JAPAN

1. Summary:
Grants are available from the European Commission to sponsor research scientists from universities and public sector laboratories on a fifteen to twenty-one month placement in Japan. Participants undertake a three-month full-time language course in Japan, followed by twelve to eighteen months full-time in a Japanese host laboratory.

The aim of the programme is to improve European research scientists' personal contacts with Japan, aiding Europe to benefit from advances in Japanese research.

Researchers will concentrate on fields in which Community programmes exist or are being explored and in which Japanese work is currently and potentially interesting.

2. Awarding Body:
Commission of the European Communities.

3. Location Restrictions:
Applicants must be EC nationals.

4. Sectoral Restrictions:
The exchange programme is intended for researchers from national laboratories and universities; private sector research institutes are excluded.

5. Size Restrictions:
None.

6. Programme Duration:
There is no specified terminal date for this programme. It is, however, subject to annual review.

7. Submission of Applications/Proposals:
The programme is open to applications on an annual basis. The 1990 application deadline was 30 April, with participants commencing their placements in Autumn 1990.

8. Other Restrictions:
Applicants should normally be between the ages of 25-35, have a reasonable command of English and have completed their doctorate degree or acquired equivalent professional experience.

Participants are required to submit regular reports and return to work in Europe immediately after participation in the programme. When selecting candidates, the Commission will consider: (a) the relevance of the research theme to current Community research programmes, or to fields which might be developed in the future; (b) the interest to Europe of current or planned Japanese work in the field; (c) the existing contacts, if any, between European and Japanese research in the field; (d) the interest of the candidate's European research institute (if applicable) in his participation in the programme and their willingness to create follow-up links. Candidates should indicate preferences for a certain laboratory in Japan, or existing contacts. However, identification of the most suitable Japanese host laboratory and the acceptance of the European scientist there will be negotiated between the Commission, the successful candidate and the Japanese authorities.

9. Eligible Expenditure:
The assistance is available towards a monthly living allowance, travel expenses between Europe and Japan, an installation allowance and language course costs.

10. Rate of Award:
Participants are paid a fixed monthly allowance of 420.000 Yen (approx. £1800) as well as travel costs, an installation allowance and fees for language courses.

11. Payment Procedure:

The living allowance is paid monthly. All other eligible expenses are covered by one-off payments.

12. Points to Note:

Participants may be placed in any national research laboratory supervised by the Japanese Science and Technology Agency, Ministry for International Trade and Industry, Ministry for Agriculture, Forestry and Fisheries, or other Ministries, or research institutes attached to national universities.

13. Application Procedure:

Application is by form available from the Commission. Applications are reviewed and selected candidates invited to Brussels for an interview. A shortlist is drawn up and reviewed in conjunction with the Japanese authorities.

14. Further Information:

Mr G Boggio
European Commission
DG XII-G-3
Rue de la Loi 200
B-1049 Brussels
Tel: (010 32 2) 235 3990/7509

YOUNG WORKER EXCHANGE PROGRAMME

1. Summary:

The Young Worker Exchange Programme is designed to enable young people to gain vocational experience in another European country. The programme aims to develop the vocational qualifications and enrich the practical experience of young people, bringing them into contact with the working environment of another EC country.

The exchanges range from short-term, lasting three weeks to three months and including study visits, work placements and a brief experience of the working environment, to longer-term work placements of four to sixteen months, preceded by a language and orientation course.

2. Awarding Body:

Commission of the European Communities.

In the UK, the programme is administered by offices of the Central Bureau for Educational Visits and Exchanges (CBEVE).

3. Location Restrictions:

Available in any Member State of the European Community. Participants must be a national of an EC Member State.

4. Sectoral Restrictions:

Application can be made by colleges or employers (in any sector) on behalf of a group of young people, or by young people themselves.

5. Size Restrictions:
To be eligible for grant aid, projects must be of a minimum duration of three weeks.

6. Programme Duration:
The programme is set to run until 31 December 1991. Before 31 March 1991, the Council will examine a proposal for a new Young Worker Exchange Programme.

7. Submission of Applications/Proposals:
Application can be made at any time.

8. Other Restrictions:
The programme is open to young people aged between 18 and 28, who are either already employed or available for employment (ie not in full-time education), and who have completed basic vocational training, or have similar work experience. Preference is given to participants who have not attended university. Individual young unemployed people are also encouraged to apply.

Projects should focus on vocational rather than social or cultural activities and may be either short or long-term. Short-term projects (3 weeks – 3 months) involve an organised programme of meetings and industrial visits. A short language course and work placement with a host employer may be included. Long-term projects involve a period of practical work experience with an employer in the host country (4 – 16 months), almost always including a period of language tuition at the outset. Work placements normally complement participants' past training and work experience.

9. Eligible Expenditure:
The Commission will contribute to the cost of accommodation, meals, language training courses (in some cases), and return travel expenses.

10. Rate of Award:
The Commission will cover general living expenses and up to 75 percent of participants' return travel expenses. Participants are expected to provide their own spending money.

11. Payment Procedure:
The European Commission's contribution will be made to the national body co-ordinating the projects.

12. Points to Note:
None.

13. Application Procedure:
Application should be made to the Central Bureau who will in turn submit it to the European Commission.

Young Worker Exchange Projects may be initiated by the Central Bureau, or arranged in collaboration with other promoting bodies and international organisations, or set up by employers, colleges or youth organisations, for a particular group of young people.

14. Further Information:

In England and Wales:
Vocational and Technical
    Education Dept.
Central Bureau for Educational
    Visits and Exchanges (CBEVE)
Seymour Mews House
Seymour Mews
London W1H 9PE
Tel: (071) 486 5101
Fax: (071) 935 5741

In Scotland:
The Central Bureau
3 Bruntsfield Crescent
Edinburgh EH10 4HD
Tel: (031) 447 8024

In Northern Ireland:
The Central Bureau
16 Malone Road
Belfast BT9 5BN
Tel: (0232) 664418/9

PART THREE

RESEARCH AND TECHNOLOGICAL DEVELOPMENT

3.0 OVERVIEW

In 1987, the Single European Act established Research and Technological Development (RTD) as a formal area of Commission responsibility, according it for the first time equal status with the Commission's traditional remit covering economic and social policy. Previously EC research funding had been restricted to areas directly associated with economic policy concerns, eg coal, steel, energy. The policy shift to extend RTD support beyond these traditional areas was intended to enhance the competitiveness of European industry by funding pre-competitive research – specifically, research which could be carried out more rationally, cost effectively and efficiently at European level. The First Framework Programme for Research and Development (1984–87) was, in effect, a probationary phase in this new sphere of Commission involvement, and was subsequently ratified by the Single Act legislation.

Reflecting the new importance given to research, Community expenditure on RTD programmes has increased considerably in recent years. The total amount of funding available over the period 1990–94 has been agreed at 8.8 billion ECU, roughly 1.75 billion ECU per annum. This accounts for 3.8 percent of the total Community budget, and represents an increase of about one-third over average annual EC expenditure on R & D in the previous five-year period.

However, the current level of EC research funding is still considered by some to be low, especially when the diverse range of research areas which have been targeted for support and the number of countries represented are taken into account. It is certainly low when compared with public sector science and technology expenditure within individual Member States. On the other hand, absolute amounts of funding allocated at EC level to certain priority fields have been sufficiently large that, within these targeted areas, the main source of public funding has been shifting from national to EC level.

To maximise the effectiveness of its limited RTD budget, the Commission awards research grants on a competitive basis. Apart from promoting specific research objectives, projects are expected to contribute to broader European objectives. Thus, projects are expected to involve transnational collaboration and co-ordination, and mobility between science and industry. A further objective associated with many of the programmes is the integration of research and technology into the context of completing the Single Market, eg agreeing European-wide standards in scientific disciplines, promoting access to expertise and equipment irrespective of location, etc. Project proposals which promote these broader objectives, not to mention the other objectives governing the operation of other EC policy instruments such as the Structural Funds (see Part One), stand the best chance of success.

The Framework Programmes

Priority research areas for EC RTD programmes are agreed in 'Framework Programmes for Research and Development'. Each Framework Programme sets out the objectives, priorities and scope of Commission support for RTD in the medium term. The First Framework Programme ran from 1984 to 1987. It was followed by the current Second Framework Programme (1987–91) which consists of eight high priority areas comprising 32 specific programmes. A Third Framework Programme was agreed in April 1990 and overlaps the Second Framework Programme by two years, running from 1990–94. The Third Framework Programme continues much of the work started under the Second Programme. It represents, however, an effort to adapt and bring up-to-date the Community's RTD activities, reflecting changes that have taken place since the Second Framework Programme was formulated.

Tables 4 and 5 list the main priority areas and respective budgets assigned to the Second and Third Framework Programmes.

As can be seen from the tables, the Third Framework Programme involves a number of shifts of emphasis. The proportion of funds targeted on Environmental Research, Biotechnology and the Mobility of Research Personnel has increased appreciably, while the level of support for Energy Research (a top priority in the mid-1970s) has fallen. Information and Communications Technologies and Materials Technologies remain the main focus of Community-funded research, accounting for over 50 percent of the total 5.7 billion ECU budget.

To concentrate the resources available under the Third Framework Programme, the 32 research programmes which were highlighted under the Second Framework Programme have been streamlined into fifteen, falling within a more limited set of six strategic sectors.

To simplify and harmonise the various research programmes and facilitate their adoption and implementation, all fifteen new programme proposals are to be based on the same 'model'. All have been proposed to run from 1990 to 1994, and it is expected that first calls for proposals will have been issued by the Spring of 1991. Brief details of each of the new programme proposals are provided in Part 4.2 – Programmes under Proposal. In a bid to introduce flexibility that will allow the Commission to fund new priority areas brought about by rapid technological change, a new method of funding 'unsolicited' project proposals has been introduced. Most funding will, however, continue to be allocated through the traditional method of selecting projects via calls for proposals.

Characteristics of Community Research Programmes

There are eight main characteristics of the Community research programmes:

1. Research programmes run for a four or five-year period with most funding allocated within the first two years.
2. Research must be innovative and pre-competitive (ie somewhere between basic fundamental research and commercial application, and at least 5 years from the market place).
3. Transnational collaboration is usually required although in cases where projects are assigned high priority by the Commission, or where

TABLE 4

Framework Programme 1987–1991		
Focal areas	**Sums in million ECU**	**Proportion of total budget (%)**
1. Quality of life	375	6.9
1.1 Health	80	
1.2 Radiation protection	34	
1.3 Environment	261	
2. Towards a large market and an information and communications society	2,275	42.3
2.1 Information technologies	1,600	
2.2 Telecommunications	550	
2.3 New services of common interest (including transport)	125	
3. Modernisation of industrial sectors	845	15.6
3.1 Science and technology for the manufacturing industry	400	
3.2 Science and technology of advanced materials	220	
3.3 Raw materials and recylcing	45	
3.4 Technical standards, measurement methods and reference materials	180	
4. Exploitation and optimum use of biological resources	280	5.2
4.1 Biotechnology	120	
4.2 Agro-industrial technologies	105	
4.3 Competitiveness of agriculture and management of agricultural resources	55	
5. Energy	1,173	21.7
5.1 Fission: nuclear safety	440	
5.2 Controlled thermonuclear fusion	611	
5.3 Non-nuclear energies and rational use of energy	122	
6. Science and technology for development	80	1.5
7. Exploitation of the sea bed and use of marine resources	80	1.5
7.1 Marine science and technology	50	
7.2 Fisheries	30	
8. Improvement of European S/T cooperation	288	5.3
8.1 Stimulation, enhancement and use of human resources	180	
8.2 Use of major installations	30	
8.3 Forecasting and assessment and other back-up measures (including statistics)	23	
8.4 Dissemination and utilisation of S/T research results	55	
Total	**5,396**	**100.0**

Source: Commission of the European Communities (DG XII)

TABLE 5

Framework Programme 1990–1994		
Focal areas	**Sums in million ECU**	**Proportion of total budget (%)**
I. Enabling technologies		
1. Information and communications technologies	2,221	38.9
— Information technologies	1,352	
— Telecommunications	489	
— Development of technological systems of general interest	380	
2. Industrial and materials technologies	888	15.6
— Industrial and materials technologies	748	
— Measurement and testing	140	
II. Management of natural resources		
3. Environment	518	9.1
— Environment	414	
— Marine science and technology	104	
4. Life sciences and technologies	741	13.0
— Biotechnology	164	
— Agricultural and agro-industrial research (incl. fisheries)	333	
— Biomedical and health research	133	
— Life sciences and technologies for developing countries	111	
5. Energy	814	14.3
— Non--nuclear energies	157	
— Nuclear fission safety	199	
— Controlled thermonuclear fusion	458	
III. Management of intellectual resources		
6. Human capital and mobility	518	9.1
Total[1]	**5,700**	**100.0**

[1] including ECU 57 million for the centralised management of the dissemination and exploitation of research results, and ECU 550 million for the Joint Research Centre (JRC)

Source: Commission of the European Communities (DG XII)

collaboration could not be justified on economic grounds (eg because of their small scale), this condition may be waived. Generally, at least two independent industrial partners from different countries must be involved in each project. Small company participation in collaborative projects is looked on particularly favourably.

4. Special funding arrangements exist to encourage partnerships between industry and higher education institutes. Funding is referred to as 'shared cost', with the Commission contributing 50 percent of industrial partner project costs and 100 percent of direct marginal costs incurred by higher education institutes.

5. Applications must generally be made in response to a call for proposals published in the Official Journal. Each call sets a strict deadline by which proposals must be submitted, usually some ten or twelve weeks from the publication date. Although calls for proposals are the predominant means of allocating research funds, the Commission has also recognised that strategic research areas may change considerably between the time a research programme is formulated and the time it is finally launched. To ensure that changes in priority areas are not overlooked, special provision exists within the Third Framework Programme (1990–94) for unsolicited project proposals to be considered in exceptional circumstances.

6. Application is made direct to the Commission, though nationally-based representatives in the relevant Government Departments may assist with proposal preparation and provide up-to-date information on programme progress, expected call dates, etc.

7. Applications are judged on a competitive basis in relation to the perceived importance of the proposed work, and the extent to which the project satisfies Community objectives.

8. In addition to funding research directly through 'shared-cost contracts', the Commission also: undertakes 'concertation actions' in which it coordinates research undertaken in different countries; provides training and mobility grants to promote scientific interchange; and funds research carried out at its own wholly-funded Joint Research Centre (JRC) based at four sites – Ispra (Italy); Geel (Belgium); Petten (Netherlands); and Karlsruhe (Germany).

Participation in EC Research Programmes

The obstacles to participating in EC research programmes are considerable – not only in terms of identifying suitable projects and partners, but also in working to the unpredictable time scale created by delays in the procedure for adopting new programmes, exacerbated by the competitive proposal selection procedure. Fortunately, much progress has been made within the past few years to minimise the difficulties participating firms face. Legislation introduced by the Single Act has speeded up the decision making process governing the adoption of new programmes, thereby making their expected start dates subject to less delay and uncertainty.

The application procedure is a further hurdle to be overcome. For most research programmes, project proposals may only be submitted within strict deadlines set by calls for proposals published in the Official Journal. Often, these calls only allow some ten to twelve weeks for submission of proposals. However, to help firms prepare for a formal call for proposals, many new programmes invite 'expressions of interest' prior to publication of the actual call. Firms which indicate an interest in participating in an RTD programme will then receive guidance on the scope of the programme and expected timing, before committing substantial resources in the preparation of a formal proposal. They are also kept informed directly about any developments in a particular research programme and receive notice of the formal calls for proposals as they are issued. Expressions of interest are also used as a feedback mechanism to assess the interest of industry in the particular area of research, and to help establish priorities in relation to specific research topics.

To ease the task of finding partners from other countries, the Commission will also try to provide a match-making service for firms who register a need. This is of particular benefit to smaller firms and can obviously bring with it new commercial opportunities quite separate from the actual research involvement.

Despite all the steps that have been taken to reduce the obstacles to participating in EC RTD programmes, there is no question that putting together a suitable proposal involving transnational collaboration requires a significant resource commitment and represents a considerable challenge. However, for those firms that do succeed, the advantages of participating in an EC RTD programme go far beyond the financial contribution offered by the Commission. Participating in a multi-national collaborative research programme gives firms access to specialists throughout Europe, access to results of research carried out by others and the acquisition of know-how. At a more indirect level it introduces firms in related areas of business to each other, providing valuable links and information for future commercial opportunities. Furthermore, for those firms willing to take the first difficult steps necessary for participation in an EC RTD programme, there is a sharp learning curve and a greater likelihood that they will be in a position to take advantage of opportunities presented in other EC programmes. In some cases, further assistance to exploit the results of Community funded R & D (ie nearer to the market place research) may be available under a nationally funded research programme. Thus although initial entry costs of participation may be high, the benefits of doing so may accrue over many years.

PART THREE

RESEARCH AND TECHNOLOGICAL DEVELOPMENT

3.1 INDUSTRIAL AND MATERIALS TECHNOLOGIES/ MEASUREMENT AND TESTING

3.1 INDUSTRIAL AND MATERIALS TECHNOLOGIES/ MEASUREMENT AND TESTING

BRITE/EURAM

1. Summary:

The BRITE/EURAM programme offers support for collaborative Research and Technological Development (RTD) projects in the fields of industrial manufacturing technologies and advanced materials applications. The programme covers the following areas: Advanced Materials Technologies; Design Methodology and Quality Assurance for Products and Processes; Application of Manufacturing Technologies; Technologies for Manufacturing Processes; Specific Activities Relating to Aeronautics. Projects may be of the following types: Industrial Applied Research (Type 1) attracting up to 90 percent of the available budget, Focussed Fundamental Research (Type 2) attracting between 7 and 10 percent of the budget, with a small proportion of the funding going towards co-ordinated activities, feasibility awards for SMEs and demonstration projects (in the latter part of the programme).

The BRITE/EURAM programme is set to run from 1 January 1989 to 31 December 1992 with a budget of 499.5 MECU.

2. Awarding Body:

Commission of the European Communities.

3. Location Restrictions:

Available in any Member State of the European Community. Organisations from the EFTA countries (Austria, Finland, Iceland, Norway, Sweden, Switzerland) may participate as additional, but not as prime partners. Partners from these countries will not, however, qualify for Community support.

4. Sectoral Restrictions:

Available to industrial organisations, research institutes and universities, established in the European Community. Projects should preferably be applicable to several industrial sectors.

Participation in Industrial Applied Research (Type 1) projects is subject to the following conditions: the contracting parties must provide a substantial part of project finance; there must be at least two legally independent industrial enterprises from at least two different Member States; universities and research institutes may only collaborate if they are in partnership with or sub-contracted to industry; within a partnership a research organisation may be classified as an independent industrial enterprise when it receives 50 percent financing in direct payments from nominated industrial sponsors involved in steering the project; research institutes whose revenue is entirely or mainly from industrial sources will be considered as industrial enterprises.

Focussed Fundamental Research (Type 2) projects are open to all organisations and must involve trans-frontier co-operation by at least two organisations in at least two Member States. To ensure an industrial focus for this research (which need not include an industrial partner), there is a requirement for industrial endorsement by nominated individuals from industry.

Projects must be endorsed by at least two independent industrial enterprises from at least two Member States.

Participation by small and medium-sized enterprises (SMEs) is particularly encouraged. SMEs may choose to act individually, as partners in their own right or as specialist subcontractors, or collectively, as part of a group of SMEs represented by another organisation (eg a research institute acting on their behalf) or by funding work of common interest within a research organisation. Where a choice has to be made between projects of similar merit, those involving SMEs will be given preference.

5. Size Restrictions:

In general, projects must be of two to four years' duration, involving a minimum of ten man-years effort and with total project costs normally between 1 and 3 MECU for Type 1 projects and 0.4 to 1 MECU in the case of Type 2 projects.

6. Programme Duration:

The programme is set to run from 1 January 1989 to 31 December 1992. The Commission has proposed a new RTD programme in the field of Industrial and Materials Technologies, to run from 1990–94 with a budget of 748 MECU.

7. Submission of Applications/Proposals:

Application is made within the deadlines specified in each of the Commission's invitations for proposals to be submitted, published in the Official Journal. Calls for proposals in relation to this programme are expected to be made annually.

No further calls relating to feasiblity awards are expected under the current programme.

Proposals for Co-ordinated Activities projects may be made at any time during the lifetime of the programme. However, it was strongly preferred that projects are submitted to meet the closing dates for Type 1 and Type 2 proposals.

8. Other Restrictions:

The Programme Technical Areas cover the following Sub-Areas:
- Advanced Materials Technologies: metallic materials and metallic matrix composites; materials for magnetic, optical, electrical and superconducting applications; high temperature non-metallic materials; polymers and organic matrix composites; materials for specialised applications.
- Design Methodology and Assurance for Products and Processes: quality, reliability and maintainability in industry; process and product assurance.
- Application of Manufacturing Technologies: advancing manufacturing practices; manufacturing processes for flexible materials.
- Technologies for Manufacturing Processes: surface techniques; shap-

ing, assembly and joining; chemical processes; particle and powder processes.
- Specific Activities Relating to Aeronautics: aerodynamics; acoustics; airborne systems and equipment; propulsion systems.

Projects must: relate to one or more of the priority themes specified in the Information Package; have a clear industrial potential and be precompetitive; be innovative and not duplicate R & D work being carried out elsewhere in the Community – if the idea is not completely new then proposers must be able to show that their project is concerned with the new application of a known technique in a product, a process development or a new material.

Proposers must demonstrate an ability to exercise a high quality of management control and convincingly describe the techniques by which this will be achieved. Proposals must demonstrate the routes of potential exploitation of results and, where appropriate, the commitment of proposers to that exploitation.

Proposers must state why they believe the project merits funding as a Community collaborative project and should reflect the European dimension by demonstrating the importance of the project to the Community as a whole.

9. Eligible Expenditure:

For organisations other than universities, eligible expenditure covers: labour (actual cost or at approved rates), travel and subsistence; consumables; equipment; computing costs; external work (sub-contracts or services); reasonable overheads. The following are not allowable: profits; marketing, distribution, advertising expenses; any interest or return on capital employed; taxes (except in limited circumstances); cost of proposal preparation; patent protection costs. Specific arrangements exist to recover non-reclaimable VAT.

Support for universities and higher education establishments may be calculated according to the marginal costs of the project (ie the actual additional direct costs of the research not met by normal recurrent expenditure, other financial sources or other third parties), unless their costing and recording systems enable them to submit and justify full costs. Each university is normally expected to operate on the basis of either marginal costs or full costs for all Community R & D programmes, and not reach a decision on a project-by-project basis. Marginal costs may include all the items listed above, although labour costs only relate to temporary additional staff specifically engaged for the research; routine and minor computing costs may not be charged; and overheads may be fixed at a percentage, corresponding to a maximum of 20 percent of all expenditure except associated contracts and VAT.

10. Rate of Award:

The rate of award for Industrial Applied Research (Type 1) projects is normally 50 percent of eligible costs; the remainder must be supplied by the contractor. Where universities and similar institutions are partners, their marginal costs form part of the total eligible costs. It is up to the partners to determine the distribution of the total EC support within the partnership.

The rate of award for universities and similar institutions is up to 100 percent of the marginal costs of the project. Co-ordination activities may attract a 100 percent contribution towards co-ordination costs; research costs are not covered.

11. Payment Procedure:

Payment is made in accordance with the agreed contract and takes the form of an advance payment following signature of the contract by all partners and the Commission, followed by periodic instalments on approval of progress reports and cost statements submitted as work progresses. Ten percent of the total financial contribution is retained (or, in the case of larger contracts, 500,000 ECUs, whichever is lower) and is paid, along with any other sums due, on approval of final technical reports and cost statements.

In all cases the Commission's contribution is made in ECUs and no liability is held for exchange losses incurred.

12. Points to Note:

Council Decision (EEC) 237/89 adopting BRITE/EURAM was published in OJ L98; 11.4.89.

The second call was published in OJ C36; 16.2.90; the deadline for applications was 14 September 1990.

Demonstration projects may be set up in the latter part of the BRITE/EURAM programme, when the results of certain projects supported by the programme will indicate the range of demonstration-type activities required.

13. Application Procedure:

The BRITE/EURAM Information Package for the Second Call for Proposals is available from the addresses below (see 14). Application is made on the appropriate form, published in the Information Package.

14. Further Information:

European Commission	Mr G A Gadge
DG XII/C2	Department of Trade & Industry
BRITE/EURAM Programme	Manufacturing Technology Division
Rue de la Loi 200	Room 517
B-1049 Brussels	Ashdown House
Tel: (010 32 2) 235 2345	123 Victoria Street
Telex:21877 COMEU B	London SW1E 6RB
Fax: (010 32 2) 235 8046	Tel: (071) 215 6336

EUREKA

1. Summary:

EUREKA is a framework, agreed between 19 European countries and the European Commission, for promoting transnational collaborative projects in advanced technology fields. Although not primarily a programme for funding R & D, participants in EUREKA projects may receive financial support related to their share of a project through the particular funding mechanism adopted by their own national governments. UK participants qualify for grants from the Department of Trade and Industry of up to 50 percent for the definition phase of a project. For subsequent phases, the level of support is negotiable.

The aim of EUREKA is to improve European competitiveness in world markets in civil applications of new technologies by encouraging industrial and technological collaboration within Europe. EUREKA projects aim to produce goods, processes and services with potential for profitable sales worldwide, using the European market as a springboard where this is helpful. EUREKA projects benefit from the information exchange process provided through the EUREKA framework and from the commitment to the development of an integrated market by EUREKA-participating countries.

2. Awarding Body:
EUREKA projects are co-ordinated by the EUREKA Secretariat, and in the UK funding is awarded by the Department of Trade and Industry.

3. Location Restrictions:
Organisations from any of the nineteen participating countries may collaborate in EUREKA projects: Austria, Belgium, Denmark, Finland, France, Germany, Greece, Iceland, Ireland, Italy, Luxembourg, Netherlands, Norway, Portugal, Spain, Sweden, Switzerland, Turkey, United Kingdom. The Commission of the European Communities is also a member of the EUREKA Initiative. Projects must involve participants from more than one EUREKA country.

4. Sectoral Restrictions:
Proposals for EUREKA projects can be submitted by any firm or institute, including small and medium-sized organisations.

There are no predetermined technological areas for EUREKA projects. It is up to the companies, universities, public or private-sector research bodies concerned to determine their particular areas of interest. Companies and research institutes identify the topics on which they wish to collaborate and seek prospective partners. They remain responsible for bringing these ideas into effect as EUREKA projects, with the assistance of national competent authorities.

5. Size Restrictions:
None.

6. Programme Duration:
There is no specified terminal date for this initiative.

7. Submission of Applications/Proposals:
Projects seeking EUREKA status may be submitted at any time. Projects are granted EUREKA status at annual Ministerial Conferences; it is possible for projects to start before status is formally confirmed.

8. Other Restrictions:
EUREKA projects generally relate to products, processes and services in the following areas of advanced technology: information technology, telecommunications, robotics, materials, advanced manufacturing, biotechnology, marine technology, lasers, environmental protection and transport technologies. Also covered are advanced technology R & D projects aimed at

the creation of the technical prerequisites for a modern infrastructure and the solution of transboundary problems.

Projects seeking EUREKA status must involve: transnational co-operation (EUREKA countries); an identifiable expected benefit from undertaking the project on a co-operative basis; the use of advanced technologies; the aim of securing a significant technological advance; appropriately qualified participants – technically and managerially; adequate financial commitment by the participants; development work carried out mainly in EUREKA countries and results exploited to their benefit.

To qualify for support collaborative research projects must be both innovative and technically realistic and have reasonable prospects of eventual exploitation. The resources devoted to the project, including managerial and technical expertise, must be sufficient for the project to be carried out effectively and to completion.

Government support will only be considered where it can be shown to influence the scope or scale of a project.

9. Eligible Expenditure:

Eligible expenditure generally relates to the directly attributable costs incurred in carrying out the project, including an agreed proportion of the salaries of personnel working directly on the project; materials consumed in the course of the project; capital equipment purchased or constructed for the project, less the estimated value to the business of the equipment at the end of the project (in certain circumstances the costs of employing capital equipment that is already owned may be supported); licensing fees paid to third parties for acquiring new technology; sub-contract charges and consultancy fees; fees for trials and testing and preparation of technical manuals; project management costs, such as travel, office space, etc that are additional to those normally involved; training that is specific to the project, including that of members of management; the cost of patenting, where this would otherwise fall on small firms; an allowance for overheads.

10. Rate of Award:

Participants in EUREKA projects are expected to find the funds they require themselves, either internally or by seeking appropriate financial partners, using private capital sources (capital markets, loans) or any public funds made available to them by their respective governments or the European Commission. Many companies participating in EUREKA projects do so without grant support, because of the non-financial benefits (see 12).

In the UK, participants may receive grants of up to 50 percent of the costs involved in the definition phase of the project. For subsequent phases, support will be negotiated; this may be on a tapering basis, for example half of eligible costs in year 1, a third in year 2, and a quarter in year 3.

11. Payment Procedure:

Payments are made retrospectively in stages, according to progress on the project.

12. Points to Note:

Projects which achieve EUREKA status benefit from a number of non-financial benefits:

- information exchange and contacts: the EUREKA framework provides for a process of information exchange on potential areas for collaboration between firms or organisations in different countries who are either seeking partners for specific projects or expressing an interest in collaboration in certain fields;
- market opening measures: EUREKA acts as a lobby or sets priorities for action by focussing on market barriers encountered by specific projects;
- prestige: the EUREKA label is highly regarded throughout Europe.

13. Application Procedure:

In the UK, application for support is by form, available from the Department of Trade and Industry. For all EUREKA projects, a proposal (agreed by all the partners) in a standard 18-point format must be submitted to the EUREKA Office. These proposals are circulated publicly for at least 45 days before confirmation of EUREKA status to allow expressions of interest from potential partners in EUREKA countries. It is up to existing participants to decide whether to invite other partners to join. It is possible to submit a proposal with partners already identified, or seeking partners.

14. Further Information:

The EUREKA Office
Department of Trade and
 Industry
Room 204
Ashdown House
123 Victoria Street
London SW1E 6RB
Tel: (071) 215 6612/3/4
Telex: 8813148
Fax: (071) 821 1298

EUREKA Secretariat
19H Avenue des Arts – BP3
B-1040 Brussels
Tel: (010 32 2) 217 0030
Telex: 29340 EUREKA B
Fax: (010 32 2) 218 7906

FOREST

1. Summary:

The FOREST programme covers the field of renewable raw materials (Forestry and Wood Products, including cork) and is a subprogramme of the Raw Materials and Recycling Programme. FOREST aims to increase the availability of forest resources, provide better quality raw materials in keeping with economic and environmental requirements, improve the international competitiveness of EC forest industries and facilitate the rational use of forestry products in the EC. The programme covers three broad areas: forest resources; wood and cork technologies; and pulp and paper manufacturing.

FOREST is set to run from 1 January 1990 to 31 December 1992 with a budget allocation of 12 MECU.

2. Awarding Body:
Commission of the European Communities.

3. Location Restrictions:
Available in any Member State of the European Community. Organisa-tions from non-Member States which have concluded framework agreements for scientific and technical co-operation with the European Communities may also participate as partners in a project, although they will not be entitled to EC funding.

4. Sectoral Restrictions:
Available to industry, public research centres and universities. Projects should, in general, be carried out by participants from more than one Member State and should include an industrial partner.

5. Size Restrictions:
None.

6. Programme Duration:
The programme is set to run from 1 January 1990 to 31 December 1992.

7. Submission of Applications/Proposals:
Application is made within the deadlines specified in each of the Commission's calls for proposals, published in the Official Journal.

8. Other Restrictions:
The programme covers the following technical areas (budget allocation in brackets):
1. Forest Resources (4 MECU): tree improvement (tree physiology and breeding); planning and management; forest protection;
2. Wood and Cork Technologies (4 MECU): quality assessment (non-destructive testing methods for assessing the quality of timber and composite wood or cork products; relation between sylvicultural practices and wood/cork properties); processing technology (improvement of processing techniques, quality improvement of timber through better drying and preservation techniques, improving and/or developing composite wood/cork products);
3. Pulp and Paper Manufacturing (4 MECU): improvement in pulping and bleaching (economic and quality improvements, chemicals derived from pulping processes); improvement in paper manufacture and coating (process management, improvement of product quality).

9. Eligible Expenditure:
For organisations other than universities, eligible expenditure covers: labour (actual cost or at approved rates), travel and subsistence, consuma-bles, equipment, computing costs, external work (sub-contracts or services), reasonable overheads. The following are not allowable: profits; marketing, distribution, advertising expenses; any interest or return on capital employed; taxes (except in limited circumstances); cost of proposal preparation; patent protection costs. Specific arrangements exist to recover non-reclaimable VAT.

Universities and higher education establishments may elect to have their support calculated according to the marginal costs of the project (ie the actual additional direct costs of the research not met by normal recurrent expenditure, other financial sources or other third parties), unless their costing and recording systems enable them to submit and justify full costs. Each university is normally expected to operate on the basis of either marginal costs or full costs for all Community R & D programmes, and not reach a decision on a project-by-project basis. Marginal costs may include all the items listed above, although labour costs may only relate to temporary additional staff specifically engaged for the research; routine and minor computing costs may not be charged; and overheads may be fixed at a percentage, corresponding to a maximum of 20 percent of all expenditure except associated contracts and VAT.

10. Rate of Award:

The rate of award is normally up to 50 percent of eligible expenditure. The remainder of the costs must be provided mainly from industrial sources. Universities and similar institutions normally receive 100 percent of the actual marginal costs incurred as additional expenditure on the R & D project.

11. Payment Procedure:

Payment is made in accordance with the agreed contract and takes the form of an advance payment following signature of the contract by all partners and the Commission, followed by periodic instalments on approval of progress reports and cost statements submitted as work progresses. Ten percent of the total financial contribution is retained (or, in the case of larger contracts, 500,000 ECUs, whichever is lower) and is paid, along with any other sums due, on approval of final technical reports and cost statements.

In all cases the Commission's contribution is made in ECUs and no liability is held for exchange losses incurred.

12. Points to Note:

Council Decision (EEC) 626/89 adopting the Raw Materials and Recycling Programme was published in OJ L359; 8.12.89.

A call for proposals was published in OJ C205; 10.8.89.

13. Application Procedure:

Application procedure is outlined in the Information Package, available from the Commission (see 14).

14. Further Information:

Matteo Donato	Mr Peter Hills
European Commission	Department of Trade and Industry
DG XII/F-5	Industrial Marterials Market Division
Rue de la Loi 200	Room 907
B-1049 Brussels	Ashdown House
Tel: (010 32 2) 235 1492/7979	123 Victoria Street
Fax: (010 32 2) 235 0145	London SW1E 6RB
Telex: COMEU B 21877	Tel: (071) 215 6117

REWARD

1. Summary:

The REWARD programme in the field of waste recycling is a subprogramme of the Raw Materials and Recycling Programme. The main objectives of REWARD are to increase the rate of waste recycling and utilisation through the development of economically viable technology, and to promote industrial competitiveness through the development of innovative technologies, the utilisation of recycled materials and the promotion of recyclable materials. The programme covers the following research areas: (1) Sampling, Analysis and Classification of Wastes; (2) Recycling Technologies; and (3) Energy Production from Waste.

REWARD is set to run from 1 January 1990 to 31 December 1992, with a budget allocation of 6 MECU.

2. Awarding Body:

Commission of the European Communities.

3. Location Restrictions:

Available in any Member State of the European Community. Organisations from non-Member States which have concluded framework agreements for scientific and technical co-operation with the European Communities may also participate as partners in a project, although they will not be entitled to EC funding.

4. Sectoral Restrictions:

Available to industry, public research centres and universities. Projects should, in general, be carried out by participants from more than one Member State and should include an industrial partner.

5. Size Restrictions:

None.

6. Programme Duration:

The programme is set to run from 1 January 1990 to 31 December 1992. The Commission has proposed a new RTD programme in the field of Industrial and Materials Technologies (1990–94) incorporating the area of Recycling.

7. Submission of Applications/Proposals:

Application under research area (2) of the programme (see 8) is made within the deadlines specified in each of the Commission's calls for proposals, published in the Official Journal. Research relating to sampling, analysis and classification of wastes and energy production from waste will be conducted through co-ordinated actions (ie the Commission will co-ordinate rather than directly fund research efforts); no calls for proposals will therefore be issued in these research areas.

8. Other Restrictions:

The programme covers the following research areas (budget allocation in brackets):

1. Sampling, Analysis and Classification of Wastes (1 MECU): waste

statistics; household and urban waste; industrial waste; emissions and residues from waste processing.
2. Recycling Technologies (4 MECU): separation and recovery; upgrading and use of reclaimed products; production of chemicals; prevention of emissions from recycling processes; upgrading of lignocellulosic waste (research will take the form of a formal concerted action); and composting.
3. Energy production from Waste (1 MECU): production and combustion of refuse derived fuels (RDF); pyrolisis and gasification.

Calls for proposals will be issued in respect of research area 2 only; research areas 1 and 3 will be implemented through co-ordination actions.

9. Eligible Expenditure:

For organisations other than universities, eligible expenditure covers: labour (actual cost or at approved rates); travel and subsistence; consumables; equipment; computing costs; external work (sub-contracts or services); reasonable overheads. The following are not allowable: profits; marketing, distribution, advertising expenses; any interest or return on capital employed; taxes (except in limited circumstances); cost of proposal preparation; patent protection costs. Specific arrangements exist to recover non-reclaimable VAT.

Universities and higher education establishments may elect to have their support calculated according to the marginal costs of the project (ie the actual additional direct costs of the research not met by normal recurrent expenditure, other financial sources or other third parties), unless their costing and recording systems enable them to submit and justify full costs. Each university is normally expected to operate on the basis of either marginal costs or full costs for all Community R & D programmes, and not reach a decision on a project-by-project basis. Marginal costs may include all the items listed above, although labour costs may only relate to temporary additional staff specifically engaged for the research; routine and minor computing costs may not be charged; and overheads may be fixed at a percentage, corresponding to a maximum of 20 percent of all expenditure except associated contracts and VAT.

10. Rate of Award:

The rate of award is normally up to 50 percent of eligible expenditure. The remainder of the costs must be provided mainly from industrial sources. Universities and similar institutions normally receive 100 percent of the actual marginal costs incurred as additional expenditure on the R & D project.

11. Payment Procedure:

Payment is made in accordance with the agreed contract and takes the form of an advance payment following signature of the contract by all partners and the Commission, followed by periodic instalments on approval of progress reports and cost statements submitted as work progresses. Ten percent of the total financial contribution is retained (or, in the case of larger contracts, 500,000 ECUs, whichever is lower) and is paid, along with any other sums due, on approval of final technical reports and cost statements.

In all cases the Commission's contribution is made in ECUs and no liability is held for exchange losses incurred.

12. Points to Note:
Council Decision (EEC) 626/89 adopting the Raw Materials and Recycling Programme was published in OJ L359; 8.12.89.

A call for proposals was published in OJ C326; 30.12.89; the deadline was 30 March 1990.

13. Application Procedure:
Application procedure is outlined in the Information Package, available from the Commission (see 14).

14. Further Information:

European Commission	Mr Peter Hills
DG XII/E-1	Department of Trade and Industry
REWARD Programme	Industrial Materials Market Division
75, Rue Montoyer	Room 907
B-1040 Brussels	Ashdown House
Tel: (010 32 2) 235 1111	123 Victoria Street
Fax: (010 32 2) 236 3024	London SW1E 6RB
Telex: 21877 COMEU B	Tel: (071) 215 6117

APPLIED METROLOGY AND CHEMICAL ANALYSIS PROGRAMME (BCR)

1. Summary:
The Applied Metrology and Chemical Analysis Programme (Community Bureau of Reference – BCR) provides support for intercomparisons and for R & D projects related to the study and improvement of measurement methods and the development of reference materials and transfer standards. The aim of the programme is to improve the reliability of chemical analyses and physical measurements (applied metrology) within the European Community, thereby obtaining better agreement between the results of different laboratories, and as a result, eliminating obstacles to the operation of the Single Market which originate from the measurements themselves.

The programme is set to run from 1 January 1988 to 31 December 1992 with a budget of 59.2 MECU.

2. Awarding Body:
Commission of the European Communities.

3. Location Restrictions:
Available in any Member State of the European Community.

The Commission may negotiate agreements with non-Member States and international organisations, in particular those countries participating in COST and those having concluded framework agreements in scientific and technical co-operation with the Community, with a view to associating them wholly or partly with the programme.

4. Sectoral Restrictions:

Available to industrial organisations, research institutes, laboratories and universities established in the Community.

Projects supported under the programme must normally involve the collaboration of organisations in at least two Member States.

5. Size Restrictions:

None.

6. Programme Duration:

The programme is set to run from 1 January 1988 to 31 December 1992. The Commission has proposed a new RTD programme in the field of Measurements & Testing, to run from 1990–94.

7. Submission of Applications/Proposals:

Application is generally made within the deadlines specified in each of the Commission's invitations to submit proposals published in the Official Journal.

A substantial proportion of the funds available has been allocated to projects submitted in response to calls issued in February 1990. Subject to the availability of funds, however, the Commission is willing to consider applications at any time (ie outwith any deadlines specified in the formal calls).

8. Other Restrictions:

Projects are chosen from those fields which are of priority importance for the Community as judged from an economic, environmental or public health view point. The priority fields are as follows: (a) analyses for food and agriculture; (b) analyses related to the environment; (c) biomedical analyses; (d) analyses of (essentially non-ferrous) metals and surface analysis of materials; (e) applied metrology (with the emphasis on the measurement and calibration of the most important parameters for test and industrial laboratories, especially for quality control).

Activities to be undertaken include in particular: execution of measurement programmes involving laboratories in several Member States (intercomparisons); improvement of methods of analysis and measurement, and of instruments necessary for high precision measurements; development of transfer standards; preparation and certification, storage and distribution of reference materials; support for setting up interlaboratory circuits for quality assurance; research grants; exchange and training of scientists associated with BCR projects; dissemination of the results of the projects; well-targeted advertising of the reference materials and promotion of their sale.

9. Eligible Expenditure:

For organisations other than universities, eligible expenditure covers: labour (actual cost or at approved rates); travel and subsistence; consumables; equipment; computing costs; external work (sub-contracts or services); project management; reasonable overheads. The following are not allowable: profits; marketing, distribution, advertising expenses; any interest or return on capital employed; taxes (except in limited circumstances); cost of proposal preparation; patent protection costs. Specific arrangements exist to recover non-reclaimable VAT.

Universities and higher education establishments may elect to have their support calculated according to the marginal costs of the project (ie the actual additional direct costs of the research not met by normal recurrent expenditure, other financial sources or other third parties), unless their costing and recording systems enable them to submit and justify full costs. Each university is normally expected to operate on the basis of either marginal costs or full costs for all Community R & D programmes, and not reach a decision on a project-by-project basis. Marginal costs may include all the items listed above, although labour costs only relate to temporary additional staff specifically engaged for the research; routine and minor computing costs may not be charged; and overheads may be fixed at a percentage, corresponding to a maximum of 20 percent of all expenditure except associated contracts and VAT.

10. Rate of Award:

The rate of award will normally be up to 50 percent of the full economic costs of the R & D project. Universities and higher education establishments may, however, attract a contribution of up to 100 percent of the actual marginal costs of the research project. Project management and preparation of synthesis reports are funded at full economic costs.

11. Payment Procedure:

Payment is made in accordance with the agreed contract and normally takes the form of an advance payment following signature of the contract by all partners and the Commission, followed by periodic instalments on approval of progress reports and cost statements submitted as work progresses. Ten percent of the total financial contribution is retained (or, in the case of larger contracts, 500,000 ECUs, whichever is lower) and is paid, along with any other sums due, on approval of final technical reports and cost statements.

In all cases the Commission's contribution is made in ECUs and no liability is held for exchange losses incurred.

12. Points to Note:

The third call for proposals under the programme was issued in February 1990 and aimed at developing activities on sub-micron and nano-metric metrology, and methodology for automated manufacturing processes.

Council Decision (EEC) 418/88 adopting the BCR programme was published in Official Journal L206; 30.07.88.

13. Application Procedure:

Application procedure is outlined in the information package for each call for proposals, available from the Commission.

14. Further Information:

Dr H Marchandise
European Commission
European Commission
DG XII (Arts Lux 3/21)

Community Bureau of Reference
Rue de la Loi 200
B-1049 Brussels
Tel: (010 32 2) 235 5014
Telex: COMEU B 21877

Dr M E Peover (Applied Metrology)
National Physical Laboratory
Teddington
Middlesex TW11 0LW
Tel: (081) 943 6039

Dr K Poulter
National Measurement System Policy Unit
Ashdown House
123 Victoria Street
London SW1E 6RB
Tel: (071) 215 6719

Dr R F Walker (Chemical Analysis)
Head of Reference Materials
Laboratory of the Government Chemist
Teddington
Middlesex TW11 0LW
Tel: (081) 943 6270

IRON AND STEEL PILOT/DEMONSTRATION PROJECTS

1. Summary:
The Iron and Steel Pilot/Demonstration Projects programme aims to complement the technical steel research activities of the European Community, through the funding of projects establishing the feasibility of innovative technologies which will lead to the industrial and commercial exploitation of production techniques, processes, plant and products. Projects should demonstrate prospects of economic viability and contribute to the achievement of improved steel quality and reduction of production costs; maintenance of traditional steel markets and the development of new markets; and adaptation of production conditions to meet increasingly stringent environmental requirements. The programme offers grants which are partially repayable in the event of commercial exploitation of the results.

2. Awarding Body:
Commission of the European Communities.

3. Locaton Restriction:
Available in any Member State of the European Community.

4. Sectoral Restrictions:
Available to any firm, research institute or other body involved in the iron

and steel industries. Preference is given to projects involving the collaboration of organisations in at least two Member States; one partner must be a steel company.

5. Size Restrictions:
None.

6. Programme Duration:
The programme is set to run from 1988–92. Applications are submitted on an annual basis.

7. Submission of Applications/Proposals:
Applications must be submitted before 1 October each year to be eligible for consideration for the coming financial year.

8. Other Restrictions:
Under guidelines published in OJ C252; 6.10.90, the following priorities were identified:

A. Production Processes: optimising existing production methods and developing new techniques which (a) reduce processing time, or improve processing plant reliability, output quality or processing line flexibility; (b) provide a more detailed knowledge of the physical and chemical phenomena of multiphase systems and develop processes giving new and improved properties; (c) achieve economies in the consumption of raw materials, manpower and energy. Research will focus on: reducing the cost of energy consumed and its effect on the environment, developing treatments for the secondary refining of liquid metal; improving measuring and analysis techniques; modelling of production processes; developing control, automation and robotisation; improving the reliability of installation; developing new processes for making/shaping steel; improving environmental quality and up-grading the value of by-products;

B. Products: optimising properties of existing products and developing new products by (a) speeding-up production, improving promotion and information provision; (b) improving consistency of quality and reliability; and (c) developing new uses for steel and the use of new steel grades. Research will concentrate on the following sectors: transport; energy; civil, plant and mechanical engineering; household and packaging; and environment. Research priorities will be: the development of steel products by existing methods and new techniques (covering forming, weldability, joining and assembly, machinability, aptitude for thermal treatment, surface treatment and coatings); the development of user properties (eg fatigue, fracture and corrosion resistance) and the development of new categories of materials.

C. Environmental Protection: improving environmental control techniques for existing processes; developing new clean technologies for steel production and processing; and upgrading the value of by-products to reduce steelplant wastes.

9. Eligible Expenditure:
Eligible expenditure is related to the type of project undertaken and is agreed on a case-by-case basis.

10. Rate of Award:

The rate of award is up to 50 percent of total project costs. In the event of commercial exploitation of a project's results, 50 percent of the award is repayable. Repayment conditions are outlined in the contract drawn up by the Commission.

11. Payment Procedure:

Payment is made in accordance with the agreed contract and will take the form of an advance payment, followed by periodic instalments as work progresses.

12. Points to Note:

Pilot projects involve the construction, operation and development of an installation, or a significant part of an installation, of a significant scale and using large components, to verify the practicability of theoretical or laboratory results and/or increase the reliability of technical and economic data needed to progress to the demonstration stage (or in certain cases, to the industrial and/or commercial stage).

Demonstration projects involve the construction and/or operation of an industrial scale installation, or a significant part of an installation, making it possible to bring together all the technical and economic data required to proceed at the least possible risk to industrial and/or commercial exploitation of the technology.

13. Application Procedure:

Proposal forms may be obtained from the address below.

14. Further Information:

P R V Evans
European Commission
DG XII/C-4
Rue de la Loi 200
B-1049 Brussels
Tel: (010 32 2) 235 3707
Telex: COMEU B 21877

RAW MATERIALS AND RECYCLING PROGRAMME

1. Summary:

The Raw Materials and Recycling programme is designed to help provide the technological base required for strategic, innovative developments in support of the supply and processing of raw materials and recycling. The programme consists of four sub-programmes: primary raw materials; recycling of non-ferrous and strategic metals; FOREST (Forestry Sectoral Research and Technology); and REWARD (Recycling of Waste Research and Development).

FOREST and REWARD are outlined in separate descriptions; this description concentrates on the primary raw materials and recycling of non-ferrous and strategic metals subprogrammes. The objective of these subprogrammes is to enhance the competitiveness of the Community's mining and metallurgical industries, by providing innovative tools in support of the supply, processing and mining of primary raw materials and of the recycling of non-ferrous and strategic metals.

The programme is implemented by means of shared-cost contracts with industry, research centres, universities and similar institutions for pre-competitive applied research. The programme is set to run from 1 January 1990 to 31 December 1992 with a total budget allocation of 45 MECU; 27 MECU has been allocated to the primary raw materials and recycling of non-ferrous metals subprogrammes.

2. Awarding Body:
Commission of the European Communities.

3. Location Restrictions:
Available in any Member State of the European Community. Organisations from non-Member States which have concluded framework agreements for scientific and technical co-operation with the European Communities may also participate as partners in a project, although they will not be entitled to EC funding.

4. Sectoral Restrictions:
Available to industry, public research centres and universities. Projects should, in general, be carried out by participants from more than one Member State and should include an industrial partner.

5. Size Restrictions:
The total cost of the project should not be less than 0.4 MECU.

6. Programme Duration:
The programme is set to run from 1 January 1990 to 31 December 1992. The Commission has proposed a new Research and Technological Development (RTD) programme in the field of Industrial and Materials Technologies (1990–94), incorporating the areas of Raw Materials and Recycling.

7. Submission of Applications/Proposals:
Application is made within the deadlines specified in each of the Commission's calls for proposals, published in the Official Journal.

8. Other Restrictions:
The programme covers the following technical areas (budget allocation in brackets):
I. Primary Raw Materials:
  (a) Exploration (7 MECU): ore genesis; geochemical methods; geophysical methods; remote sensing and multi-data correlation; drilling technology;
  (b) Mining Technology (7 MECU): development of new mining methods and improvement of existing ones; rock fracturing; support systems; load and transportation systems; modelling and simulations in mining operations; specific equipment for small-size mines;
  (c) Mineral processing and extractive metallurgy (7 MECU): process

innovation and intensification; processing of high purity metals and multi-element compounds; industrial minerals; treatment of metallurgical residues and tailings; modelling, simulation and automatic control in mineral processing and extractive metallurgy.

Iron ore, fossil fuels and building materials are excluded.

II. Recycling of Non-Ferrous and Strategic Metals: characterisation and classification of secondary materials and physical separation and concentration (2 MECU); advanced pyrometallurgical processes (1 MECU); advanced hydrometallurgical processes (2 MECU); refining technologies and instrumentation on process control (1 MECU).

9. Eligible Expenditure:

For organisations other than universities, eligible expenditure covers: labour (actual cost or at approved rates); travel and subsistence; consumables; equipment; computing costs; external work (sub-contracts or services); reasonable overheads. The following are not allowable: profits; marketing, distribution, advertising expenses; any interest or return on capital employed; taxes (except in limited circumstances); cost of proposal preparation; patent protection costs. Specific arrangements exist to recover non-reclaimable VAT.

Universities and higher education establishments may elect to have their support calculated according to the marginal costs of the project (ie the actual additional direct costs of the research not met by normal recurrent expenditure, other financial sources or other third parties), unless their costing and recording systems enable them to submit and justify full costs. Each university is normally expected to operate on the basis of either marginal costs or full costs for all Community R & D programmes, and not reach a decision on a project-by-project basis. Marginal costs may include all the items listed above, although labour costs may only relate to temporary additional staff specifically engaged for the research; routine and minor computing costs may not be charged; and overheads may be fixed at a percentage, corresponding to a maximum of 20 percent of all expenditure except associated contracts and VAT.

10. Rate of Award:

The rate of award is normally up to 50 percent of eligible expenditure. The remainder of the costs must be provided mainly from industrial sources. Universities and similar institutions normally receive 100 percent of the actual marginal costs incurred as additional expenditure on the R & D project.

11. Payment Procedure:

Payment is made in accordance with the agreed contract and takes the form of an advance payment following signature of the contract by all partners and the Commission, followed by periodic instalments on approval of progress reports and cost statements submitted as work progresses. Ten percent of the total financial contribution is retained (or, in the case of larger contracts, 500,000 ECUs, whichever is lower) and is paid, along with any other sums due, on approval of final technical reports and cost statements.

In all cases the Commission's contribution is made in ECUs and no liability is held for exchange losses incurred.

12. Points to Note:
Council Decision (EEC) 626/89 adopting the programme was published in OJ L359; 8.12.89.

A call for proposals was published in OJ No C205; 10.8.89.

13. Application Procedure:
Application procedure is outlined in the Information Package, available from the Commission.

14. Further Information:

Matteo Donato
European Commission
DG XII/C-5
Rue de la Loi 200
B-1049 Brussels
Tel: (010 32 2) 235 3955
Fax: (010 32 2) 235 8046
Telex: COMEU B 21877

Mr Peter Hills
Department of Trade and Industry
Industrial Materials Market Division
Room 907
Ashdown House
123 Victoria Street
London SW1E 6RB
Tel: (071) 215 6117

STEEL RESEARCH PROGRAMME

1. Summary:
Under Article 55 of the European Coal and Steel Community (ECSC) Treaty, the European Commission is empowered to provide financial support for collaborative steel process and product oriented research, concentrating on the priority technological needs of the steel industry.

Within the Steel Research Programme, specific project areas are laid down in medium-term guidelines, in order to direct support to projects of specific interest to the Community. Under the current guidelines covering the period 1991–95, the major objectives identified are: the achievement of improved steel quality and reduction of production costs; maintenance of traditional steel markets and the development of new markets; and adaption of production conditions to meet increasingly stringent environmental requirements (see 8 for further details).

Applications are considered on an annual basis and must be submitted by 1 September to be considered for support in the following financial year.

2. Awarding Body:
Commission of the European Communities.

3. Location Restrictions:
Available in any Member State of the European Community.

4. Sectoral Restrictions:
Available to any enterprise, research institute or individual. Projects supported under this programme generally involve collaborative research.

Applicants do not need to be directly connected with the iron and steel industry but research projects must be of interest to a large number of undertakings in this sector.

5. Size Restrictions:

Where a project involves only one organisation, total project costs should not exceed 1 MECU over three years. Preference will be given to large scale transnational projects of major industrial importance, requiring budgets greater than 1 MECU.

6. Programme Duration:

There is no specified terminal date for this scheme. The current guidelines for steel research projects cover the period 1991-95.

7. Submission of Applications/Proposals:

Applications should be submitted before 1 September each year to be considered for support in the following financial year.

8. Other Restrictions:

Priorities identified for the period 1991–95 are:

A. Production Processes: optimising existing production methods and developing new techniques which (a) reduce processing time, or improve processing plant reliability, output quality or processing line flexibility; (b) provide a more detailed knowledge of the physical and chemical phenomena of multiphase systems and develop processes giving new and improved properties; (c) achieve economies in the consumption of raw materials, manpower and energy. Research will focus on: reducing the cost of energy consumed and its effect on the environment, developing treatments for the secondary refining of liquid metal; improving measuring and analysis techniques; modelling of production processes; developing control, automation and robotisation; improving the reliability of installation; developing new processes for making/shaping steel; improving environmental quality and up-grading the value of by-products;

B. Products: optimising properties of existing products and developing new products by (a) speeding-up production, improving promotion and information provision; (b) improving consistency of quality and reliability; and (c) developing new uses for steel and the use of new steel grades. Research will concentrate on the following sectors: transport; energy; civil, plant and mechanical engineering; household and packaging; and environment. Research priorities will be: the development of steel products by existing methods and new techniques (covering forming, weldability, joining and assembly, machinability, aptitude for thermal treatment, surface treatment and coatings); the development of user properties (eg fatigue, fracture and corrosion resistance) and the development of new categories of materials.

C. Environmental Protection: improving environmental control techniques for existing processes; developing new clean technologies for steel production and processing; and upgrading the value of by-products to reduce steelplant wastes.

9. Eligible Expenditure:

Eligible expenditure includes: the cost of equipment and apparatus (the rate of depreciation charged to research costs is generally 20 percent of the purchase price per estimated year of use); gross salaries and statutory charges on all staff directly employed (both full and part-time) on the research; operational costs directly chargeable to the project; a fixed allowance of 30 percent of gross personnel costs for other expenditure not specified elsewhere (eg travel, administrative, etc.).

10. Rate of Award:

As a general rule, the Commission contributes approximately 60 percent of estimated project costs.

11. Payment Procedure:

The Commission makes an advance payment, followed by half-yearly instalments, but normally not more than 90 percent of its total share until the closure of the contract.

12. Points to Note:

The guidelines for the programme for 1991-95 were published in Official Journal No. C252; 6.10.90.

13. Application Procedures:

The procedure applicable to the lodging and consideration of applications, the terms and conditions of aid, and the obligations of the beneficiary as regards protection and dissemination of research results are laid down in a communication published in Official Journal C159; 24.06.82.

14. Further Information:

P R V Evans
European Commission
DG XII C/4
Rue de la Loi 200
B-1049 Brussels
Tel: (010 32 2) 235 3707
Telex: COMEU B 21877

PART THREE

RESEARCH AND TECHNOLOGICAL DEVELOPMENT

3.2 INNOVATION/RESEARCH DISSEMINATION AND EVALUATION

3.2 INNOVATION/RESEARCH DISSEMINATION
AND EVALUATION

MONITOR

1. Summary:

The MONITOR programme supports strategic analysis, forecasting and evaluation projects concerned with new developments in the area of research and technology. The programme's broad aim is to identify new directions and priorities for Community research and technological development policy and to help highlight the relationship between R & D and other common policies. MONITOR comprises three activities: SAST – strategic analysis; FAST – forecasting; and SPEAR – activities in support of the evaluation of R & D programmes (see 8 for further details).

MONITOR will be implemented through transnational collaborative projects carried out by experts and organisations on contract, or through scientific and professional networks. MONITOR will run from 1989 to 1992 with a total budget allocation of 22 MECU.

2. Awarding Body:

Commission of the European Communities.

3. Location Restrictions:

Available in any Member State of the European Community. International organisations, organisations in non-Member States participating in European co-operation in the field of scientific and technological research (COST), and those European countries which have concluded framework agreements in scientific and technical co-operation with the Community, may also participate in the programme on a case-by-case basis, although they will not be eligible for Commission funding.

4. Sectoral Restrictions:

The implementation of the programme will involve research centres or research teams from the Community countries which specialise in strategic analyses, forecasting and the evaluation of R & D programmes.

5. Size Restrictions:

None.

6. Programme Duration:

The programme is set to run from 1989 to 1992.

7. Submission of Applications/Proposals:

A call for expressions of interest (in contract work, research networks, workshop participation, conferences etc) was published in OJ No C144; 10.6.89.

8. Other Restrictions:

The programme comprises the following three activities (estimated funding in brackets):

    1. SAST – strategic analysis (3.1 MECU): aims to clarify the Commun-

ity's strategic orientations in the field of science and technology. More specifically, the aim is to set out policy options for a given problem, and give recommendations for action. Research activities will last from a few months up to twelve to eighteen months.

2. FAST – forecasting (4.5 MECU): the aim is to provide the Community with global long-term analyses consisting of forecasting reports on major topics, applied assessment studies and synthesis reports analysing major topics and key forecasting studies worldwide. Research activities will last for up to one or two years.

3. SPEAR – support studies for the evaluation of Community R & D (1.8 MECU): the aim to provide the Commission with improved theoretical and methodological tools to evaluate the social and economic impact of its R & D programmes – through horizontal evaluations (covering particular activities or mechanisms common to several programmes) and methodological studies of evaluation techniques.

In respect of SAST and SPEAR, the Commission will establish an annual calendar of priority activities. In respect of FAST, a biennial work programme will be established by the Commission.

9. Eligible Expenditure:
Eligible expenditure relates to the total costs of the research undertaken.

10. Rate of Award:
The Commission will pay up to 100 percent of the cost of research undertaken.

11. Payment Procedure:
Details of the payment procedure in each case are available from the European Commission.

12. Points to Note:
Council Decision (EEC) 414/89 adopting MONITOR was published in Official Journal L200; 13.07.89.

13. Application Procedure:
An information package and standard forms for expressions of interest are available on request from the Commission.

14. Further Information:

Herbert Allgeier
European Commission
DG XII
Directorate H – Monitor
Rue de la Loi 200
B-1049 Brussels
Tel: (010 32 2) 235 4055

Mr B Arthur
Department of Trade & Industry
Ashdown House
123 Victoria Street
London SW1E 6RB
Tel: (071) 215 6699

SCIENCE

1. Summary:

SCIENCE (plan to stimulate the international co-operation and interchange needed by European research scientists) is a programme of funding which aims to improve the overall scientific and technical quality of R & D throughout the European Community and contribute thereby to the reduction of scientific and technical development disparities between different Member States. Specific objectives of SCIENCE are to promote training through research, to improve the mobility of scientists throughout the Community, to develop and support intra-European scientific and technical co-operation on high-quality projects, and to promote the establishment of intra-European co-operation and interchange networks.

SCIENCE consists of a range of incentives including research bursaries, research grants, grants for high-level courses, contracts encouraging the twinning of laboratories, and operations contracts including equipment and accompanying measures where appropriate. It covers all fields of science and technology (the exact and natural sciences).

The SCIENCE programme is set to run from 1 January 1988 to 31 December 1992 with a budget of 167 MECU.

2. Awarding Body:

Commission of the European Communities.

3. Location Restrictions:

Available in any Member State of the European Community. It should be noted, however, that activities eligible for funding under the programme must involve cross-national co-operation or interchange.

European non-Member States and international organisations, particularly those taking part in European Co-operation in the field of Scientific and Technical Research (COST) and European countries which have concluded scientific and technical framework co-operation agreements with the EC, may participate in SCIENCE.

4. Sectoral Restrictions:

Available to research scientists, and teams of research and development organisations, whether in the public sector or in industry.

Measures to stimulate interchange and co-operation apply to all fields relevant to the exact and natural sciences such as mathematics; physics; chemistry; life sciences; earth sciences and ocean sciences; scientific instrumentation; engineering sciences.

5. Size Restrictions:

There are no specified size restrictions but some of the activities supported under the programme are restricted in terms of their duration.

6. Programme Duration:

The programme is set to run from 1 January 1988 to 31 December 1992.

7. Submission of Applications/Proposals:

The SCIENCE programme is open to application on a continuous basis.

Proposals are examined by the Committee for the European Development of Science and Technology (CODEST) which meets four times a year.

Application must be made and approval given before the project is started as any expenditure made prior to formal approval will not be eligible for support.

8. Other Restrictions:

The SCIENCE Plan will be implemented by means of the following:
- Research bursaries: to enable scientists to acquire additional training by participating in a research project in a laboratory in a Community country other than their own for a period of at least one and at most two years.
- Research grants: to cover the cost to the laboratories concerned of the transfer or secondment of a scientist from one Community country to another, either to join a research team, or to enable a graduate to specialise before joining a university or industrial research laboratory. Funding covers: short stays; mobility and research costs associated with a longer-term secondment; mobility and research costs associated with attendance at longer training courses; subsidies to extend specialised high-level courses to scientists from different Member States.
- Twinning of laboratories in different countries.
- Development of multidisciplinary, multinational operations: to enable associated research teams to have enough resources (including equipment) and to be able to bring together the best expertise available in different countries and disciplines, in order to achieve a predetermined objective or to undertake jointly a predetermined scientific task.

All the results belong equally to the partners in a project. Projects are chosen essentially on the basis of their quality, the extent to which they are multidisciplinary, innovative, and contribute to breaking down barriers within the Community. Where scientific and technical quality is comparable, particular attention is given to projects likely to reduce scientific and technical disparities between Member States and thereby to contribute to economic and social cohesion within the European Community.

9. Eligible Expenditure:

Eligible expenditure varies depending on the type of researcher involved and the objective of the research bursary/grant. These might include funding for the following: to enable a researcher to make short-stay visits (15 days to 2 months) to another EC country; mobility costs (travel, subsistence, removal, etc.) and possibly the salary of a researcher seconded to, or assimilated in a research team in another EC country over a six month to three year period; mobility and research-related work costs of scientists employed in industry who undertake lengthy training courses (1–3 years) in a public sector laboratory in a different EC country (salary costs are met by the industrial employer); subsidies to bodies offering high level training courses.

In the case of laboratory twinning, support could cover the costs of meetings, of undertaking joint experiments, exchanging results, adding to their equipment, or strengthening their teams by temporarily taking on other scientists.

10. Rate of Award:
The level of financial support is 100 percent of approved expenditure.

11. Payment Procedure:
Payment is normally made in stages as expenditure is defrayed. Typically for a two-year project, 25 percent would be given on signature of the support contract, 50 percent in equal amounts at six-monthly intervals (upon submission of claims detailing expenditure) and the remainder upon completion of the project.

12. Points to Note:
Council Decision (EEC) 419/88 adopting SCIENCE was published in OJ L206; 30.7.88.

The Commission will also undertake a series of consultations, surveys and seminars with the co-operation of Community scientific and technical circles in order to analyse and evaluate scientific and technical needs and opportunities, with the aim of providing more detail to the content of the SCIENCE Plan.

A Stimulation Plan for Economic Science (SPES) was adopted by the Council of Ministers in February 1989 (Council Decision (EEC) 118/89; OJ L44; 16.2.89) with the aim of stimulating co-operation between and the interchange of researchers in economic science. SPES is set to run for four years from 1 January 1989, with a budget allocation of 10 MECU. Topics of research include: the EC's internal market programme and issues of microeconomic analysis; European integration economics; the determinants of economic growth in Western Europe; monetary, macroeconomic and fiscal policy co-ordination issues; trade policy problems and the role of Western Europe in the international division of labour; employment, health and social policy issues; relevant methodological and modelling problems, the setting up of statistical concepts and adequate technical, social and economic indicators, as well as precise economic models; microeconomics; problems with the evaluation of the economic impact of environmental risks; and the problems of economic relations between Western and Eastern Europe.

13. Application Procedure:
Applications for research bursaries/grants, laboratory twinning and operations contracts are made on the appropriate form, available from the address below. Interested applicants should also obtain more detailed information from the Commission.

14. Further Information:
Louis Bellemin	Mr M Tagney
European Commission	Department of Education & Science
DG XII	Elizabeth House
Directorate HI SDM 1/85	York Road
'Stimulation Plan'	London SE1 7PH
Rue de la Loi 200	Tel: (071) 934 9000
B-1049 Brussels	
Tel: (010 32 2) 235 3696	

SPRINT

1. Summary:
SPRINT (Strategic Programme for Innovation and Technology Transfer) provides financial assistance for the following broad actions (see 8 for further details).

(A) Strengthening of the innovation services infrastructure in Europe;

(B) Supporting intra-Community pilot projects for information transfer;

(C) Improving the innovation environment.

SPRINT has been adopted to run from 1 January 1989 to 31 December 1993 with a budget of 90 MECU.

2. Awarding Body:
Commission of the European Communities.

3. Location Restrictions:
Available in any Member State of the European Community. A significant part of the budget will be targeted to benefit regions designated under Objective 1 (lagging in development) or Objective 2 (in industrial decline) of the EC's Structural Funds.

4. Sectoral Restrictions:
Projects, other than studies and services, must involve the participation of organisations from at least two different Member States.

5. Size Restrictions:
None.

6. Programme Duration:
SPRINT has been adopted to run from 1 January 1989 to 31 December 1993.

7. Submission of Applications/Proposals:
Application is made within the deadlines specified in each of the Commission's invitations for proposals to be submitted, published in the Official Journal.

A series of calls for proposals was published in OJ C186; 27.7.90, with deadlines between October and December 1990 (see 12 for further details).

8. Other Restrictions:
Priority lines of action for SPRINT are as follows:

- A. Strengthening the European infrastructure for innovation services by the establishment of intra-Community networks, in particular this involves: (1) consolidation of existing networks, formation of new networks, strengthening intra-Community co-operation, and introduction of linkage mechanisms between the various networks; (2) network support measures – actions of information, awareness, promotion and the transfer of know-how in innovation management and related measures, specific instruments to enhance the effectiveness of networks, and the launching of innovations emerging from networks by improving the dialogue between sources of funding, technical experts and innovators identified by the networks.

- B. Supporting specific projects for intra-Community innovation transfer, particularly by means of transnational projects, accompanying measures to heighten awareness of new technologies and to train companies adopting them, the provision of technical support for potential users and support for the effective execution of projects, particularly by mobilising public and private sector funding. Projects under action B should promote the development of the sectors and the use of the technologies concerned. They must meet, wholly or in part, the following criteria: be model projects employing a systematic overall approach to the introduction of technological change; provide an optimum combination of skills through various forms of co-operation; involve industrial sectors or technologies chosen for their economic impact; contribute to reducing regional technological disparities; be based on and enhance the use of existing infrastructures; include follow-up and evaluation provisions.

- C. Improving the innovation environment through a European Innovation Monitoring System and evaluation of support measures, and strengthening concertation and the exchange of experience in the field of innovation policy and technology transfer, with the particular aim of establishing a favourable regulatory, legal, economic and fiscal environment.

9. Eligible Expenditure:
Eligible expenditure covers the cost of the specific project.

10. Rate of Award:
The rate of award is generally up to 50 percent of eligible project costs although, in exceptional cases, a higher contribution is possible, in particular for the purposes of taking account of the specific difficulties encountered by Objective 1 and 2 regions in taking part in transnational activities.

The Community's financial contribution will be adapted to the characteristics of each specific project. It may take the form of a direct or indirect subsidy, an advance on own capital, or any other appropriate form. As a percentage of total costs, this contribution will be lower the greater the proximity of the action or project is to the market.

11. Payment Procedure:
Payment procedure varies according to the type of project being undertaken.

12. Points to Note:
The 1990 series of calls for proposals covered the following fields:

1. Transnational technology transfer networks, ie the establishment of co-operation schemes between technology and innovation management advisory services located in different Member States (including venture capital clubs);

2. The development of a European Innovation Monitoring System (EIMS), involving the translation of survey and research results on

innovation and technology transfer onto databases, suitable for use in policy decision making and information dissemination;

3. A science park consultancy scheme – either giving advice to science park promoters, or receiving advice from the selected panel of experts;

4. Organising transnational seminars for innovation support service (ISS) suppliers, eg management consultants, university/industry liaison offices concerned with research exploitation, seed and venture capital companies, chambers of commerce etc;

5. Network support measures: organising guided group visits, professional exchanges, technology transfer meetings and investment fora – all for ISS organisations;

6. The definition phase of technology transfer projects – preference will be given to projects focusing on the application of broad spectrum technologies in traditional industrial sectors, sectors with a low technology intensity or sectors with a high social utility/visibility, where these technologies are not yet used.

Council Decision (EEC) 286/89 adopting SPRINT was published in Official Journal L112; 25.4.89.

13. Application Procedure:
Application procedure is outlined in each call for proposals.

14. Further Information:

Mr Robin Miege
European Commission
DG XIII/C/2
Batiment Jean Monnet
Rue Alcide de Gasperi
L-2920 Luxembourg
Tel: (010 35 2) 4301 4180
Telex: 2752 EURDOC LU

Mr Matthew Porter
Department of Trade and Industry
Ashdown House
123 Victoria Street
London SW1E 6RB
Tel: (071) 215 6638

VALUE

1. Summary:
The VALUE programme offers financial support for the dissemination and utilisation of results from Community scientific and technological research. The first part of the programme will be implemented through two subprogrammes covering (I) dissemination and utilisation of the results of Community research and technological development (RTD) activities and (II) the creation of a computer communications network between European research centres (see 8 for further details).

VALUE is implemented through calls for proposals or tenders (restricted or public), contracts for studies and services to be carried out on behalf of the Commission, subsidies and shared-cost contracts, and support for European co-operation networks.

VALUE is set to run from 1 January 1989 to 31 December 1991 with a budget allocation of 38 MECU.

2. Awarding Body:
Commission of the European Communities.

3. Location Restrictions:
Available in any Member State of the European Community. The Commission is authorised to negotiate with third countries taking part in COST (European Co-operation in the field of Scientific and Technical research), with a view to associating them with the programme. It is also authorised to establish appropriate links with EUREKA. Commission funding is, however, restricted to expenditure incurred by organisations established within the Member States.

4. Sectoral Restrictions:
The programme is open to industrial firms, including small and medium-sized enterprises, universities, research institutes, individuals, or combinations thereof.

5. Size Restrictions:
None.

6. Programme Duration:
The programme is set to run from 1 January 1989 to 31 December 1991.

7. Submission of Applications/Proposals:
Application must be made, where appropriate, within the deadlines specified in each of the Commission's calls for proposals or tenders to be submitted, published in the Official Journal. Proposals may be submitted at any time. A call for tenders relating to the preparation and distribution of brochures describing EC scientific and technical publications was published in OJ C319; 19.12.90; with a deadline of 15 February 1991.

8. Other Restrictions:
The general objective of VALUE is to promote the effective utilisation of the results of RTD activities in a bid to attain the goals of the framework programme, to strengthen the scientific and technological basis of European industry, to make industry more competitive at the international level, and to contribute to the completion of the single internal market. Subprogramme I of VALUE (estimated funding - 28 MECU) covers the dissemination and utilisation of the results of Community RTD activities and involves the following lines of action: collection and dissemination of information relating to existing or planned RTD programmes; identification, characterisation and screening to establish their suitability for dissemination or exploitation of the results of relevant RTD activities; action on legal protection of the results; dissemination of results which need not be protected; and promotion of the exploitation of relevant results.

Subprogramme II (estimated funding - 8 MECU) covers Computer communications networks and involves the following lines of action: general support for the development of computer communications networks in the field of RTD; work on requirements for confidentiality and integrity of Community RTD information.

9. Eligible Expenditure:

For organisations other than universities, eligible expenditure covers: labour (actual cost or at approved rates); travel and subsistence; consumables; equipment; computing costs; external work (sub-contracts or services), reasonable overheads. The following are not allowable: profits; marketing, distribution, advertising expenses; any interest or return on capital employed; taxes (except in limited circumstances); cost of proposal preparation; patent protection costs. Specific arrangements exist to recover non-reclaimable VAT.

Universities and higher education establishments may elect to have their support calculated according to the marginal costs of the project (ie the actual additional direct costs of the research not met by normal recurrent expenditure, other financial sources or other third parties), unless their costing and recording systems enable them to submit and justify full costs. Each university is normally expected to operate on the basis of either marginal costs or full costs for all Community R & D programmes, and not reach a decision on a project-by-project basis. Marginal costs may include all the items listed above, although labour costs only relate to temporary additional staff specifically engaged for the research; routine and minor computing costs may not be charged; and overheads may be fixed at a percentage, corresponding to a maximum of 20 percent of all expenditure except associated contracts and VAT.

10. Rate of Award:

The rate of award is normally up to 50 percent of the full economic costs of the R & D project. Universities and higher education establishments may, however, attract a contribution of up to 100 percent of the actual marginal costs of the research project.

11. Payment Procedure:

Payment is made in accordance with the agreed contract and takes the form of an advance payment following signature of the contract by all partners and the Commission, followed by periodic instalments on approval of progress reports and cost statements submitted as work progresses. Ten percent of the total financial contribution is retained (or, in the case of larger contracts, 500,000 ECUs, whichever is lower) and is paid, along with any other sums due, on approval of final technical reports and cost statements.

In all cases the Commission's contribution is made in ECUs and no liability is held for exchange losses incurred.

12. Points to Note:

VALUE aims to ease and accelerate the circulation of information related to Community RTD work and results in order to increase the efficiency of the Research and Technical Development (RTD) work itself and to stimulate the process of innovation and industrial exploitation in Europe.

The European Commission will study, select and apply methods for the efficient dissemination and take-up of technological innovations. It will apply the accumulated experience and best practice of both European and international experts in this field. In its exploitation work, the Commission will take into consideration the legitimate interests of the contractors.

The Commission may also nominate bodies to be its correspondents for the local promotion of the objectives of the programme in Member States or regions where the infrastructure for these activities needs to be developed.

Council Decision (EEC) 412/89 adopting VALUE was published in Official Journal No L200; 13.7.89.

The first call for tenders was issued in OJ No C92; 13.4.89. This was followed by a call for proposals relating to the RTD information service (CORDIS), published in OJ C203; 8.8.89; an invitation to tender for the selection of experts and consultants in the field of RTD results utilisation; published in OJ C229; 6.9.89; a restricted call relating to the promotion of the exploitation of RTD results in OJ C134; 1.6.90; and a call for tenders relating to the continued implementation of the RTD-Results database, published in OJ C264; 19.10.90.

13. Application Procedures:
Application procedure is outlined when a call for proposals is issued.

14. Further Information:

Jean Noel Durvy
European Commission
DG XIII – VALUE Programme
Batiment Jean Monnet
Rue Alcide de Gaspari
L-2920 Luxembourg
Tel: (010 352) 4301 3610
Fax: (010 352) 4301 4129
Telex: 2752 EURDOC LU

Dr P Brooke
Department of Trade & Industry
Kingsgate House
66/74 Victoria Street
London SW1E 6SW
Tel: (071) 215 6611

ACCESS TO LARGE SCALE FACILITIES

1. Summary:
An experimental Community Plan to support and facilitate access to large-scale scientific and technical facilities and installations situated in the European Community has been adopted to run for four years from 1 January 1989. Under the Plan, Community support is available for between one and four years to operators of large-scale scientific and/or technical facilities. In return they must allow free access to the facility for European researchers who would not normally have such access, and provide them with the same scientific, technical and logistic back-up as their normal users.

2. Awarding Body:
Commission of the European Communities.

3. Location Restrictions:
Available in any Member State of the European Community. Scientists or

research workers acquiring access to a facility as a result of financial support under the Plan must be nationals of a Member State.

4. Sectoral Restrictions:

The support is available to any organisation within the Community which possesses major scientific and technical equipment or an installation of interest to the exact and natural sciences, and to any researcher or engineer who is a national of one of the Member States and who is currently working in a public or private sector laboratory in one of the Member States. All fields of the exact and natural sciences are eligible.

5. Size Restrictions:

The support is available for at least one and not more than four years to operators of a large-scale scientific and/or technical facility or a group of smaller facilities which, put together, have the capacity of a large-scale facility.

6. Programme Duration:

The Plan is set to run from 1 January 1989 to 31 December 1992.

7. Submission of Applications/Proposals:

Application must be made within the deadlines specified in each of the Commission's calls for tenders, published in the Official Journal. The Commission also ensures that scientists and research workers who could potentially benefit under the Plan are informed of the possibilities likely to become available.

8. Other Restrictions:

Support is given only to provide access to a scientific facility for scientists or research workers not normally enjoying access to the facility in question. The criteria used to select the facilities to receive Community support are as follows:

- Quality of the facility: specific characteristics; originality or uniqueness, up-to-dateness; range of experiments or tests possible; back-up and technical support available.
- Interest shown by potential users: priority is given to researchers from Member States other than that in which the major installation is situated.
- Cost/benefit ratio of Community support: the number and quality of opportunities made available at the facility in return for Community support.
- Value to the Community: importance of the facility in respect of the Community's overall scientific and technical potential; value of the experimental opportunities made available in terms of achieving the Community's scientific and technical objectives (potential links with sectoral R & D objectives); value of the facility in terms of strengthening the scientific and technical potential of certain countries or regions of the Community.

9. Eligible Expenditure:

Eligible expenditure relates to the following: the operating costs of the facilities and, if necessary, the cost of adaptations and/or special features to meet the objectives of the Plan; incidental expenditure arising from the operations; expenditure incurred by the scientist or research workers, including expenditure on mobility and travel.·

10. Rate of Award:
The assessment and value of Community support is based upon an evaluation of the proposal put forward in relation to the selection criteria (see 8).

11. Payment Procedure:
Details of payment procedure are available from the European Commission.

12. Points to Note:
The precise objectives of the Plan are as follows: to encourage access by researchers who are nationals of Member States to major scientific and technical installations within the Community to which they would not normally enjoy access; to increase training opportunities available to European researchers so as to enable them to make better use of major scientific and technical installations; to develop the use of large-scale scientific and technical facilities within the Community, where necessary by adaptation and/or the addition of special features.

The programme was adopted by Council Decision (EC) 238/89 in Official Journal L98; 11.4.89.

Under a call for tenders published in OJ C93; 14.4.89, the deadline for preliminary applications from operators of large-scale facilities was 1 October 1989.

13. Application Procedure:
Application forms are available from the address below. Preliminary proposals from operators of large-scale facilities submitted under calls for tenders must be accompanied by expressions of interest from potential users.

14. Further Information:

Louis Bellemin
European Commission
DG XII-H-I
(Large-scale facilities plan)
Rue de la Loi 200
B-1049 Brussels
Tel: (010 32 2) 235 3696

Mr M Tagney
Department of Education & Science
Elizabeth House
York Road
London SE1 7PH
Tel: (071) 934 9000

PART THREE

RESEARCH AND TECHNOLOGICAL DEVELOPMENT

3.3 INFORMATION TECHNOLOGY/COMMUNICATIONS

151

3.3 INFORMATION TECHNOLOGY/COMMUNICATIONS

DOSES

1. Summary:
DOSES offers support into the research and development of Statistical Expert Systems. The programme addresses the exploitation of advanced information technologies in the field of statistics, especially the application of expert systems technology to the whole chain of statistical data processing. DOSES consists of two parts: the organisation of co-ordinated projects (Part 1); and shared-cost R & D projects meriting priority in the field of official statistics (Part II).

DOSES is set to run from 1 January 1989 to 31 December 1992 with a budget allocation of 4 MECU.

2. Awarding Body:
Commission of the European Communities.

3. Location Restrictions:
Available in any Member State of the European Community. Agreements may also be negotiated with European third countries and with international organisations, particularly the OECD and its member countries, with a view to their full or partial integration into the programme.

4. Sectoral Restrictions:
Available to research organisations, companies and other organisations within the Community. Part II projects had to involve the participation of at least two partners, who are independent of each other and not both established in the same Member State.

5. Size Restrictions:
None.

6. Programme Duration:
The DOSES programme is set to run from 1 January 1989 to 31 December 1992. A successor programme is currently under discussion.

7. Submission of Applications/Proposals:
Proposals for projects under Part I may be submitted throughout the lifetime of the programme. The budget for Part II projects has now been fully committed.

8. Other Restrictions:
The DOSES programme is being implemented in two parts as follows (allocated budget in brackets):
- Part I Co-ordinated projects covering: subjects which are intrinsically international in character; problems common to various Member States (and possibly the Commission) which may therefore benefit from a co-ordinated approach; problems which must be solved for purposes of harmonisation; problems arising in connection with the processing of confidential data. The emphasis will be on projects able to

produce results in two to three years and on projects requiring the use of techniques associated with the study of artificial intelligence (0.5 MECU).

- Part II Jointly funded projects in the following areas: (1) vertical study (preparation of a complete system for automated information processing, from collection to dissemination, in a specific field); (2) documentation of data and statistical methods; (3) access to statistical information; (4) forecasting (3 MECU). The budget for this part of the programme has now been fully allocated.

9. Eligible Expenditure:

In relation to Part I, co-ordinated projects, the Commission provides a framework within which projects can be selected on the basis of proposals submitted by the interested parties; eligible expenditure relates to the organisation costs of these projects.

For organisations other than universities, eligible expenditure in relation to Part II projects covers: labour (actual cost or at approved rates), travel and subsistence, consumables, equipment, computing costs, external work (subcontracts or services), reasonable overheads. Not allowable are profits; marketing, distribution, advertising expenses, any interest or return on capital employed; taxes (except in limited circumstances), cost of proposal preparation, patent protection costs. Specific arrangements exist to deal with VAT paid in connection with the project, but which cannot be reclaimed from national authorities by the usual means.

Universities and higher education establishments may elect to have their support calculated according to the marginal costs of the project (ie the actual additional direct costs of the research not met by normal recurrent expenditure, other financial sources or other third parties), unless their costing and recording systems enable them to submit and justify full costs. Each university is normally expected to operate on the basis of either marginal costs or full costs for all Community R & D programmes, and not reach a decision on a project-by-project basis. Marginal costs may include all the items listed above for other organisations, except that: labour costs only relate to temporary additional staff specifically engaged for the research; routine and minor computing costs may not be charged; overheads may be fixed at a percentage, corresponding to a maximum of 20 percent of all expenditure, except associated contracts and VAT.

10. Rate of Award:

Financial assistance to help organise Part I co-ordinated projects is available at the discretion of the Commission.

The rate of award for Part II projects is normally up to 50 percent of the full economic costs of the R & D project. Universities and higher education establishments may, however, attract a contribution of up to 100 percent of the actual marginal costs of the project.

11. Payment Procedure:

Payment procedure is detailed in the calls for proposals and the DOSES Information Pack.

12. Points to Note:
Council Decision (EEC) 415/89 adopting DOSES was published in OJ L200; 13.7.89.

13. Application Procedure:
Application procedure is outlined in the calls for proposals and the Information Pack.

14. Further Information:

Daniel Defays	Mr P B Kenny
European Commission	Head of Methodology
DG XIII – DOSES	Branch A3
Batiment Jean Monnet	Central Statistical Office
Rue Alcide de Gasperi	Millbank Tower ·
L-2920 Luxembourg	London SW1P 4QU
Tel: (010 352) 4301 2854	Tel: (071) 217 4209
Telex: 3423 COMEUR LU	Fax: (071) 217 4338

EUROTRA

1. Summary:
The EUROTRA programme supports research and development into a machine translation system of advanced design, capable of dealing with all the official languages of the Community. The programme has now reached its final phase involving the development of an operational EUROTRA system. The objective of this stage of the programme is to develop suitable conditions for the transition to an operational EUROTRA system, advancement of work on lexicography and terminology, and the setting-up of training and co-operative projects. Priority action lines include: system development, testing and research environment; language-specific research and development work; linguistic research of general interest; research into advanced system architectures; re-usability of lexical and terminological resources; standards for textual, lexical and terminological data; education and training; and programme evaluation.

This phase of the programme is set to run for two years from 26 November 1990, with a budget allocation of 10 MECU. It follows on from the previous phase which created the system prototype which is to be further developed.

2. Awarding Body:
Commission of the European Communities.

3. Location Restrictions:
Available in any Member State of the European Community. Participation is also open, subject to appropriate conditions, to organisations in non-Member States which have concluded framework agreements for scientific and technical co-operation with the European Community, and countries

participating in COST (European Cooperation in the field of Scientific and Technological Research).

4. Sectoral Restrictions:

Action Line 1 (system development) will be undertaken by industrial contractors on the basis of calls for tenders. Action Line 2 (language research) will be carried out by national research teams in Member States. Action Lines 3 – 5 inclusive (linguistic research of general interest, advanced system architectures and re-usability of lexical resources) will be carried out as co-operative ventures between industries, research centres and EURO-TRA teams. Contractors will be selected on a call for proposals basis. Action Line 6 will be undertaken by professional associations and standards organisations.

5. Size Restrictions:

None.

6. Programme Duration:

EUROTRA is set to run for two years from 26 November 1990. The Commission has proposed a new Research and Technological Development (RTD) programme in the field of Telematic Systems of General Interest (1990-94), incorporating the area of linguistic research and engineering. This will build on the results of the current EUROTRA Programme.

7. Submission of Applications/Proposals:

Application should be made within the deadlines specified in each of the Commission's calls for proposals, published in the Official Journal. Calls for proposals will be issued in relation to Action Lines 1, 3, 4 and 5 of the programme.

8. Other Restrictions:

Priority Action Lines under EUROTRA are:
1. System development, testing and research environment: the environment should have a powerful and user-friendly formalism for describing linguistic facts; a special-purpose data management system for the creation and maintenance of large-scale dictionaries; an efficient rule interpreter; and a set of testing tools with special attention to interactive on-line testing and correction of dictionaries/grammars;
2. Language-specific research and development work: review and extension of the existing implementations; relayed transfer;
3. Linguistic research of general interest: general linguistic research to increase the interlinguality of the interface structure and reduce overgeneration; use of subject-field specific knowledge; use of text and discourse type-specific constraints to reduce overgeneration;
4. Research into advanced system architectures;
5. Re-usability of lexical and terminological resources: development of methods and tools for the conversion of the formalised parts of existing dictionaries; research into the utilisation of non-formalised portions;
6. Standards for textual, lexical and terminological data;

7. Education and training – research grants for post-graduate students to participate in R & D work outlined above.

9. Eligible Expenditure:

The Commission pays the cost of the central EUROTRA team in Luxembourg and shares the cost of the work undertaken in Member States, with those States contributing the balance of the funds.

10. Rate of Award:

The rate of award for Action Line 1 (system development, testing and research environment) is 100 percent. The rate of award for Action Lines 3–5 inclusive (linguistic research of general interest, advanced systems architectures, re-usability of lexical and terminological resources) is up to 50 percent of total expenditure. This percentage may vary according to the nature and development stage of the research. Universities and research institutes may opt for 100 percent funding of the marginal costs of the project.

11. Payment Procedure:

Payment is made in stages as work progresses.

12. Points to Note:

Council Decision (EEC) 752/82 adopting EUROTRA was published in OJ L317; 13.11.82.

13. Application Procedure:

Application procedure is outlined when a call for proposals is issued.

14. Further Information:

Sergei Perschke
European Commission
DG XIII-B-EUROTRA
Batiment Jean Monnet
L-2920 Luxembourg
Tel: (010 35 2) 4301 3423

Dr N Ostler
Department of Trade & Industry
Ashdown House
123 Victoria Street
London SW1E 6RB
Tel: (071) 215 8317

MEDIA

1. Summary:

The MEDIA programme (Measures to Encourage the Development of the Industry of Audiovisual Production) consists of a package of pilot schemes intended to assist the promotion of the European audiovisual industry through co-operative actions with various EC (and non-EC) media bodies.

Pilot schemes include the provision of financial aid, support services and training programmes aimed at improving the quality and competitiveness of the European film and television industries, and assisting with distribution, production and training costs. The schemes include: the European Film Distribution Office (EFDO); Broadcasting Across the Barriers of European

Language (BABEL); the European Organisation for an Audio-Visual Independent Market (EURO-AIM); the MEDIA Investment Club, the SCRIPT Development Fund; the European Centre for Animation Films (CARTOON) and the European Audiovisual Entrepreneurs (EAVE). The pilot phase of MEDIA ran until the end of 1990. The main phase is proposed to run for five years from 1 January 1991.

2. Awarding Body:
Commission of the European Communities, in conjunction with the film and television industries of EC Member States.

3. Location Restrictions:
Available throughout the European Community, non-Member States may also participate.

4. Sectoral Restrictions:
MEDIA is open to producers and script-writers in the audio-visual industries.

5. Size Restrictions:
The European Film Distribution Office (EFDO) provides loans to assist with the distribution costs of low-budget films (ie with production costs of up to 2.25 MECU) and films with a minimum feature length of 60 minutes. Under the proposed extension of MEDIA, films with production costs of up to 4.5 MECU may receive assistance.
No size restrictions are specified under other pilot schemes.

6. Programme Duration:
The pilot phase of MEDIA ran until the end of 1990. The main phase of the programme is proposed to run for five years from 1 January 1991, to continue support for the schemes initiated under the pilot phase.

7. Submission of Applications/Proposals:
Deadlines for applications to the European Film Distribution Office (EFDO) will be announced in professional international film publications. Further information on application submission for the other MEDIA schemes can be obtained from the Commission.

8. Other Restrictions:
MEDIA covers the following pilot schemes:
  – I. EFDO (Film Distribution Office): assistance towards distribution costs of 'low-budget' EC films (documentary, animation or feature), proposed for release in at least three countries by three different distributors. Support covers costs of dubbing/subtitling, printing, copying and promotion and is intended to supplement the distributors' own investment, becoming repayable if the film breaks even.
  – II. BABEL (Multi-lingual broadcasting): an alliance between the EC, European Broadcasting Union and the European Alliance for Television and Culture (AETC) offers donations for the dubbing and subtitling of television programmes. Priority is given to projects involving less commonly used EC languages.
  – III. EURO-AIM (Audio-visual Markets): provides a range of services

(technical, legal and commercial) assisting independent producers with marketing, promoting and selling their productions. These include shared screening facilities and the EURO-AIM MEDIA database.

- IV. The Media Investment Club unites industry, commerce and finance in an investment aid scheme offering reimbursable loans/subsidies supporting the production of programmes involving advanced technologies (eg digital and HDTV, computer graphics) and training in these technologies.
- V. The SCRIPT Development Fund provides financial assistance for the writing and development of quality fiction scripts on topics likely to attract audiences in at least two different European countries, repayable when the script reaches the production stage and written off if scripts prove to be unsuccessful. Submissions may be made by individuals or teams. The SCRIPT Development Fund is a financial partnership between MEDIA 92, The British Academy of Film and Television Arts (BAFTA), the British Film Institute (BFI), the BBC, ITV and Channel 4.
- VI. CARTOON (Animation films): promotes the development of animation techniques and a co-operation network between European animation studios and also provides seed capital for the scripting, preparation and production of pilot films.
- VII. EAVE (Audiovisual Entrepreneurs): organises training sessions for independent producers (in association with the EC COMETT programme).

Under the main phase of MEDIA, support for these schemes will be continued under the following headings: Distribution Mechanisms (EFDO, EVE, BABEL, EURO-AIM); Improvement of Production Conditions (SCRIPT, CARTOON, MEDIA Investment Club); Stimulation of financial investment; other measures; and promotion of co-operation with professional circles in central and Eastern European countries.

9. Eligible Expenditure:

Eligible expenditure relates to the type of project undertaken.

10. Rate of Award:

Support from EFDO (Film Distribution Office) may be for up to 50 percent of distribution costs; up to a maximum of 70,000 ECU per film and country (repayable if the film breaks even).

Under the SCRIPT Development Fund, subsidies of up to 37,500 ECU are available; repayable if the script reaches the production stage; producers should contribute at least 20 percent of total development costs.

BABEL (Multi-lingual broadcasting) offers financial support covering total project costs of dubbing or subtitling.

11. Payment Procedure:

Payment procedure varies depending on the project undertaken.

12. Points to Note:

Other projects encompassed by MEDIA include: a European video cassette film distribution network (EVE); and a project in collaboration with the European Regional Development Fund developing production facilities in the less favoured regions of Europe.

13. Application Procedure:
Details of the application procedure for all schemes can be obtained from the European Commission or the Producers' Association.

14. Further Information:

European Commission
DG X – MEDIA Programme
Rue de la Loi 200
B-1049 Brussels
Tel: (010 32 2) 235 11 11
Telex: 21877 COMEU B

Lori Keating
Producers' Association
Paramount House
162–170 Wardour Street
London W1V 4LA
Tel: (071) 437 7700
Fax: (071) 734 4564

RACE

1. Summary:
The RACE programme (Research and Development Programme in Advanced Communications Technologies for Europe) supports projects which are designed to bring about the Community-wide introduction of Integrated Broadband Communication (IBC) by 1995, taking into account the evolving Integrated Services Digital Network (ISDN) and national introduction strategies. RACE covers the following three areas: IBC Development and Implementation Strategies; IBC Technologies; Pre-normative Functional Integration.

The programme is set to run from 1 June 1987 to 31 May 1992 with a budget allocation of 550 MECU. This has now been almost completely allocated.

2. Awarding Body:
Commission of the European Communities.

3. Location Restrictions:
Available in any Member State of the European Community.

Where framework agreements for scientific and technical co-operation between non-Member European countries and the European Communities have been concluded, organisations and undertakings in these countries may become partners in a RACE project.

4. Sectoral Restrictions:
Available to network operators, research establishments, undertakings, including small and medium-sized enterprises, and other bodies established in the European Community.

Projects must involve the participation of at least two independent industrial partners not all established in the same Member State. In exceptional cases concerning projects considered indispensable for implementing key requirements of the Workplan, where a proposal would involve unreasonable burdens on participants (especially SMEs and research establishments), only one independent industrial partner, more than one independent industrial partner established in the same Member State, or where an open tendering procedure would be unjustified on grounds of cost or efficiency, or where the Community's contribution is less than 1 MECU, support may be offered outwith the normal tendering procedure and collaboration requirements may be relaxed.

5. Size Restrictions:
None.

6. Programme Duration:
The programme is set to run from 1 June 1987 until 31 May 1992. A follow-on programme, RACE II, has been proposed to run from 1991 until 1994, with a budget allocation of 489 MECU.

7. Submission of Applications/Proposals:
Application is made within the deadlines specified in each of the Commission's calls for proposals to be submitted, published in the Official Journal. The next call for proposals may be issued when the follow-on programme has been approved.

8. Other Restrictions:
RACE covers pre-competitive and pre-normative R & D in advanced telecommunications technologies, aimed at the introduction of Integrated Broadband Communications.
  The programme is structured into three main parts:
  - Part I: IBC Development and Implementation Strategies relating to the development of functional specifications, systems and operations research towards the definition of proposals for IBC standards; concepts and conventions conforming to an open systems approach, and analytical work required for establishing interoperability for IBC equipment and services;
  - Part II: IBC Technologies covering the technological co-operation in pre-competitive R & D addressing key requirements of new technology for the low cost realisation of IBC equipment and services;
  - Part III: Pre-Normative Functional Integration relating to co-operation in the realisation of an 'open verification environment' designed to assess functions, operational concepts and experimental equipment with respect to specifications and standardisation proposals arising from Part I.

RACE II is proposed to focus on eight priority areas: IBC R & D; Intelligence in Networks/flexible communications resource management; mobile and personal communications; image and data communications; integrated services technologies; information security technologies; advanced communications experiments; and test infrastructures and interworking (horizontal R & D supporting other priority areas).

9. Eligible Expenditure:
Eligible expenditure relates to the following allowable costs: labour and certain related overheads; travel, subsistence and relocation; services such as translation, dataprocessing and consultancy; subcontracting and third party participation; materials and durable equipment; and other costs such as patents and know-how acquired for the purposes of the project.

10. Rate of Award:
The rate of award is up to 50 percent of eligible expenditure.

11. Payment Procedure:
Payment is made in instalments. An advance payment is made following notification of the date work will commence. Subsequent instalments will be equal to 50 percent of the actual costs incurred. The advance payment and all instalments other than the last are subject to a maximum cumulative total of 80 percent of the Commission's maximum financial contribution. The final payment is made following acceptance of the final report and consolidated statement of costs incurred. However, if the difference between the total contribution and the 80 percent maximum is higher than 500,000 ECU, the amount retained is limited to 500,000 ECU.

12. Points to Note:
The Commission will ensure close co-ordination with the ESPRIT programme, EUREKA projects and/or other European transnational co-operation projects and national actions.

In order to make optimal use of research facilities and human resources, experts from one organisation can be associated with a RACE project carried out by another organisation where this is agreeable to both parties. The various parties would contribute as follows: parent organisations, release from current duties and 50 percent of the salary; host organisations, costs of providing the work place and operational expenses, RACE, 50 percent of the salary and additional costs associated with the secondment according to the allowable costs for officials on secondment from the country of origin. The secondment must be proposed jointly by parent and host organisation.

Council Decision adopting the RACE programme (EEC) 28/88 was published in Official Journal No L16; 21.1.88.

13. Application Procedure:
Full details of the procedure for submitting proposals when calls are issued are available from the European Commission. Potential applicants registering as interested parties will automatically be sent information when calls are issued. The Department of Trade and Industry can give specialist advice to bidders from UK companies, but requests for bulk information should be directed to the Commission.

14. Further Information:

RACE Central Office
European Commission
DG XIII
Directorate F/RACE TR61
Rue de la Loi 200
B-1049 Brussels
Tel: (010 32 2) 235 9235
Telex: 22045 RACE B

Mr French
Department of Trade and Industry
Telecommunications & Posts Division
Room 415
Kingsgate House
66-74 Victoria Street
London SW1E 6SW
Tel: (071) 215 8193
Fax: (071) 931 7194

PART THREE

RESEARCH AND TECHNOLOGICAL DEVELOPMENT

3.4 ENERGY

3.4.1 NUCLEAR ENERGY

3.4.1 NUCLEAR ENERGY

SCA-RS

1. Summary:
Financial support is available within the Action Research Programme on Reactor Safety (SCA-RS) for research in the following areas: Light Water Reactors; Liquid Metal Fast Breeder Reactors. The objectives are to support research on reactor safety covering priority themes within the research areas, to stimulate collaboration among national organisations, and to promote integration of research performed in national laboratories with that carried out in the Joint Research Centre.

The programme is set to run from 1 January 1988 to 31 December 1991.

2. Awarding Body:
Commission of the European Communities.

3. Location Restrictions:
Available in any Member State of the European Community.

4. Sectoral Restrictions:
Participation in the present research is open to any Community national organisation.

5. Size Restrictions:
Within each research area an upper limit of expenditure is stipulated for individual priority themes. However, there is no specified upper or lower limit on the size of the project acceptable within the programme.

6. Programme Duration:
The programme is set to run from 1 January 1988 to 31 December 1991. The Commission has proposed a new programme in the field of Nuclear Fission, to run from 1990. The programme will cover reactor safety and radiation protection research.

7. Submission of Applications/Proposals:
Application is made within the deadlines specified in each of the Commission's invitations for proposals to be submitted, published in the Official Journal.

8. Other Restrictions:
The research areas within the programme are as follows:
- Light Water Reactors (LWR): reliability and risk evaluation; Project for Inspection of Steel Components (PISC); study of abnormal behaviour of cooling systems; source term;
- Liquid Metal Fast Breeder Reactors (LMFBR): accident modelling; Post Accident Heat Removal (PAHR) in pile.

The criteria used for project selection are the adequacy to fulfil technical requirements; the technical and scientific level; the feasibility in the proposed time schedule; the scientific background of the proposing organisation;

multinationality; the availability of experimental equipment; cost versus benefit.

As part of the SCA-RS programme, the Commission launched an action covering the following LWR source term areas: thermochemical data (providing laboratory measurements of the thermochemical properties of selected compounds of relevance to LWR source term analysis and not available in the open literature); code package for source term predictions (providing the Community with a system code for the prediction of source terms associated with severe accidents in LWR, which would also be applied for interpretation of the Phebus FP in pile tests).

This action was started in 1989 with a provisional budget of approximately 600,000 ECU, continued in 1990 and 1991 with a supplementary yearly budget. Calls for participation were issued in 1989 and 1990.

9. Eligible Expenditure:

For organisations other than universities, eligible expenditure covers: labour (actual cost or at approved rates); travel and subsistence; consumables; equipment; computing costs; external work (sub-contracts or services); reasonable overheads. The following are not allowable: profits; marketing, distribution, advertising expenses; any interest or return on capital employed; taxes (except in limited circumstances); cost of proposal preparation; patent protection costs. Specific arrangements exist to recover non-reclaimable VAT.

Universities and higher education establishments may elect to have their support calculated according to the marginal costs of the project (ie the actual additional direct costs of the research not met by normal recurrent expenditure, other financial sources or other third parties), unless their costing and recording systems enable them to submit and justify full costs. Each university is normally expected to operate on the basis of either marginal costs or full costs for all Community R & D programmes, and not reach a decision on a project-by-project basis. Marginal costs may include all the items listed above, although labour costs only relate to temporary additional staff specifically engaged for the research; routine and minor computing costs may not be charged; and overheads may be fixed at a percentage, corresponding to a maximum of 20 percent of all expenditure except associated contracts and VAT.

10. Rate of Award:

The rate of award is normally up to 50 percent of the full economic costs of the R & D project. Universities and higher education establishments may, however, attract a contribution of up to 100 percent of the actual marginal costs of the research project. In addition, an overhead of 40 percent of the total marginal costs is allowable.

11. Payment Procedure:

Payment is made in accordance with the agreed contract and takes the form of an advance payment following signature of the contract by all partners and the Commission, followed by periodic instalments on approval of progress reports and cost statements submitted as work progresses. Ten percent of the total financial contribution is retained (or, in the case of larger contracts,

500,000 ECUs, whichever is lower) and is paid, along with any other sums due, on approval of final technical reports and cost statements.

In all cases the Commission's contribution is made in ECUs and no liability is held for exchange losses incurred.

12. Points to Note:

Council Decision (EEC) 521/88 adopting SCA-RS was published in OJ L286; 20.10.88.

The most recent call for participation in an action dealing with LWR source term was published in OJ C103; 25.4.90.

13. Application Procedure:

Interested organisations should contact one of the addresses below.

14. Further Information:

European Commission
Institute of Safety Technology – Building 6
Joint Research Centre – Ispra Site
I-21020 Ispra (VA)
Italy
Tel: (010 39) 332 789 593 – A. Markovina – for LWR proposals
Tel: (010 39) 332 789 871 – O. Simoni – for LMFBR proposals
Telex: 380042/380058
Fax: (010 39) 332 789 045

Department of Energy
Atomic Energy Division
1 Palace Street
London SW1E 5HE
Tel: (071) 238 3000

TELEMAN

1. Summary:

The TELEMAN programme offers support for research and training projects in the field of remote handling in nuclear hazardous and disordered environments. The programme is implemented through research and development actions, concerted actions, studies and co-ordination activities. Training/mobility grants are included to facilitate the assembly of relevant skills at appropriate locations for the work of the projects, and to promote effective diffusion of knowledge.

The objective of TELEMAN is to reinforce the scientific and technical base used for the design of nuclear remote handling equipment – tele-operators – especially mechanical arms to which a variety of tools and sensors can be attached, manipulators attached to moveable gantries and partially autonomous vehicles equipped for specialised jobs.

The technical content of the programme covers: I Tele-operator component and subsystem development; II Environmental tolerance; III Research machine projects; IV Product evaluation and studies.

TELEMAN is set to run from 18 July 1989 until 31 December 1993 with a budget allocation of 19 MECU.

2. Awarding Body:
Commission of the European Communities.

3. Location Restrictions:
Available in any Member State of the European Community.

Once firmly established the programme may be extended to EFTA countries, although they will not be entitled to EC funding.

4. Sectoral Restrictions:
Preference is given to projects in which industry, universities and research organisations from Community countries collaborate, and where participants come from more than one Member State. Help with choosing a partner is available from the Commission. The participation of small and medium-sized enterprises is particularly encouraged.

5. Size Restrictions:
None, although the recommended project size has a total cost of between 0.3 and 2 MECU.

6. Programme Duration:
The programme is set to run from 18 July 1989 to 31 December 1993.

7. Submission of Applications/Proposals:
Application is made within the deadlines specified in each of the Commission's invitations to submit proposals, published in the Official Journal. The first call for proposals (covering sections I and II of the programme) was published in OJ C242; 22.9.89. The second call for proposals covered sections III and IV of the programme.

8. Other Restrictions:
TELEMAN covers the following areas (budget allocation in brackets):

    I. Tele-operator component and subsystem development (8.8 MECU): R&D on the utilisation, modification and, where necessary, the development of sensors, perception and decision-making systems, information transmission and engineering for tele-operator mobility and dexterity in nuclear environments.

    II. Environmental tolerance (2.5 MECU): research to be carried out throughout the life of the programme on the adaptation of sensors and electronic hardware to nuclear environments, the development of machine monitoring systems and design strategies that permit easy repair or recovery of stranded machines.

    III. Research machine projects (6.4 MECU): products of research on components and subsystems will be demonstrated by incorporating them into existing or new research machines. Development will focus on tele-operators that typify nuclear industry requirements (eg intelligent manipulators for cranes for use in high radiation fields, and a mobile platform for information gathering).

IV. Product evaluation and studies (1.3 MECU): end-users of TELE-MAN will be encouraged to test and evaluate the practicality and reliability of the products of the programme in realistic environments to guide the subsequent commercialisation of successful products by industry. Studies will cover the application of new technologies, new uses for computer-assisted tele-operators, the evolution of guidelines and standards and programme development.

TELEMAN will, in particular, help the nuclear industry to comply with the requirements that workers be exposed to the minimum practicable amount of radiation without compromising inspection, maintenance and repair operations.

9. Eligible Expenditure:
Eligible expenditure relates to the total cost of the project.

10. Rate of Award:
The rate of award for research contracts is up to 50 percent of project costs.

11. Payment Procedure:
Payment procedure is outlined in the Information Pack available from the Commission.

12. Points to Note:
The first call for proposals was published in OJ C242; 22.9.89. This call covered areas I and II of the programme, and allocated a maximum of 10 MECU.

Council Decision (Euratom) 464/89 adopting TELEMAN was published in Official Journal No L226; 3.8.89.

13. Application Procedure:
Application procedure is outlined in the Information Pack available from the Commission.

14. Further Information:

Herman de Nordwall	Mr P Agrell
European Commission	Department of Energy
DG XII	1 Palace Street
Rue de la Loi 200	London SW1E 5HE
B-1049 Brussels	Tel: (071) 238 3778
Tel: (010 32 2) 235 5355	

DECOMMISSIONING OF NUCLEAR INSTALLATIONS

1. Summary:
Under the research and technological development programme concerned with the Decommissioning of Nuclear Installations, financial support is available for: A. selected R&D projects; B. projects concerned with the identification of guiding principles in relation to a number of key areas; and C. testing of new techniques in practice (see 8).

The aim of the programme is to promote the joint development of a system of management of decommissioned nuclear installations and of the radioactive wastes produced in their dismantling which will provide the best possible protection for mankind and the environment throughout the decommissioning process. The programme is being implemented through research contracts, concerted actions, studies, co-ordination activities; secondment, training and mobility grants will also be available.

The programme has been agreed to run from 1 January 1989 to 31 December 1993 with a budget allocation of 31.5 MECU.

2. Awarding Body:
Commission of the European Communities.

3. Location Restrictions:
Available in any Member State of the European Communities.

The Commission may also negotiate agreements or contracts with a third State, an international organisation or a national of a third State, with a view to associating them wholly or partly with the programme.

4. Sectoral Restrictions:
Research projects may be submitted by industrial organisations, research institutes and universities established in the Community. SMEs are encouraged to participate in the programme.

Where appropriate, research projects should be carried out by participants in more than one Member State and such proposals will be given priority by the Commission.

5. Size Restrictions:
None.

6. Programme Duration:
The programme has been agreed to run from 1 January 1989 to 31 December 1993.

7. Submission of Applications/Proposals:
Application is made within the deadlines specified in each of the Commission's invitations for proposals to be submitted, published in the Official Journal. A call for proposals relating to section C (testing of new techniques in practice) was published in OJ C24; 31.1.91; with a deadline of 31 March 1991.

8. Other Restrictions:
Activities eligible for support include (indicative budget allocations in brackets):

A. Research and development projects concerned with long-term integrity of buildings and systems; decontamination for decommissioning purposes; dismantling techniques; treatment of specific waste materials (steel, concrete, graphite); qualification and adaptation of remote-controlled semi-autonomous manipulator systems; estimation of quantities of radioactive wastes arising from decommissioning (8.4 MECU).

B. Identification of guiding principles relating to the design and operation of nuclear installations with a view to simplifying their subsequent decommissioning; minimising occupational radiation exposures during decommissioning; the technical elements of a Community policy in this field (1.1 MECU).

C. Testing of new techniques in practice within the framework of large-scale decommissioning operations (16.6 MECU), mainly focusing on a few, already selected, pilot dismantling projects (see 12), but including complementary tests performed in other nuclear installations (4.3 MECU).

The secondment of research staff from other Member States, to the pilot dismantling projects, will also be promoted within this area (1.1 MECU).

9. Eligible Expenditure:

For organisations other than universities, eligible expenditure covers: labour (actual cost or at approved rates); travel and subsistence; consumables; equipment; computing costs; external work (sub-contracts or services); reasonable overheads. The following are not allowable: profits; marketing, distribution, advertising expenses; any interest or return on capital employed; taxes (except in limited circumstances); cost of proposal preparation; patent protection costs. Specific arrangements exist to recover non-reclaimable VAT.

Universities and higher education establishments may elect to have their support calculated according to the marginal costs of the project (ie the actual additional direct costs of the research not met by normal recurrent expenditure, other financial sources or other third parties), unless their costing and recording systems enable them to submit and justify full costs. Each university is normally expected to operate on the basis of either marginal costs or full costs for all Community R & D programmes, and not reach a decision on a project-by-project basis. Marginal costs may include all the items listed above, although labour costs only relate to temporary additional staff specifically engaged for the research; routine and minor computing costs may not be charged; and overheads may be fixed at a percentage, corresponding to a maximum of 20 percent of all expenditure except associated contracts and VAT.

10. Rate of Award:

The rate of award is up to 50 percent of the full economic costs of research undertaken by commercial undertakings and 100 percent of the marginal costs of research undertaken by universities and higher education institutes.

11. Payment Procedure:

Payment is made in accordance with the agreed contract and takes the form of an advance payment following signature of the contract by all partners and the Commission, followed by periodic instalments on approval of progress reports and cost statements submitted as work progresses. Ten percent of the total financial contribution is retained (or, in the case of larger contracts, 500,000 ECUs, whichever is lower) and is paid, along with any other sums due, on approval of final technical reports and cost statements.

In all cases the Commission's contribution is made in ECUs and no liability is held for exchange losses incurred.

12. Points to Note:
Council Decision (EURATOM) 239/89 adopting the Decommissioning of Nuclear Installations Programme was published in OJ L98; 11.4.89.

Under the call for proposals published in June 1989 (OJ No C196; 13.06.89), applications were invited in respect of Section A (all areas) and part of Section C (alternative large-scale tests to be performed in nuclear installations other than the already selected pilot dismantling projects), secondments of staff to the pilot dismantling projects and, within the framework of the pilot dismantling projects, the large-scale testing of appropriate new techniques developed in Member States.

13. Application Procedure:
Application procedure is outlined in the call for proposals and in the Information Pack.

14. Further Information:
Mr B Huber
European Commission
Division XII/D/2 (ARTS 2/37)
Rue de la Loi 200
B-1049 Brussels
Tel: (010 32 2) 235 4084
Telex: 21877 COMEU B
Fax: (010 32 2) 236 2006

Mr P Agrell
Department of Energy
1 Palace Street
London SW1E 5HE
Tel: (071) 238 3778

MANAGEMENT AND STORAGE OF RADIOACTIVE WASTE

1. Summary:
The research and technical development programme in the field of Management and Storage of Radioactive Waste is aimed at perfecting and demonstrating a system for managing the radioactive waste produced by the nuclear industry ensuring, at the various stages, the best possible protection of man and environment. Part A covers waste management and associated R & D actions, Part B covers the construction and/or operation of underground facilities open to Community joint activities.

The programme is carried out by means of research contracts, study contracts, co-ordination projects and training and mobility grants, and is set to run for five years from 1 January 1990, with a budget allocation of 79.6 MECU.

2. Awarding Body:
Commission of the European Communities.

3. Location Restrictions:
Available in any Member State of the European Community.

4. Sectoral Restrictions:
The programme will be implemented mainly through research contracts

with public organisations or private firms, including small and medium-sized enterprises.

5. Size Restrictions:
None.

6. Programme Duration:
The programme is set to run from 1 January 1990 to 31 December 1994.

7. Submission of Applications/Proposals:
Application is made within the deadlines specified in each of the Commission's invitations for proposals to be submitted, published in the Official Journal.

8. Other Restrictions:
The programme will cover the following tasks/projects (budget allocation in brackets):
- Part A: Waste management and associated R & D actions: 1. System studies and harmonisation of waste management practices and policies (5.4 MECU); 2. Treatment of radioactive waste (7.5 MECU); 3. Safety of the multi-barrier system of geological disposal (39.2 MECU);
- Part B: Construction and/or operation of underground facilities open to Community joint activities (27.5 MECU): 1. Pilot underground facility in the Asse salt mine in the Federal Republic of Germany; 2. Pilot underground facility in the agrillaceous layer under the Mol nuclear site in Belgium; 3. Underground validation facility in France; 4. Underground validation facility in the United Kingdom. Other projects may be added in the course of the programme.

9. Eligible Expenditure:
For organisations other than universities, eligible expenditure covers: labour (actual cost or at approved rates), travel and subsistence, consumables, equipment, computing costs, external work (sub-contracts or services), reasonable overheads. The following are not allowable: profits; marketing, distribution, advertising expenses; any interest or return on capital employed; taxes (except in limited circumstances); cost of proposal preparation; patent protection costs. Specific arrangements exist to recover non-reclaimable VAT.

Universities and higher education establishments may elect to have their support calculated according to the marginal costs of the project (ie the actual additional direct costs of the research not met by normal recurrent expenditure, other financial sources or other third parties), unless their costing and recording systems enable them to submit and justify full costs. Each university is normally expected to operate on the basis of either marginal costs or full costs for all Community R & D programmes, and not reach a decision on a project-by-project basis. Marginal costs may include all the items listed above, although labour costs only relate to temporary additional staff specifically engaged for the research; routine and minor computing costs may not be charged; and overheads may be fixed at a percentage, corresponding to a maximum of 20 percent of all expenditure except associated contracts and VAT.

10. Rate of Award:

The rate of award is normally up to 50 percent of the full economic costs of the R & D project. Universities and higher education establishments may, however, attract a contribution of up to 100 percent of the actual marginal costs of the research project.

11. Payment Procedure:

Payment is made in accordance with the agreed contract and takes the form of an advance payment following signature of the contract by all partners and the Commission, followed by periodic instalments on approval of progress reports and cost statements submitted as work progresses. Ten percent of the total financial contribution is retained (or, in the case of larger contracts, 500,000 ECUs, whichever is lower) and is paid, along with any other sums due, on approval of final technical reports and cost statements.

In all cases the Commission's contribution is made in ECUs and no liability is held for exchange losses incurred.

12. Points to Note:

Council Decision (EURATOM) 664/89 adopting the Management and Storage of Radioactive Waste Programme was published in OJ L395; 30.12.89.

A call for proposals was published in OJ C55; 7.3.90 relating to Part A of the programme.

13. Application Procedure:

Application procedure is detailed in each call for tenders.

14. Further Information:

Mr Serge Orlowski
European Commission
DG XII
Rue de la Loi 200
B-1049 Brussels
Tel: (010 32 2) 235 4063
Telex: 21877 COMEU B

Research and Assessments Branch
Radioactive Substances Division
H M Inspectorate of Pollution
Romney House
43 Marsham Street
London SW1 3PY
Tel: (071) 276 8090

PART THREE

RESEARCH AND TECHNOLOGICAL DEVELOPMENT

3.4 ENERGY

3.4.2 NON-NUCLEAR ENERGY

3.4.2 NON-NUCLEAR ENERGY

THERMIE

1. Summary:
The THERMIE programme offers financial support for projects promoting energy technology (ie projects designed to develop and promote innovative technologies whose implementation entails a large element of risk).

THERMIE covers the following fields of application: rational use of energy; renewable energy sources; coal and other solid fuels; and hydrocarbons. Support is available for innovatory projects, dissemination projects, and targeted projects instigated by the European Commission (see 8 for further details).

THERMIE is set to run from 1990 to 1994, with a budget allocation of 350 MECU over the first three years. A further 350 MECU has been proposed for the final two years of the programme.

2. Awarding Body:
Commission of the European Communities.

3. Location Restrictions:
Available in any Member State of the European Community. Projects implemented in less developed regions are particularly encouraged.

Projects must generally be carried out within Community territory. However, if it is in the interests of the Community to have all or part of a project carried out in a non-Member State, because of the special characteristics of the project, it may also qualify.

4. Sectoral Restrictions:
Projects may be submitted by persons or undertakings established within the Community. Preference is given to projects proposed by small and medium-sized enterprises or by an association of such enterprises. Projects must be proposed by persons prepared to disseminate the techniques, processes or products.

Projects costing over 6 MECU must, as a general rule, be submitted by two independent promoters in different Member States. Projects with a total cost of less than 6 MECU may be proposed by single organisations, although projects proposed by independent organisations in two or more Member States are also encouraged.

5. Size Restrictions:
None.

6. Programme Duration:
THERMIE is set to run until 31 December 1994.

7. Submission of Applications/Proposals:
Application is made within the deadlines specified in each of the

Commission's invitations for proposals to be submitted, published in the Official Journal.

Under the second call (OJ No 215; 30.8.90), proposals had to be submitted by 7 January 1991.

8. Other Restrictions:

Support may be granted for:

- Innovatory projects implementing innovatory techniques, processes or products for which the R & D stage has been completed, or new applications of established techniques, products or processes; projects should prove the viability of new technologies by applying them on a sufficiently large scale for the first time;
- Dissemination projects for the techniques, processes or products referred to above; projects must be designed to encourage preliminary applications of tested new technologies, either under different economic or geographic conditions or with technical modifications, provided they still entail some risk.
- Targeted projects: where the EC considers it necessary, and especially where a need is not being met or where a significant technological advance could be achieved, it will itself take the initiative to encourage or co-ordinate the setting-up of specific projects.

THERMIE covers the following fields and sectors of application:

- Rational Use of Energy: in buildings; industry; energy industry, electricity and heat; transport and urban infrastructure.
- Renewable Energy Sources: solar energy (thermal and photovoltaic applications); energy from biomass, agricultural products and waste; geothermal energy; hydroelectric energy; wind energy.
- Coal and Other Solid Fuels: combustion; conversion; waste; gasification integrated with a combined gas/steam cycle.
- Hydrocarbons: innovatory projects relating to onshore and offshore exploration, production, transportation and storage of oil and natural gas; refining projects are excluded, as are dissemination projects.

Projects must appear technically and economically viable, must offer appropriate solutions for protection of the environment and safety, be difficult to finance because of technical or economic risks and be designed to encourage propagation of the technology on the market.

9. Eligible Expenditure:

Support may be granted for an entire project, for novel elements of a project, or for different stages of a project.

10. Rate of Award:

The rates of award are determined separately for each project and may be up to 40 percent of eligible costs for Innovatory or Targeted projects, and up to 35 percent of eligible costs for Dissemination projects.

11. Payment Procedure:

Payment procedure is detailed in an Information Pack accompanying each call for proposals, but is normally 30 percent on signing of the contract, 50 percent phased throughout the project, and the final 20 percent on submission of a satisfactory final report.

12. Points to Note:

Council Decision (EEC) 2008/90 adopting THERMIE was published in OJ L185; 17.7.90.

The first call (OJ C77; 27.3.90) covered the rational use of energy, biomass, solar energy, wind/diesel systems, solid fuels and hydrocarbons. A total of 55 MECU was allocated to projects under this call.

An invitation to tender for assistance with the implementation of THERMIE, encouraging the application and market penetration of energy technologies, was published in OJ C188; 28.7.90; deadline 10 September 1990.

The Commission may undertake associated measures to encourage the application and marketing of energy technologies – eg evaluating and analysing market features and potential (including any feasibility studies); circulating information and results of projects; monitoring, auditing projects and sectoral energy units; areas of technological co-operation; encouraging industrial co-operation with third countries; training staff; using regional institutions to help with these activities.

The Commission may require all or part of the financial support granted to be repaid if the contractor responsible for implementing a project receiving assistance does not use the successful technique, process or product, or facilitate its use and allow the results obtained to be disseminated.

13. Application Procedure:

Application procedure is outlined in the Information Packs accompanying each call for proposals.

14. Further Information:

Michael Thomas Gowen
European Commission
DG XVII
Energy Technology
Rue de la Loi 200
B-1049 Brussels
Tel: (010 32 2) 236 0436
Telex: 21877 COMEU-B
Fax: (010 32 2) 235 0150

UK contacts are as follows:
General Enquiries:
David Wallace
Department of Energy
1 Palace Street
London SW1E 5HE
Tel: (071) 238 3010
Tel: (0235) 432621 – Richard Shock
(Rational Use of Energy)
Tel: (0235) 433561 – Arthur Hollis
(Renewables)
Tel: (071) 238 3011 – Alan Heyes
(Solid Fuels)
Tel: (041) 242 5762 – Brian Darbyshire
(Hydrocarbons)

COAL RESEARCH PROGRAMME

1. Summary:
Under Article 55 of the European Coal and Steel Community (ECSC) Treaty the European Commission is empowered to provide financial support for technical coal research projects relating to the production and increased use of coal and to occupational safety in the coal industry.

Within the Coal Research Programme, specific project areas are laid down in medium-term guidelines in order to direct support to projects of specific interest to the Community. Under the current guidelines, laid down for the period 1990 to 1995, two major sectors of the coal industry have been selected for research projects: mining engineering, and product upgrading. It is planned to give special emphasis to problems of environmental protection in the 1991 programme.

2. Awarding Body:
Commission of the European Communities.

3. Location Restrictions:
Available in any Member State of the European Community.

4. Sectoral Restrictions:
Available to any enterprise, research institute or individual. Applicants do not need to be directly connected with the coal industry but research projects must be of interest to a large number of undertakings in the coal sector.

5. Size Restrictions:
There are no formal restrictions, but projects should not exceed five years in duration.

6. Programme Duration:
There is no specified terminal date for this scheme.

7. Submission of Applications/Proposals:
Applications should be submitted before 1 September each year in order to be effective the following year.

8. Other Restrictions:
Under the 1990 to 1995 guidelines, eligible projects can relate to mining engineering or product upgrading. Within mining engineering, the following research fields are included: development work (relating to new pits or the extension of existing pits); mine gases, ventilation, climate; methods of working and techniques of coal-winning; mine infrastructure; modern management. Projects concerned with product upgrading may relate to: coal preparation; metallurgical uses of coal; combustion of coal; coal upgrading and conversion.

The criteria used for the selection of research projects are as follows:
- the objectives of the common energy policy and of the common general research policy (with particular reference to energy research); the interest of the research for the Community; the value of the research; the repercussions on the environment; the lead time between the completion of the research and its practical application.

9. Eligible Expenditure:

Eligible expenditure includes: the cost of equipment and apparatus (the rate of depreciation charged to research costs is generally 20 percent of the purchase price per estimated year of use); gross salaries and statutory charges on all staff directly employed (both full and part-time) on the research; operational costs directly chargeable to the project; a fixed allowance of 30 percent of gross personnel costs for other expenditure not specified elsewhere (eg travel, administrative, etc.).

10. Rate of Award:

As a general rule, the Commission contributes approximately 60 percent of estimated project costs. The extent of the contribution may vary from one project to another and will depend on the value of the research, its importance in the context of general objectives and on whether the research is initiated by the applicant or the Commission.

11. Payment Procedure:

The Commission will pay an advance on request, followed by half-yearly instalments, but normally not more than 90 percent of its total share until the closure of accounts.

12. Points to Note:

The objectives of ECSC coal research are to: reduce production costs; concentrate R & D efforts on projects with the best prospects of technical and economic results; assure the optimal use of R & D resources through close collaboration/rapid dissemination of research results; maintain the technological lead position of engineering/mining machinery manufacturers; optimise colliery management through improved systems; transfer best practice to difficult geological situations; improve raw coal quality; increase the share of coal in the heat market; develop the coking plant of the year 2000; optimise coal utilisation processes to improve the public acceptance of coal; work towards the clean utilisation of coal.

The 1990-95 guidelines were published in Official Journal No C52; 1.03.89.

13. Application Procedures:

The procedure applicable to the lodging and consideration of applications, the terms and conditions of aid, and the obligations of the beneficiary as regards protection and dissemination of research results are laid down in a communication published in Official Journal No C159; 24.06.82.

14. Further Information:

James Keith Wilkinson
European Commission
Energy Technology Directorate
XVII/D/2
Rue de la Loi 200
B-1049 Brussels
Tel: (010 32 2) 235 5576

PART THREE

RESEARCH AND TECHNOLOGICAL DEVELOPMENT

3.5 ENVIRONMENTAL RESEARCH

3.5 ENVIRONMENTAL RESEARCH

ACE

1. Summary:
The ACE programme (Action by the Community relating to the Environment) offers financial assistance for demonstration projects aimed at developing: (a) new clean technologies; (b) techniques for recycling and re-using waste; (c) techniques for locating and restoring sites contaminated by hazardous wastes and/or substances; (d) techniques and methods for measuring and monitoring the quality of the natural environment.

Also eligible are projects for the conservation of nature (especially (e) seriously threatened biotopes which are the habitat of endangered bird species) and (f) projects for the protection or re-establishment of land threatened or damaged by fire, erosion and desertification.

The four-year programme (1987-1991) has a budget allocation of 24 MECU.

2. Awarding Body:
Commission of the European Communities.

3. Location Restrictions:
Available in any Member State of the European Community.

4. Sectoral Restrictions:
Available to any natural persons, or legal persons constituted in accordance with the law of the Member States, who are responsible for the project.

5. Size Restrictions:
None.

6. Programme Duration:
The programme is set to run from 30 July 1987 until 29 July 1991.

The Commission has proposed a new Research and Technical Development (RTD) programme in the field of the environment, to run from 1990-94. The topics it will cover include: participation in global change programmes; technologies and engineering for the environment; research on economic and social aspects of environmental issues, and integrated research projects.

7. Submission of Applications/Proposals:
Application is made within the deadlines specified in each of the Commission's invitations to submit proposals, published in the Official Journal.

A specific call relating to plastics and tyre recycling was published in OJ C134; 1.6.90; deadline 30 June 1991.

It is unlikely that there will be any further calls for proposals in relation to areas (a) and (b).

Project proposals relating to (e) and (f) may be submitted to the

Department of Environment at any time although they are considered by the Commission in batches.

8. Other Restrictions:

Projects must satisfy the following conditions: be based on completed R & D; relate to full-size installations or the development of ready to apply techniques; exploit innovatory techniques, processes or products which are still untested or not yet in existence in the EC; offer promising prospects of industrial, economic and commercial viability and for the dissemination of similar projects; present financing difficulties due to the considerable technical and economic risks involved.

Projects (a) to (c) (new clean technologies, recycling and re-using waste, location and restoration of contaminated sites) must concern installations or processes which seriously harm the environment.

Projects in (d) (measurement and monitoring of the natural environment) must cover the major air, water and soil pollutants and contribute towards harmonisation of methods of measurement and the compatibility of measurement results obtained within the Community.

9. Eligible Expenditure:

Eligible expenditure relates to total project costs, excluding the costs of building and land.

10. Rate of Award:

The rates of award are as follows: up to 30 percent for projects relating to clean technologies, waste recycling and the restoration of, contaminated sites (a–c); up to 50 percent for projects relating to measurement techniques, seriously threatened biotopes, and land reclamation (d–f) with, exceptionally, 75 percent awarded in respect of (e) – seriously threatened biotopes.

The actual level of the Community's contribution is determined by the extent to which it is shown that the project is of interest to the Community in terms of protection of the environment and/or management of natural resources.

In the event of the commercial exploitation of the results of a project, the Community may request repayment of its financial contribution in accordance with arrangements to be laid down in the contract.

11. Payment Procedure:

An advance payment is made on signature of the contract. Advances are also paid, as specified in the contract, on the basis of technical reports on the progress of the work (together with a statement of expenditure) to be submitted every six months, a final report on the work carried out, a final report on the evaluation of the results obtained, and a full statement of expenditure closing the accounts.

12. Points to Note:

Projects under headings (a) to (d) which are eligible for financial support under other Community programmes are excluded.

The contractor remains the owner of patentable inventions and of the know-how obtained during the course of the project. He must, however, undertake to disseminate directly, with or without the collaboration of the

Community, the results of the project and to exploit or facilitate exploitation of the successfully demonstrated technique, process or product. The contractor must provide the EC with technical reports on the progress of the work, accompanied by statements of expenditure (every 6 months), a final report and a report for publication purposes, and a full statement of expenditure closing his accounts at the end of the project.

Council Regulation (EEC) 2242/87 adopting ACE was published in OJ L207; 29.7.87.

13. Application Procedure:

Application in relation to demonstration projects in areas (a) to (d) are submitted to the Commission in response to a call for proposals published in the Official Journal. Application procedures are outlined in each call for proposals.

Proposals relating to projects in areas (e) and (f) are submitted to the Department of the Environment before being submitted to the Commission.

14. Further Information:

Department of the Environment   Eusebio Murillo-Matilla
Room A3.04   European Commission
Romney House   DG XI/A/3
43 Marsham Street   ACE Programme
London SW1P 3PY   Rue de la Loi 200
Tel: (071) 276 8388   B-1049 Brussels
                                 Tel: (010 32 2) 236 13 88

MEDSPA

1. Summary:

MEDSPA (Environmental Protection in the Mediterranean) is a co-ordinated international action programme aimed at tackling the environmental problems of the Mediterranean region. Participation in the programme is open to organisations from any Member State. Action under MEDSPA complements that undertaken by the Community Structural Funds and Financial Instruments, and includes subsidies for pilot/demonstration schemes and projects other than infrastructure projects, interest rebates for infrastructure projects, and repayable advances.

Priority areas identified include waste management (including toxic waste and sewage sludge), water treatment and nature conservation (see 8 for further details). The programme is set to run for ten years, from 1990 to 1999, and is divided into two phases. By the end of 1994, priority areas for the second phase will be reassessed.

2. Awarding Body:

Commission of the European Communities. Action under MEDSPA complements other Community programmes pursuing similar objectives, in particular: the Structural Funds (ERDF, EAGGF (Guidance Section), ESF);

the Community Financial Instruments (the EIB, ECSC Loans); the Integrated Mediterranean Programmes (IMPs); the Community Research and Technological Development programmes (in particular ACE); Community action for the protection of forests; co-operation agreements with non-Member States; instruments providing regional and multilateral co-operation; and ecology in the developing countries.

3. Location Restrictions:

Project proposals are accepted from organisations located in any Member State of the European Community, and may concern any part of the Mediterranean region (ie both EC and non-EC regions, and those territories of Spain and Portugal south of the river Tagus) irrespective of whether they border on the Mediterranean.

4. Sectoral Restrictions:

The programme is open to organisations in any Member State, but preference is given to actions conducted jointly by several Mediterranean partners, those concerning the southern side of the Mediterranean and those of interest to several countries in the region.

5. Size Restrictions:

None.

6. Programme Duration:

The programme is set to run from 1990 to 1999.

7. Submission of Applications/Proposals:

Application must be made and approval given before any work on a project is undertaken or expenditure is incurred. Application is made within the deadlines specified in the calls for proposals published in the Official Journal.

8. Other Restrictions:

Projects should present financial difficulties such that they would not be carried out without public sector national or community aid.

Priority areas identified are as follows:

1. Management of waste (water and solid) in coastal towns with less than 100,000 inhabitants and on small islands;
2. Management of dangerous and toxic waste and sewage sludge;
3. Treatment of ballast or tank-washing water, and oil and chemical residues from maritime activities;
4. Integrated management of characteristic coastal ecosystems.

9. Eligible Expenditure:

Eligible expenditure relates to the type of work undertaken. Assistance may be granted to a project in its entirety or to different phases of a project.

10. Rate of Award:

The rate of award is: up to 50 percent of total costs in the case of public investment projects and pilot/demonstration projects; up to 30 percent of total costs in the case of private investment projects; and up to 100 percent of total costs for measures designed to provide the information required for implementation of the action or of technical assistance measures initiated by the Commission.

11. Payment Procedure:
Payment procedure is agreed in relation to the type of work undertaken.

12. Points to Note:
The programme is undertaken in co-operation with other international bodies with similar objectives in the region, particularly the specialised UN agencies, such as Mediterranean Action Plan (MAP) and the World Bank.

An invitation to submit proposals for demonstration projects, projects raising public awareness and data management projects was published in OJ S54; 17.3.89. The priorities identified for 1989 were: the upgrading and management of sensitive ecosystems typical of the Mediterranean region; protection of indigenous fauna and flora; management of wastes in small-scale human settlements; treatment and utilisation of agricultural waste; the rehabilitation of areas contaminated by dangerous and toxic wastes, and the treatment of residues from those areas.

A further call was published in OJ C41; 21.2.90.

13. Application Procedure:
Application procedure is outlined in each call for proposals published in the Official Journal.

14. Further Information:
Mr Zampetti
European Commission
DG XI – Task Force MEDSPA
10 Rue Guimard
B-1040 Brussels
Tel: (010 32 2) 235 1774
Fax: (010 32 2) 235 4947

PILOT CONSERVATION PROJECTS (ARCHITECTURAL HERITAGE)

1. Summary:
Assistance is available for pilot projects to conserve and promote the European Community's architectural heritage. Support is given to projects concerned with the conservation of monuments/sites, in rural or urban areas, illustrating some aspects of the national, regional or local architectural heritage of the Community by reason of their artistic value, historic interest and socio-economic influence in bearing witness to the living and working conditions of a given section of the population.

Within a four-year (1989–1992) plan designed to make more efficient use of the Community's resources and to lead to more positive action in the architectural heritage sector, emphasis is to be given each year to a theme depicting the functional relationships between the relevant monuments/sites, the environment and the public.

In 1991, the theme is: testimonies to productive activities in industry, agriculture and crafts.

2. Awarding Body:
Commission of the European Communities.

3. Location Restrictions:
Available in any Member State of the European Community. The Commission is considering extending the programme to cover projects in Central and Eastern Europe.

4. Sectoral Restrictions:
Available to any individual or body in possession of, or responsible for a monument or site of European renown which illustrates some aspects of the national or regional architectural heritage of the Community.

5. Size Restrictions:
The maximum project cost eligible for grant aid is 5 MECU.

6. Programme Duration:
The programme is currently operating under a four-year plan covering 1989-1992.

7. Submission of Applications/Proposals:
Application must be made within the deadlines specified in each of the Commission's annual invitations for proposals to be submitted, published in the Official Journal. The call relating to the 1991 round of awards was published in OJ C304; 4.12.90; with a deadline of 20 February 1991.

Application must normally be made and grant approved before work on the project is begun as no grant will be paid in respect of expenditure incurred prior to approval.

8. Other Restrictions:
The following themes will be highlighted over the coming years:
- 1991 Testimonies to productive activities in industry, agriculture, crafts etc, ie monuments and sites which have served as workplaces and whose importance to European heritage is clearly establishd. This may relate to architecture, or to the historic and social significance of the monument or site, or to its contents (tools, machines etc).
- 1992 Upgrading of public spaces in historic centres as part of a restoration project: to upgrade urban centres, setting out to restore the link between historic buildings and their environment, and giving a new purpose to the complex in keeping with its architectural and historic character.

Priority will be given to projects which provide novel solutions: (1) allowing the conservation of technical equipment 'in situ'; or (2) using a monument or disused site for a new purpose compatible with its architectural characteristics.

The provision of financial support is conditional on the following: the applicant must allow the conservation/restoration work to be inspected; the grant must be used entirely for the conservation/restoration work, which must be completed by a specified date; the applicant must ensure that the

Commission's financial contribution to the project is made known to the general public; and applications must not be submitted for projects which have already received Community financial support in previous years.

9. Eligible Expenditure:

Eligible expenditure covers the total approved conservation costs of the project. Modernisation work, technical improvements and new construction work are not eligible.

10. Rate of Award:

The rate of award varies according to the size of the project as follows: up to 25 percent for projects with a total investment of up to 750,000 ECU (maximum grant 130,000 ECU); up to 10 percent for projects costing between 750,000 ECU and 2.5 MECU (maximum grant 150,000 ECU); and up to 5 percent for projects costing between 2.5 and 5 MECU (maximum grant 125,000 ECU).

11. Payment Procedure:

Payment procedure will be arranged by individual contracts with successful applicants. The Commission grant will not be definitively paid until such time as the relevant regional or national organisation has accepted the conservation works.

12. Points to Note:

In 1989, the scheme concerned emerging civil and religious monuments/ sites (ie monuments and sites, archaeological sites, historic gardens which are of exceptional interest due to their historical message or their architectural value); in 1990 it covered historic buildings and groups of buildings which define and characterise an urban or rural pattern: individual buildings and complexes which by their nature form and define the character of a town or village, and reflect its historical continuity.

13. Application Procedure:

Application is made direct to the European Commission on a standard form, available from the Commission or the relevant regional address below, and must include descriptions of the monument and the project. Adequate documentation providing a clear explanation of the monument or site and the work to be carried out must be enclosed. A copy of the application must be sent at the same time to the relevant UK national organisation (see 14).

14. Further Information:

In England:
English Heritage
Historic Buildings & Monuments
   Commission for England
Fortress House
23–25 Savile Row
London W1X 1AB
Tel: (071) 734 6010

In Scotland:
Scottish Office Environment
   Department
Historic Buildings and Monuments
20 Brandon Street
Edinburgh EH3 5RA
Tel: (031) 224 2946/2906

In Wales:
CADW
Welsh Historic Monuments
Brunel House
2 Fitzalan Place
Cardiff CF2 1UY
Tel: (0222) 465511

European Commission
Cultural Action Division
(Office 0/16, 70 rue Joseph)
Rue de la Loi 200
B-1049 Brussels
Tel: (010 32 2) 235 3844

In Northern Ireland:
Department of the Environment
Conservation Service
Calvert House
23 Castle Place
Belfast BT1 1FY
Tel: (0232) 230560

PART THREE

RESEARCH AND TECHNOLOGICAL DEVELOPMENT

3.6 BIOTECHNOLOGY/HEALTHCARE

3.6 BIOTECHNOLOGY/HEALTHCARE

BRIDGE

1. Summary:

The BRIDGE (Biotechnology Research for Innovation, Development and Growth in Europe) programme offers support for two types of transnational projects in the field of biotechnology: 'N' projects for the integration of research efforts in areas where the main bottlenecks result from gaps in basic knowledge (ie information infrastructure, enabling technologies, cellular biology, pre-normative research); and 'T' projects for the removal of important bottlenecks resulting from structural and scale constraints. The programme involves research and training actions, and concertation actions to develop the work begun under the Biotechnology Research Action Programme (BAP).

BRIDGE is set to run from 1 January 1990 until 31 December 1993 with a budget allocation of 100 MECU.

2. Awarding Body:

Commission of the European Communities.

3. Locaton Restrictions:

Available in any Member State of the European Community. Organisations from non-member European States which have concluded framework agreements in scientific and technical co-operation with the Community, and from COST participating States may also participate, although they will not be eligible for EC funding.

4. Sectoral Restrictions:

Research projects can be undertaken by industrial organisations, research laboratories, university institutes, or combinations of these. Projects should involve at least three contractors from different Member States and should exploit converging contributions from different fields, disciplines and techniques in an integrated manner. Priority is given to projects with commitment from industry, in cash or in kind, and in particular from small and medium-sized enterprises.

Training grants are available to scientists at various levels (whether or not currently employed) who hold the required qualifications and who wish to undertake research in a laboratory located in one of the Member States other than the trainee's country of origin or residence.

5. Size Restrictions:

None.

6. Programme Duration:

BRIDGE is set to run from 1 January 1990 to 31 December 1993. The Commission has proposed a new RTD programme in the field of Biotechnology to run from 1990-94 covering molecular approaches; cellular and organism approaches; and ecology and population biology.

7. Submission of Applications/Proposals:

Application is made within the deadlines specified in each of the Commission's calls for proposals published in the Official Journal.

A call for proposals was published in OJ C201; 19.8.90; relating to a 'T' project on animal cell biotechnology. The deadline was 31 December 1990. No further calls for proposals are expected. Application in relation to training courses can be made throughout the programme – details are available from the addresses below.

8. Other Restrictions:

Action I covers two types of research projects:

- – 'N' projects for the integration in adapted Community structures (European Laboratories Without Walls: ELWW) of research efforts in areas where the main bottlenecks result from gaps in basic knowledge.
- – 'T' projects for the removal, through a significant investment of skills and resources, of important bottlenecks resulting from structural and scale constraints.

Action I, Research and Training, will cover the following areas (budget allocation in brackets – to be divided equally between 'N' and 'T' projects):

- – A. Information infrastructure (7 MECU): culture collections; processing and analysis of bio(techno)logical data.
- – B. Enabling technologies (27 MECU): protein design/molecular modelling; biotransformation; gene mapping, genome sequencing, novel cloning techniques.
- – C. Cellular biology (27 MECU): physiology and molecular genetics of industrial micro-organisms; basic biotechnology of plants and associated organisms; biotechnology of animal cells.
- – D. Pre-normative research (15.5 MECU): safety assessments associated with the release of genetically engineered organisms; in vitro evaluation of the toxicity and pharmacological activity of molecules.

Action II, Concertation Activities (budget allocation 9.5 MECU), will cover the following tasks: monitoring developments in biotechnology, particularly in R & D, and assessing their implications; identifying possible ways of improving the development of biotechnology in Europe, the effectiveness and coherence of biotechnology programmes; disseminating knowledge and increasing public awareness, investigating the wider implications of biotechnology R & D for consumers, society, the environment and development, identifying the need for and promoting greater activity in the small firm sector. Concertation activities will continue the work begun under BAP, the previous Biotechnology Research Action Programme, and will specifically involve in-house analysis, the setting-up and exploitation of an organised information base, and missions.

9. Eligible Expenditure:

For organisations other than universities, eligible expenditure covers: labour (actual cost or at approved rates); travel and subsistence; consumables; equipment; computing costs; external work (sub-contracts or services); reasonable overheads. The following are not allowable: profits; marketing, distribution, advertising expenses; any interest or return on capital employed; taxes (except in limited circumstances); cost of proposal preparation; patent protection costs. Specific arrangements exist to recover non-reclaimable VAT.

Universities and higher education establishments may elect to have their support calculated according to the marginal costs of the project (ie the actual additional direct costs of the research not met by normal recurrent expenditure, other financial sources or other third parties), unless their costing and recording systems enable them to submit and justify full costs. Each university is normally expected to operate on the basis of either marginal costs or full costs for all Community R & D programmes, and not reach a decision on a project-by-project basis. Marginal costs may include all the items listed above, although labour costs only relate to temporary additional staff specifically engaged for the research; routine and minor computing costs may not be charged; and overheads may be fixed at a percentage, corresponding to a maximum of 20 percent of all expenditure except associated contracts and VAT.

10. Rate of Award:

The rate of award is in relation to research contracts normally up to 50 percent of the full economic costs of the R & D project. Universities and higher education establishments may, however, attract a contribution of up to 100 percent of the actual marginal costs of the research project.

The Community contribution to 'N' projects shall not exceed 400,000 ECU per project per year. The Community contribution to 'T' projects may vary from 1 – 3 MECU per project per year.

Information on the rate of award in relation to training grants is available from the Commission.

11. Payment Procedure:

Payment is made in accordance with the agreed contract and takes the form of an advance payment following signature of the contract by all partners and the Commission, followed by periodic instalments on approval of progress reports and cost statements submitted as work progresses. Ten percent of the total financial contribution is retained (or, in the case of larger contracts, 500,000 ECUs, whichever is lower) and is paid, along with any other sums due, on approval of final technical reports and cost statements.

In all cases the Commission's contribution is made in ECUs and no liability is held for exchange losses incurred.

12. Points to Note:

Council Decision EEC/621/89 adopting BRIDGE was published in OJ L360; 9.12.89.

The European Parliament has proposed (OJ C318; 20.12.89) that a minimum of 5 percent of the total BRIDGE budget be allocated to parallel research projects in the form of social-sciences research into the possible effects of the generic technologies and techniques to be supported under BRIDGE. It has been proposed that social-sciences research be a separate subprogramme within BRIDGE, with its own budget of not less than 5 MECU.

13. Application Procedure:
Application forms and further information can be obtained from the Commission.

14. Further Information:
For research projects:

Dr Dreux de Nettancourt	Mr Tony Lott
European Commission	Laboratory of the Government Chemist
DG XII/F	Queens Road
Biotechnology Division	Teddington
Rue de la Loi 200	Middlesex TW11 0LY
B-1049 Brussels	Tel: (081) 943 7338
Tel: (010 32 2) 235 4044	Telex: 931 213 476 GC G
Telex: 21877 COMEU B	Fax: (081) 943 2767
Fax: (010 32 2) 235 5365	

For training grants:
Mrs Mongini
Address as above
Tel: (010 32 2) 235 8596

For information on Concertation Activities:
Mark Cantley
Address as above
Tel: (010 32 2) 235 8145

HUMAN GENOME ANALYSIS

1. Summary:
The Human Genome Analysis Programme supports pre-competitive research intended to allow the use and improvement of new biotechnologies in the study of the human genome, for a better understanding of the mechanisms of the genetic function, and the prevention and treatment of human diseases.

The primary short-term objective is that the programme should establish European networks of laboratories working in the fields of the human genetic map; ordered clone libraries of human DNA and cDNA sequencing; improvement of the methods and basis for the study of the human genome; all using data processing facilities for data handling and developing integrated databases.

Alteration of germ cells or any stage of embryo development with the aim of modifying human genetic characteristics in a hereditary manner is specifically excluded from the programme.

The programme will be carried out through research contracts, support to centralised facilities and networks, training contracts and grants, courses, consultations with national experts, organisation of study-group meetings, participation in seminars and symposia, publications, studies, dissemination of results to all interested groups, and the organisation of public presentations.

The programme has been adopted to run for a period of two years from 29 June 1990, with a budget allocation of 14 MECU.

2. Awarding Body:
Commission of the European Communities.

3. Location Restrictions:
Available in any Member State of the European Communities.

Participation is also open, subject to appropriate conditions, to organisations in non-Member States which have concluded framework agreements for scientific and technical co-operation with the European Community. No Community financing will be available to such organisations; they will also be expected to contribute to general administrative costs.

4. Sectoral Restrictions:
Participants may be research institutes, universities, private enterprises, or combinations of these. Projects must be carried out by participants from more than one country, including at least two independent partners from two Member States.

5. Size Restrictions:
None.

6. Programme Duration:
The programme has been adopted to run for a period of two years from 29 June 1990.

7. Submission of Applications/Proposals:
Proposals must be submitted within the deadlines specified in each of the Commission's calls for proposals, published in the Official Journal. The first call was published in OJ C250; 4.10.90 and covered clone libraries/'contig' mapping, data handling and databases; and improvement of the methods and basis for the study of the human genome. The deadline for proposals was 15 January 1991.

8. Other Restrictions:
The programme covers the following research areas (budget allocation in brackets):

(1) Improvement of the human genetic map (3.3 MECU): establishment of a Europe-wide network (extending worldwide) for the collection and mapping of the DNA of large families, in order to provide research scientists with well-characterised genetic material and sets of probes to determine the location of the relative positions of genes on chromosomes.

(2) Setting up of ordered clone libraries of human DNA (3.4 MECU): setting up of a European network of laboratories working on establishing overlapping clone libraries, and support for limited sequencing of cDNA.

(3) Improvement of the methods and basis for study of the human genome (2.2 MECU): new biochemical reagents; improved methods

for the detection and localisation of genetic markers; development of new vectors for the cloning of large DNA fragments and of procedures for the transfection of chromosomes, development of model systems for the reproducible and stable expression of medically important genes ('in vivo' and 'in vitro') and of new computer software for the storage and manipulation of data from genome sequencing and mapping.

(4) Training (1.9 MECU): setting up of a training programme to assist with technology transfer of molecular genetics methods, in particular to Member States in which these techniques are currently underdeveloped.

The research will require the development of integrated databases to serve European networks. (A budget of 2.2 MECU has been allocated to this area.) A further 1 MECU has been allocated to an investigation of the ethical, social and legal aspects of human genome analysis.

9. Eligible Expenditure:

Eligible expenditure relates to the costs of individual projects.

10. Rate of Award:

For shared-cost contracts, the rate of award will be up to 50 percent of total expenditure (in other cases, EC participation may be up to 100 percent of total costs). In the case of universities and research institutes the Commission may bear up to 100 percent of marginal costs incurred.

11. Payment Procedure:

Payment procedure is determined on a case-by-case basis at the time of contract negotiation.

12. Points to Note:

Council Decision (EEC) 395/90 adopting the Human Genome Analysis Programme was published in OJ L196; 26.7.90.

Research contracts can only be drawn up if the contracting parties undertake to abstain from all research seeking to modify the genetic constitution of human beings by alteration of germ cells or of any stage of embryo development which may make these alterations hereditary.

The contracts regulate the granting of licences arising out of research projects, and in particular there is no right to exploit any property rights in respect of human DNA on an exclusive basis.

In addition, the Commission reserves the right to publish the results of research performed within the scope of the contracts.

13. Application Procedures:

Application procedure will be outlined in the Information Pack which will be issued when a call for proposals is published.

14. Further Information:
Anthony Dickens
European Commission
DG XII – Human Genome Analysis
Rue de la Loi 200
B-1049 Brussels
Tel: (010 32 2) 235 0032

RADIATION PROTECTION PROGRAMME

1. Summary:
The Radiation Protection Programme provides support for research projects in the following areas (see 8 for further details):
A. Human exposure to radiation and radioactivity;
B. Consequences of radiation exposure to man; their assessment, prevention and treatment;
C. Risks and management of radiation exposure.
The programme will be implemented through research contracts, study contracts and co-ordinating actions; particular emphasis will be placed on awards for training and mobility grants.
The programme is set to run from 1 January 1990 to 31 December 1991 with a budget allocation of 21.2 MECU.

2. Awarding Body:
Commission of the European Communities.

3. Location Restrictions:
Available in any Member State of the European Community.

4. Sectoral Restrictions:
Participants may be from public or private research organisations, including universities, established in the Community. Projects will normally be carried out by participants from more than one Member State.

5. Size Restrictions:
None.

6. Programme Duration:
The programme is set to run from 1 January 1990 to 31 December 1991.
The Commission has proposed a new RTD programme in the field of Nuclear Fission to run from 1990-94. The programme will cover Radiation Protection Research and Reactor Safety.

7. Submission of Applications/Proposals:
Application is made within the deadlines specified in each of the Commission's invitation for proposals to be submitted, published in the Official Journal.

8. Other Restrictions:

The programme deals with the following subject areas (budget allocation in brackets):

- A. Human exposure to radiation and radioactivity (7.4 MECU): measurement of radiation dose and its interpretation; transfer and behaviour of radionuclides in the environment.
- B. Consequences of radiation exposure to man; their assessmet, prevention and treatment (7.4 MECU): stochastic effects of radiation; non-stochastic effects of radiation; radiation effects on the developing organism.
- C. Risks and management of radiation exposure (6.4 MECU): assessment of human exposure and risks; optimisation and management of radiation protection. The information resulting from the implementation of the research activities will be made accessible on an equal basis to all Member States. Licences and/or other rights developed in the framework of the programme are subject to Community rules, taking into account contractual agreements.

9. Eligible Expenditure:

For organisations other than universities, eligible expenditure covers: labour (actual cost or at approved rates); travel and subsistence; consumables; equipment; computing costs; external work (sub-contracts or services); reasonable overheads. The following are not allowable: profits; marketing, distribution, advertising expenses; any interest or return on capital employed; taxes (except in limited circumstances); cost of proposal preparation; patent protection costs. Specific arrangements exist to recover VAT paid in connection with the project, but which cannot be reclaime from national authorities by the usual means.

Universities and higher education establishments may elect to have their support calculated according to the marginal costs of the project (ie the actual additional direct costs of the research not met by normal recurrent expenditure, other financial sources of other third parties), unless their costing and recording systems enable them to submit and justify full costs.

Each university is normally expected to operate on the basis of either marginal costs or full costs for all Community R & D programmes, and not reach a decision on a project-by-project basis. Marginal costs may include all the items listed above for other organisations, except that labour costs only relate to temporary additional staff specifically engaged for the research; routine and minor computing costs may not be charged; overheads may be fixed at a percentage, corresponding to a maximum of 20 percent of all expenditure, except associated contracts and VAT.

10. Rate of Award:

The rate of award is normally up to 50 percent of the full economic costs of the R & D project. Universities and higher education establishments may, however, attract a contribution of up to 100 percent of the actual marginal costs of the research project.

11. Payment Procedure:

Payment is made in accordance with the agreed contract and takes the form of an advance payment following signature of the contract by all partners and the Commission, followed by periodic instalments on approval of progress reports and cost statements submitted as work progresses. Ten percent of the total financial contribution is retained (or, in the case of larger contracts, 500,000 ECUs, whichever is lower) and is paid, along with any other sums due, on approval of final technical reports and cost statements.

In all cases the Commission's contribution is made in ECUs and no liability is held for exchange losses incurred.

12. Points to Note:

Council Decision (EURATOM) 416/89 adopting the Radiation Protection Research Programme was published in OJ L200; 13.7.90.

A call for proposals relating to all areas of the programme was published in OJ C236; 14.9.89; deadline 31 January 1990.

13. Application Procedure:

Application details and an application form were included in the Radiation Protection Programme Information Package.

14. Further Information:

Mr Georg Gerber
European Commission
DG XII/D-4
Rue de la Loi 200
B-1049 Brussels
Belgium
Tel: (010 32 2) 235 4045

Mr I Wilson
Department of Health
Alexander Fleming House
Elephant and Castle
London SE1 6BY
Tel: (071) 407 5522 Ext.7018

PART THREE

RESEARCH AND TECHNOLOGICAL DEVELOPMENT

3.7 AGRICULTURE AND FISHERIES RESEARCH

3.7 AGRICULTURE AND FISHERIES RESEARCH

FAR

1. Summary:

The Fisheries Research programme (FAR) supports research and co-ordination activities in the following broad areas (see 8 for further details): Fisheries Management; Fishing Methods; Aquaculture; Upgrading of Fishery Products. Research programmes are implemented by means of shared-cost contracts; co-ordination activities are carried out by means of seminars, conferences, study visits, exchanges of researchers and working meetings of scientific experts and by collating, analysing and publishing, as appropriate, the results.

The programme has been adopted to run from 1988 to 1992 with a budget allocation of 30 MECU.

2. Awarding Body:

Commission of the European Communities.

3. Location Restrictions:

Available in any Member State of the European Community.

4. Sectoral Restrictions:

Project proposals may be submitted by any legal entity, research or industrial organisation, or higher education institute or university established within a Member State.

5. Size Restrictions:

None.

6. Programme Duration:

The programme has been adopted to run from 1 January 1988 to 31 December 1992.

7. Submission of Applications/Proposals:

Application for research contracts is made within the deadlines specified in each of the Commission's invitations for proposals to be submitted, published in the Official Journal.

8. Other Restrictions:

The research programme covers the following specific areas:
- Fisheries Management: research on the abundance and distribution of important stocks: R & D of multi-species biological models; development of a multi-disciplinary approach to fisheries management, initial analysis of the structure of fleets, undertakings, and the market; research on specific environmental problems (pollution, diseases, parasites).
- Fishing Techniques: development of fuel-saving and species selective gear; improvement of static gear.
- Aquaculture: study of early growth stages of reared species, including shellfish farming and cost-effectiveness of fish feeds; identification and

  treatment of diseases; genetic research and conservation of gametes;
  research on the interaction between the fish-farming environment and
  the species farmed.
  – Upgrading of Fishery Products: improved techniques for handling,
    storing, processing and packaging; enhancement of landing values;
    recovery of edible protein and other components from fish and
    shellfish.
Proposals are treated confidentially and judged on their value to the
Community, their scientific merit and their innovative approach.

9. Eligible Expenditure:

For organisations other than universities, eligible expenditure covers
labour (actual cost or at approved rates); travel and subsistence; consumables; equipment; computing costs; external work (sub-contracts or services);
reasonable overheads. The following are not allowable: profits; marketing,
distribution, advertising expenses; any interest or return on capital employed;
taxes (except in limited circumstances); cost of proposal preparation; patent
protection costs. Specific arrangements exist to recover non-reclaimable
VAT.

Universities and higher education establishments may elect to have their
support calculated according to the marginal costs of the project (ie the
actual additional direct costs of the research not met by normal recurrent
expenditure, other financial sources or other third parties), unless their
costing and recording systems enable them to submit and justify full costs.
Each university is normally expected to operate on the basis of either
marginal or full costs for all Community R & D programmes in which they
are involved. Marginal costs may include all the items listed above, although
labour costs only relate to temporary additional staff specifically engaged for
the research; routine and minor computing costs may not be charged; and
overheads may be fixed at a percentage, corresponding to a maximum of 20
percent of all expenditure except associated contracts and VAT.

10. Rate of Award:

The rate of award is normally up to 50 percent of the full economic costs
of the R & D project. Universities and higher education establishments may,
however, attract a contribution of up to 100 percent of the actual marginal
costs of the research project. With respect to co-ordination activities the
Commission funds the organisational costs.

11. Payment Procedure:

Payment is made in accordance with the agreed contract and takes the form
of an advance payment following signature of the contract by all partners and
the Commission, followed by periodic instalments on approval of progress
reports and cost statements submitted as work progresses. Ten percent of the
total financial contribution is retained (or, in the case of larger contracts,
500,000 ECUs, whichever is lower) and is paid, along with any other sums
due, on approval of final technical reports and cost statements.

In all cases the Commission's contribution is made in ECUs and no
liability is held for exchange losses incurred.

12. Points to Note:

The programme embraces both research and co-ordination activities. Research activities are detailed in section 8. Co-ordination activities cover specific activities within the same broad areas as follows:

- Fisheries Management: development of simple methods for evaluating stock; co-ordination of research into the capacity of fleets, the choice of statistical parameters and collection of data; methodology for collecting and processing basic data; co-ordination of data relating to environmental factors (pollution, diseases, parasites).
- Fishing Techniques: testing techniques and instrumentation; fuel saving, selectivity of fishing gear; catch quality.
- Aquaculture: co-ordination of data on the mass production of live foods for aquaculture species; low-cost rearing and on-growing of mollusc spat; genetics of cultivable invertebrate aquatic species; smolt quality until release into the sea; effectiveness and profitability of fish-farming techniques and structures; aquaculture and environment.
- Upgrading Fishery Products: standardisation and development of analytical methods for fishery products; consumer response and demand studies.

Council Decision (EEC) 534/87 adopting the programme was published in Official Journal L314; 4.11.87.

A call for research proposals (covering all areas of the programme) was published in OJ No C313; 13.12.89.

13. Application Procedure:

Application procedure is outlined in the Information Pack attached to each call for proposals.

14. Further Information:

Jean-Paul Repussard
European Commission
DG XIV, FAR Programme
Rue de la Loi 200
B-1049 Brussels
Tel: (010 32 2) 235 9302
Telex: 21877 B
Fax: (010 32 2) 235 2569

Mr D A Earey
Ministry of Agriculture, Fisheries
  and Food
Nobel House, Room 411
17 Smith Square
London SW1P 3JR
Tel: (071) 238 5891

MAST

1. Summary:

The MAST (Marine Science and Technology) programme offers support for research and technology development projects in the field of marine science and technology. The aim of the programme is to contribute to establishing a scientific and technological basis for the exploration, exploitation, management and protection of European, coastal and regional seas, through the co-ordination of on-going activities in the Member States and the support of transnational R & D activities.

MAST comprises four main headings (see 8 for further details): Basic and Applied Marine Science; Coastal Zone Science and Engineering; Marine Technology; Supporting Initiatives. The programme is implemented through research contracts, co-ordination activities (including concerted actions), supporting initiatives, study contracts and training and exchange of staff.

MAST is set to run from 1989–92 with a budget allocation of 50 MECU.

2. Awarding Body:
Commission of the European Communities.

3. Location Restrictions:
Available in any Member State of the European Community.

Organisations in non-Member States which have concluded framework agreements for scientific and technical co-operation with the European Communities and from countries participating in COST (European Co-operation in the Field of Scientific and Technological Research), may also participate in the programme on a case-by-case basis, although they will not be eligible for funding from the Commission.

4. Sectoral Restrictions:
The programme is open to industrial firms, including small and medium-sized enterprises, universities, research institutions and individuals, or any combination thereof. Projects involving research centres (and/or universities) and industry are particularly welcome, and mandatory for marine technology projects. These projects should, in general, be carried out by participants from more than one Member State.

5. Size Restrictions:
None.

6. Programme Duration:
The MAST programme is set to run from 28 June 1989 to 27 June 1992. The Commission recently proposed a new Research and Technological Development programme (RTD) in the field of Marine Science and Technology (MAST II), to run from 1990–94.

The proposed programme will build on work undertaken through MAST, introducing new topics and extending the programme's geographical coverage.

7. Submission of Applications/Proposals:
Application is made within the deadlines specified in the Commission's invitation for proposals to be submitted, published in the Official Journal.

8. Other Restrictions:
MAST covers four main fields, each of which has a number of sub-fields (funding allocation in brackets):
- Basic and Applied Marine Science (15 – 17.5 MECU): including (1) Modelling (continental shelf and regional seas, coastal waters, ecosystem models, modelling co-ordination); (2) Oceanography (circulation

and exchange of water masses, biogeochemical cycles and fluxes, interface and boundary processes, biological processes, sedimentary processes).

- Coastal Zone Science and Engineering (7.5 - 10 MECU): coastal morphodynamics, coastal ecosystems, meteomarine predictions, coastal engineering.
- Marine Technology (15 - 17.5 MECU): instrumentation for science, generic enabling technologies, design aspects of large facilities, studies on the outlook for the 1990s.
- Supporting Initiatives (5 - 7.5 MECU): European ocean data and information network, research vessel co-ordination, advanced training, surveying for resource evaluation, preparation of norms and standards, marine polar and marine lithospheric research.

9. Eligible Expenditure:

For organisations other than universities, eligible expenditure covers: labour (actual cost or at approved rates); travel and subsistence; consumables; equipment; computing costs; external work (sub-contracts or services); reasonable overheads. The following are not allowable: profits; marketing, distribution, advertising expenses; any interest or return on capital employed; taxes (except in limited circumstances); cost of proposal preparation; patent protection costs. Specific arrangements exist to recover non-reclaimable VAT.

Universities and higher education establishments may elect to have their support calculated according to the marginal costs of the project (ie the actual additional direct costs of the research not met by normal recurrent expenditure, other financial sources or other third parties), unless their costing and recording systems enable them to submit and justify full costs. Each university is normally expected to operate on the basis of either marginal costs or full costs for all Community R & D programmes, and not reach a decision on a project-by-project basis. Marginal costs may include all the items listed above, although labour costs only relate to temporary additional staff specifically engaged for the research; routine and minor computing costs may not be charged; overheads may be fixed at a percentage, corresponding to a maximum of 20 percent of all expenditure, except associated contracts and VAT.

10. Rate of Award:

The rate of award is normally up to 50 percent of the full economic costs of the R & D project. Universities and higher education establishments may, however, attract a contribution of up to 100 percent of the actual marginal costs of the research project.

11. Payment Procedure:

Payment is made in accordance with the agreed contract and takes the form of an advance payment following signature of the contract by all partners and the Commission, followed by periodic instalments on approval of progress reports and cost statements submitted as work progresses. Ten percent of the total financial contribution is retained (or, in the case of larger contracts,

500,000 ECUs, whichever is lower) and is paid, along with any other sums due, on approval of final technical reports and cost statements.

In all cases the Commission's contribution is made in ECUs and no liability is held for exchange losses incurred.

12. Points to Note:

The MAST Regulation (EEC) 413/89 was published in OJ No L200; 13.7.89. The first call for proposals was published in OJ No C75; 23.3.89.

A call for tenders concerning feasibility studies, site proposals and market analyses for large acoustic underwater calibration facilities was published in OJ C127; 23.5.90; deadline 20 July 1990.

13. Application Procedure:

Application procedure and further information on the programme is outlined in the MAST Information Pack, available from the European Commission. General enquiries may be directed to the Department of Education and Science.

14. Further Information:

Dr J Boissonnas	Mr Martin Sharpe
European Commission	Department of Education and Science
DG XII/E	Elizabeth House
Rue de la Loi 200	York Road
B-1049 Brussels	London SE1 7PH
Tel: (010 32 2) 235 6787	Tel: (071) 934 9378
Telex: 21877 COMEU B	
Fax: (010 32 2) 236 3024	

AGRICULTURAL RESEARCH PROGRAMME

1. Summary:

The Agricultural Research Programme (CAMAR) supports shared-cost contracts, pilot activities and coordination activities in the field of the Competitiveness of Agriculture and the Management of Agricultural Resources.

The programme aims to help farmers adapt to the new situation created by over production and a restrictive policy on prices and markets; maintain incomes from holdings and encourage structural reform whilst controlling output and reducing production costs; care for and improve the agricultural structure in regions which have been slow to develop; conserve natural resources and the countryside; develop agricultural information services and infrastructures to improve the dissemination of research results within and between Member States.

The programme is set to run for five years (1989–1993), with a budget allocation of 55 MECU. Approximately 75 percent of the budget will be allocated to agricultural research contracts.

2. Awarding Body:
Commission of the European Communities.

3. Location Restrictions:
Available in any Member State of the European Community.

4. Sectoral Restrictions:
The programme is open to national and regional institutions such as universities, research centres and agencies involved in R & D for agriculture. Commercial operations with a contribution to make to research and development may also be included. Projects must involve participants from more than one Member State.

5. Size Restrictions:
None.

6. Programme Duration:
The programme is set to run from 26 February 1989 to 25 February 1993. The Commission has proposed a new RTD programme in the field of Agriculture and Agro-Industry, to run from 1990–94.

7. Submission of Applications/Proposals:
Application for research contracts is made within the deadline specified in each of the Commission's invitations for proposals published in the Official Journal.

A call was published in OJ C269; 21.10.89 covering all areas of the programme; deadline 31 December 1991.

The selection procedure will operate on three occasions before 31 December 1991.

High priority projects will be implemented by the Commission.

8. Other Restrictions:
Emphasis is placed on the following topics (budget allocation in brackets): conversion and diversification, including extensification of production, reduction of costs and protection of the rural environment (34 MECU); product quality and research for new uses for traditional products, aspects of plant and animal health (20.9 MECU); socio-economic aspects and specific actions for regions lagging behind in development (18.3 MECU); and methods and services to disseminate agricultural research information (particularly from this programme) (5.3 MECU).

Co-ordination activities have been allocated a budget of 16.2 MECU, and 5.3 MECU have been allocated to training and mobility grants. High priority pilot projects undertaken by the Commission will respond to particular technical problems relating to the Common Agricultural Policy, possibilities to apply promising research results in farming practice, and the need to demonstrate to farmers the real scope for improving production by adopting and exploiting new techniques derived from research results and from new technology.

9. Eligible Expenditure:
Eligible expenditure relates to the total cost of the project.

10. Rate of Award:

The rate of award in relation to research projects is up to 50 percent of total project costs; high priority pilot projects may qualify for over 50 percent of total costs.

11. Payment Procedure:

Payment is made in accordance with the agreed contract and takes the form of an advance payment following signature of the contract by all partners and the Commission, followed by periodic instalments on approval of progress reports and cost statements submitted as work progresses. Ten percent of the total financial contribution is retained (or, in the case of larger contracts, 500,000 ECUs, whichever is lower) and is paid, along with any other sums due, on approval of final technical reports and cost statements. In all cases the Commission's contribution is made in ECUs and no liability is held for exchange losses incurred.

12. Points to Note:

Co-ordination activities will serve the needs of research and high-priority activities. Seminars and workshops will bring together scientists to address a limited number of agricultural research problems of particular importance to the Community and the Common Agricultural Policy. Such activities will prepare for later collaboration which will avoid duplication of research and ensure more rapid dissemination of results and other information. The programme encourages laboratory twinning and training of scientists working on techniques and methods of interest to the EC.

Council Decision (EEC) 84/90 adopting the Agricultural Research Programme was published in OJ L58; 7.3.90.

13. Application Procedure:

Application procedure is detailed in the Information Pack and in the calls for proposals.

14. Further Information:

Mrs A Dumoulin
European Commission
DG VI/F/11-3
Rue de la Loi 200
B-1049 Brussels
Tel: (010 32 2) 235 8939
Fax: (010 32 2) 236 3029
Telex: 22037 AGREC B

Mr R L Bedford
Ministry of Agriculture, Fisheries
  and Food
Nobel House
17 Smith Square
London SW1P 3JR
Tel: (071) 238 5600

PART THREE

RESEARCH AND TECHNOLOGICAL DEVELOPMENT

3.8 TRANSPORT RESEARCH

3.8 TRANSPORT AND RESEARCH

EURET

1. Summary:
The EURET programme supports research and technological development projects in the field of transport. Research should contribute towards the standardisation of equipment and systems, have an added Community dimension, and be in one of the following fields: optimum network exploitation; logistics; and the reduction of harmful externalities (eg pollution, accidents) (see 8 for further details).

The programme will be implemented by means of shared-cost research contracts and concerted actions (where the Commission co-ordinates rather than directly funds research).

EURET is set to run from 1 March 1990 to 28 February 1994, with a budget allocation of 25 MECU.

2. Awarding Body:
Commission of the European Communities.

3. Location Restrictions:
Available in any Member State of the European Community. The Commission may negotiate agreements with non-Member States and international organisations, in particular those countries participating in COST and those which have concluded framework agreements for scientific and technical co-operation with the Community (particularly EFTA countries), with a view to associating them wholly or partly with the programme.

4. Sectoral Restrictions:
Available to universities, research organisations and industrial companies (including small and medium-sized enterprises), individuals or any combination thereof established in the Community. Projects must normally involve the collaboration of organisations in at least two Member States.

5. Size Restrictions:
None.

6. Programme Duration:
The EURET programme is set to run from 1 March 1990 to 28 February 1994.

7. Submission of Applications/Proposals:
Proposals must be submitted within the deadlines specified in each of the Commission's call for proposals, published in the Official Journal.

A call for expressions of interest in EURET was published in OJ C146; 15.6.90. The first general call for proposals was published in OJ C9; 15.1.91; with a deadline of 15 April 1991.

8. Other Restrictions:
EURET covers three sub-programmes (budget allocation in brackets):
  1. Optimum network exploitation: Cost-benefit and multi-criteria analy-

sis for new road construction (0.5 MECU); European rail traffic management conception (5 MECU); design and assessment of a vessel traffic management system (3 MECU); trials in automated air/ground data exchange for air traffic management systems in Europe (5 MECU); study on the controller work station in air traffic management systems in Europe (3 MECU);

2. Logistics: Economic scenario and demand projections for freight transport in the Community (0.5 MECU); economic and technical research on the transfer of goods-design and evaluation of rapid transfer systems (3 MECU); optimisation of manpower in maritime transport (3 MECU); taking human factors into consideration in man/ship system (1 MECU);

3. Reduction of harmful externalities: improved methods for evaluating the road safety of car and trailer trains (0.5 MECU); assessment of the driving safety of possible truck and trailer combinations (0.5 MECU).

9. Eligible Expenditure:

For organisations other than universities, eligible expenditure covers: labour (actual cost or at approved rates); travel and subsistence; consumables; equipment; computing costs; external work (sub-contracts or services); reasonable overheads. The following are not allowable: profits; marketing, distribution, advertising expenses; any interest or return on capital employed; taxes (except in limited circumstances); cost of proposal preparation; patent protection costs. Specific arrangements exist to recover non-reclaimable VAT.

Universities and higher education establishments may elect to have their support calculated according to the marginal costs of the project (ie the actual additional direct costs of the research not met by normal recurrent expenditure, other financial sources or other third parties), unless their costing and recording systems enable them to submit and justify full costs. Each university is normally expected to operate on the basis of either marginal costs or full costs for all Community R & D programmes, and not reach a decision on a project-by-project basis. Marginal costs may include all the items listed above, although labour costs may only relate to temporary additional staff specifically engaged for the research; routine and minor computing costs may not be charged; and overheads may be fixed at a percentage, corresponding to a maximum of 20 percent of all expenditure except associated contracts and VAT.

10. Rate of Award:

The rate of award is normally up to 50 percent of total expenditure for shared-cost contracts, but this percentage may be varied according to the nature and stage of development of the research. Universities and research institutes may attract a contribution of up to 100 percent of actual marginal costs of the research project.

11. Payment Procedure:

Payment is made in accordance with the agreed contract and takes the form of an advance payment following signature of the contract by all partners and the Commission, followed by periodic instalments on approval of progress reports and cost statements submitted as work progresses. Ten percent of the total financial contribution is retained (or, in the case of larger contracts, 500,000 ECUs, whichever is lower) and is paid, along with any other sums due, on approval of final technical reports and cost statements.

In all cases the Commission's contribution is made in ECUs and no liability is held for exchange losses incurred.

12. Further Information:
The EURET proposal was published in OJ C318; 20.12.89.

13. Application Procedure:
Application procedure will be outlined in the Information Pack accompanying the Commission's call for proposals.

14. Further Information:

Mr F Fabre
European Commission
DG VII/B-3 (B-34 02/13)
Rue de la Loi 200
B-1049 Brussels
Tel: (010 32 2) 235 3999
Fax: (010 32 2) 235 0133
Telex: 21877 COMEUR B

Mrs Anthea Nicholson
Department of Transport
Room P2/046A
2 Marsham Street
London SW1P 3EB
Tel: (071) 276 5802

PART FOUR

CURRENTLY INACTIVE EC PROGRAMMES

PART FOUR

CURRENTLY INACTIVE EC PROGRAMMES

4.1 PROGRAMMES WITH FULLY ALLOCATED BUDGETS

4.1 PROGRAMMES WITH FULLY ALLOCATED BUDGETS

Introduction

Funding for most EC research programmes is allocated on the basis of a limited number of calls for project proposals issued within the first year or two following adoption of each programme. This results in budgets becoming fully allocated early on within each programme, in effect closing the programme to any new participants. In most cases, new research programmes continuing or extending areas of research have been proposed under the Third Framework Programme for Research and Technological Development (RTD) (1990–94) and will introduce new research programmes which will overlap existing programmes.

This section provides brief details of existing programmes whose budgets are now fully allocated and, where information is available, any proposals to continue or extend these programmes.

AIM (Advanced Informatics in Medicine)

AIM provided support for precompetitive research and development concerned with the application of information technology and telecommunications applied to health care. The objectives of the programme were to promote the competitiveness of the Community's health service providers and industries, improve health-care standard and to progress the standardisation of computerised information. The areas covered included: the development of a common conceptual framework for cooperation; medical informatics environment; data structures and medical records; communication and functional integration; integration of knowledge-based systems into health care; advanced instrumentation, equipment and services for health care and medical research environments; and non-technological factors.

AIM ran from 1 June 1988 to 31 May 1990. A new RTD programme in the field of Telematic Systems of General Interest (1990–94) (see page 239) incorporating the topic of health care has been proposed by the Commission. This will build on the exploratory work carried out under the AIM programme.

Council Decision (EEC) 577/88 adopting AIM was published in OJ L314; 22.11.88.

DELTA (Development of European Learning Through Technological Advance)

DELTA funded pre-normative and pre-competitive collaborative research related to the development of techniques, tools and infrastructures required to support advanced learning, particularly open and distance learning. Specifically DELTA exploited advances in Information Technology and Telecommunications for the support of learning. The areas covered in the initial Exploratory Action were: Learning Systems Research; Collaborative

Development of Advanced Learning Technology; Testing and Validation; Interoperability; Investigation of Related Factors.

The DELTA Exploratory Action phase ran from 1 June 1988 to 31 May 1990 with a budget of 20 MECU. The European Commission proposal for a new RTD programme in the field of Telematic Systems of General Interest (1990–94) (see page 239) incorporated the area of distance learning, and will build on the exploratory work carried out under DELTA.

Council Decision (EEC) 417/88 adopting DELTA was published in Official Journal No L200; 30.07.88.

DRIVE (Dedicated Road Infrastructure for Vehicle Safety)

DRIVE funded pre-competitive collaborative R & D involving the application of information technology and telecommunications to road transport. The programme entailed: research, development and assessment of a range of Road Transport Informatics (RTI) technologies; the evaluation of strategic choices of candidate systems; and a significant amount of standardisation work. The aim of the programme was to improve road safety and transport efficiency, and reduce vehicle emissions and noise pollution.

DRIVE ran from 1 June 1988 to 31 May 1991, with a budget allocation of 60 MECU. The European Commission proposal for a new RTD programme in the field of Telematic Systems of General Interest (1990–94) (see page 239) incorporates the topic of road transport, and will build on the work carried out under DRIVE.

Council Decision (EEC) 416/88 adopting DRIVE was published in OJ L206; 30.7.88.

ECLAIR (European Collaborative Linkage of Agriculture and Industry through Research)

ECLAIR supports precompetitive research and technological development projects in biotechnology and other advanced technologies. The programme aims to improve the interface of agriculture and industry by exploiting existing expertise in biotechnology and the life sciences. Though not supporting the development of marketable products or processes, ECLAIR supports research for clear-cut agricultural and/or industrial applications or objectives. Separate grants were available to cover training and mobility expenses.

ECLAIR was adopted to run from 1 July 1988 to 30 June 1993. The 80 MECU budget has, however, now been fully allocated. A new programme in the field of agriculture and and agro-industry has been proposed to run from 1990–94, covering related research areas (see page 233).

Council Decision (EEC) 160/89 adopting ECLAIR was published in Official Journal L60; 3.3.89.

EPOCH (Climatology and Natural Hazards)

EPOCH supports research projects in the following areas: past climates and climate change; climate processes and models; climatic impacts and climate-related hazards; seismic hazard. The programme has been implemented through research contracts, concerted actions, coordination activities, education and training activities, studies and assessments.

EPOCH was adopted to run from 20 November 1989 to 19 November 1993. The 40 MECU budget has now been fully allocated. A new Environment programme has been proposed to run from 1990–94 with a budget of 414 MECU and will cover similar topics to EPOCH (see page 235). Council Decision (EEC) 625/89 adopting EPOCH was published in OJ L359; 8.12.89.

ESPRIT II (European Strategic Programme for Research and Development in Information Technologies)

Within the second phase of the ESPRIT programme financial assistance was available to encourage and promote precompetitive, collaborative RTD in information technologies in the following three sectors: Microelectronics and Peripheral Technologies; Information Processing Systems; IT Application Technologies.

ESPRIT II was adopted to run from 1 December 1987 until 31 December 1992. The budget of 1,600 MECU has now been fully allocated, and no further calls for proposals are expected under this phase of the programme. A follow-up programme has been proposed (see page 236).

Council Decision (EEC) 279/88 adopting ESPRIT was published in OJ L118; 6.5.88.

FLAIR (Food-Linked Agro-Industrial Research)

FLAIR supports pre-competitive research and development projects in the field of food technology, aiming to improve Europe's competitiveness in the food industry and food safety and quality for the consumer, and strengthen the food science and technology infrastructures in Europe.

FLAIR was adopted to run from mid-1989 to mid-1993 with a budget of 25 MECU, and is being implemented by means of research contracts, research projects carried out by Commission establishments (concerted actions) and by training/mobility grants.

The funding for research contracts has now been fully allocated; however, applications for training and mobility grants may be submitted at any time. Council Decision (EEC) 411/89 adopting FLAIR was published in Official Journal No L200; 13.7.89.

JOULE (Joint Opportunities for Unconventional or Long-Term Energy Supply)

JOULE supports specific research and technological development projects in the field of energy – non-nuclear energies and rational use of energy. JOULE covers the following subprogrammes: models for energy and environment; rational use of energy; energy from fossil sources; renewable energies. The programme is being carried out by means of shared-cost research and study contracts, coordination projects and training mobility grants.

JOULE was adopted to run from 1 January 1989 to 31 March 1992 with a budget allocation of 122 MECU. No further calls for proposals will be issued under JOULE, but a new programme of Non-Nuclear Energy RTD has been proposed (see page 238). This will overlap the current JOULE programme.

Council Decision (EEC) 236/89 adopting JOULE was published in Official Journal No L98;11.4.89.

STEP (Science and Technology for Environmental Protection)

STEP provides support for research projects covering the following nine areas: environment and human health; assessment of risks associated with chemicals; atmospheric processes and air quality; water quality; soil and groundwater protection; ecosystem research; protection and conservation of the European cultural heritage; technologies for environmental protection; major technological hazards; and fire safety.

The programme is being implemented through research contracts, concerted actions, coordination activities, education and training activities and studies and assessments.

STEP was adopted to run from 20 November 1989 to 19 November 1993 with a budget allocation of 75 MECU. This budget has now been fully allocated and no further calls for proposals are expected. A new Environment Programme has been proposed to run from 1990–94 with a budget of 414 MECU and will cover similar topics to STEP (see page 235).

Council Decision (EEC) 625/89 adopting STEP was published in OJ L359; 8.12.89.

Science and Technology for Development

The Science and Technology for Development programme promotes increased scientific cooperation between the European Community and developing countries. The programme supports specialist research in areas important for the economic and social progress of developing countries and comprises two subprogrammes:

1. Tropical and Subtropical Agriculture covering: the improvement of agricultural products; conservation and optimum use of the environment; agricultural engineering and post-harvest technology; and production systems.
2. Medicine, Health and Nutrition in tropical and subtropical areas.

The programme was adopted to run from 1 January 1987 to 31 December 1991 with a budget of 80 MECU. This budget has been fully allocated. The Commission has proposed a new programme in the field of Life Sciences and Technologies for Developing Countries, covering the same topics (see page 237). This new programme is proposed to run from 1990–94 with a budget of 111 MECU. Council Decision (EEC) 590/87 adopting the Science and Technology for Development programme was published in OJ L355; 17.12.87.

CURRENTLY INACTIVE EC PROGRAMMES

4.2 PROGRAMMES UNDER PROPOSAL

4.2 PROGRAMMES UNDER PROPOSAL

Introduction

Fifteen separate research programmes have been agreed to run under the Third Framework Programme (1990-94). Many of these programmes overlap and/or extend work already being funded under the Second Framework Programme (1987-91). In an effort to simplify and harmonise the various research programmes and to facilitate their implementation, the fifteen programme proposals are all based on the same model. Most programme proposals have been published in Official Journal No C174; 16.07.90. The only exceptions are the programmes concerning Controlled Thermonuclear Fusion and Nuclear Fission Safety which were published in Official Journals Nos C261; 16.10.90 and C247; 2.10.90 respectively.

All fifteen programmes have been agreed to run for five years from 1990 to 1994. Calls for project proposals under each programme are expected to be published separately in the spring of 1991. Most funding will be allocated to the best proposals submitted in response to the published calls. However, provision exists under the Third Framework Programme for 'unsolicited' proposals to be taken into consideration in exceptional circumstances, provided they are highly original and innovative.

Brief descriptions of each of the fifteen programme areas proposed under the Third Framework Programme and their links with existing EC-funded Research and Technological Development (RTD) programmes are provided in the remainder of this section.

Agriculture and Agro-Industry Programme

The proposed new programme in the field of Agriculture and Agro-Industry will support research in the following fields (percentage of the 333 MECU budget allocation in brackets):

1. Primary production in agriculture, forestry, aquaculture and fishing (25-30 percent): aims to adapt primary production to market conditions, provide the scientific and technical basis for correcting imbalances and facilitating diversification;
2. Inputs to agriculture, forestry, aquaculture and fishing (20-25 percent): aims to reduce inputs and production costs, and develop environmentally friendly inputs to crop production;
3. Processing of biological raw materials from agriculture, forestry, aquaculture and fishing (30-35 percent): to provide the basic procedure for developing new applications for biological materials;
4. End use and products (15-20 percent): to generate a better knowledge of the characteristics consumers and industry require from final products based on biological material.

This new programme will cover related areas to ECLAIR (see page 228). ECLAIR has been adopted to run from 1988-93, the budget has, however, now been fully allocated.

Biomedicine and Health Programme

The proposed new programme in the field of Biomedicine and Health will cover the following research topics (percentage of the 133 MECU budget allocation in brackets):

1. Harmonisation of methodologies and protocols in epidemiological, biological and clinical research (20–25 percent);
2. Diseases of great socio-economic impact (45–50 percent): AIDS, cancer, cardiovascular disease, mental illness and neurological disorders and mental handicap; ageing and age-related health problems and disabilities;
3. Human Genome Analysis (30–35 percent): building on the work undertaken under the current Human Genome Analysis Programme (1990–92) (see page 236).

Biotechnology Programme

The proposed new programme in the field of Biotechnology will cover the following research topics (percentage of the 164 MECU budget allocation in brackets):

1. Molecular approaches (35–40 percent): protein structure and function, structure and function of genes, expression of genes;
2. Cellular and organism approaches (45–55 percent): cellular regeneration, reproduction and development of living organisms, metabolism of animals, plants and microbes, essential physiological tracts, communication systems within living matter;
3. Ecology and population biology (10–15 percent): ecological implications of biotechnology, conservation of genetic resources.

The new programme will complement and extend work carried out under the current BRIDGE programme (1990–93) (see page 197).

Communications Technologies Programme

The proposed Communications Technologies programme will focus on the following eight priority areas (percentage of the 489 MECU budget allocation in brackets):

1. IBC (Integrated Broadband Communications) R & D (20–24 percent);
2. Intelligence in Networks/Flexible Communications Resource Management (6–8 percent);
3. Mobile and Personal Communications (8–10 percent);
4. Image and Data Communications (11–16 percent);
5. Integrated Services Technologies (6–8 percent);
6. Information Security Technologies (6–8 percent);
7. Advanced Communications Experiments (20–25 percent);
8. Test Infrastructures and Interworking (horizontal R & D supporting other priority areas) (1–3 percent).

The programme will distinguish three main types of work in these areas: the development of implementation strategies for IBC systems, services and applications; advanced communications technologies; and validation of standards and common functional specifications for IBC, involving the use of experimental equipment and services to address generic applications.

The new programme will follow on from the current RACE programme (1987–92) (see page 160).

Controlled Thermonuclear Fusion Programme

The proposed new programme in the field of Controlled Thermonuclear Fusion will have a budget of 458 MECU.

The long-term objective of the programme is the creation of safe, environmentally sound prototype reactors. The programme will encompass work undertaken in all Member States of the Community and aims to lead eventually towards a prototype commercial reactor, following development of an experimental reactor (Next Step) and a demonstration reactor (DEMO).

The first priority will be to provide a scientific and technological base and prepare industry for the construction of a 'Next Step' device. Four areas will be covered: 'Next Step' design; long-term technical developments; Joint European Torus (JET); and a support programme. It will be implemented through shared-cost research and technological development contracts, the JET Joint Undertaking, accompanying measures and concerted actions.

Environment Programme

The proposed new programme in the field of the Environment will focus on large-scale projects which complement ongoing environment research programmes and can respond rapidly to new problems raised by global change. The programme has been allocated a budget of 414 MECU.

The following fields will be covered (percentage of budget in brackets):

1. Participation in Global Change Programmes (35–45 percent): coordination of national programmes within the framework of large international ones, covering: natural and anthropogenic climatic change; the impact of climatic change; the depletion of stratospheric ozone and its consequences; tropospheric physics and chemistry, biogeochemical cycles; ecosystems dynamics.
2. Technologies and Engineering for the Environment (20–25 percent): promoting better environmental quality standards through pre-competitive technological innovation in environmental monitoring; the development of techniques and systems to protect and rehabilitate the environment.
3. Research on the economic aspects of environmental issues (5–10 percent): addressing critical areas of environmental social science and environmental economics research.
4. Integrated research projects (25–35 percent): solving problems of

transnational interest; addressing regional issues or issues of immediate relevance to EC policy.

This programme will build on work carried out under STEP (1989–93) (see page 230) and EPOCH (1989–93) (see page 228), whose budgets have now been fully allocated.

Human Capital and Mobility Programme

The proposed new programme in the field of Human Capital and Mobility has as its goal to increase qualitatively and quantitatively the human resources in research and development, to meet Member States' needs over the coming years. This will be achieved by a training programme, increasing the mobility of researchers across Europe's advanced research centres. Unlike other research programmes, it will not pursue sectoral objectives through targeted research.

The programme will have a budget of 518 MECU and involve granting fellowships to promising young researchers to enable them to spend a period (normally two years) in a high level research centre in another Member State.

This new programme will be carried out in co-ordination with action carried out under the SCIENCE Programme (1987–91) (see page 139).

Industrial and Materials Technologies Programme

The proposed programme in the field of Industrial and Materials Technologies will cover the following areas:

1. Materials: raw materials – improving existing processes and mastering new technologies; recycling – reinforcing the scope and effectiveness of recycling technologies; and new and improved materials – production and quality control technologies for conventional mass commodity materials.
2. Design and Manufacturing: research will be directed at advanced enabling disciplines, eg mechanics, optics, acoustics, fluid dynamics and process engineering and their integration into new technological developments.

   The programme will build on the work undertaken through the current BRITE/EURAM (1989–92) (see page 113) and the Raw Materials and Recycling Programme (1990–92) (see page 129).

Information Technology Programme

The proposed Information Technology Programme will focus on the development of a new generation of IT under the following five areas (percentage of the 1352 MECU budget allocation in brackets):

1. Microelectronics (27–31 percent);
2. Information Processing Systems and Software (23–27 percent);
3. Advanced Business and Home Systems and Peripherals (15–19 percent);

4. Computer Integrated Manufacturing and Engineering (17-21 percent);
5. Basic Research (9-11 percent).

Accompanying measures will include technology transfer and training activities carried out in each of the five areas and actions aimed at increasing the participation of peripheral EC regions in Community R & D programmes.

The new programme will follow on from ESPRIT II (1987-90), whose budget has been fully allocated (see page 229).

Life Sciences and Technologies for Developing Countries Programme

The proposed new Life Sciences and Technologies for Developing Countries Programme will concentrates on two areas (estimated percentage of the 111 MECU budget in brackets):

1. Agriculture (63-69 percent): covers reduction of food shortages; agricultural production of high economic value;
2. Medicine, health and nutrition (31-37 percent): covers the prevention and treatment of the predominant diseases in developing countries; health care systems appropriate to the rural or urban environment of developing countries.

This new programme will build on work carried out under the current Science and Technology for Development Programme (1987-91) whose budget has now been fully allocated (see page 230).

Marine Science and Technology Progamme

The proposed new programme in the field of Marine Science and Technology will cover the following fields (percentage of the 104 MECU budget allocation in brackets):

1. Marine Science (45-50 percent): including ocean circulation systems; dynamics of water masses; biogeochemical processes, hydrothermal activity; the global carbon cycle in coastal, continental and deep seas; rates of exchange of substances at interactive sites; mathematical models for biological processes and marine geosciences.
2. Coastal engineering (15-20 percent): research into currents; waves; behaviour of sediments; changes in the sea floor; coastline morphology, the impact of waves and other coastal processes on breakwaters and other structures, and improvement of beach nourishment.
3. Marine Technology (30-35 percent): development of new sensors, (quasi) real-time data transmission and two-way communication links, measurement and sampling instruments; underwater acoustics; actions to develop enabling technologies; studies of the exploitation of natural chemical substances in the marine environment, and of the exploitation of marine mineral resources.

The programme will build on work undertaken through the current MAST programme (1989-92) (see page 211) introducing new topics and expanding the programme's geographical coverage.

Measurements and Testing Programme

The proposed new Measurements and Testing Programme aims to improve measurements, technical tests and chemical analyses wherever they are not sufficiently reliable and wherever the various laboratories do not agree on results, to establish the common standards required for the operation of the Single European Market. The programme is divided into four areas (percentage of the 140 MECU budget allocation in brackets):

1. Support for Regulations and Directives (15-25 percent);
2. Sectoral testing problems (15-25 percent);
3. Support for means of calibration (25-35 percent);
4. Development of new methods of measurement (25-35 percent).

The programme will cover similar areas of activity as the Applied Metrology and Chemical Analysis Programme (1988-92) (see page 124).

Non-Nuclear Energies Programme

The proposed new programme in the field of Non-Nuclear Energies will cover the following fields (percentage of the 157 MECU budget allocation in brackets):

1. Analysis of strategies and modelling (5-7 percent): the use of models to assess the strategic role of energy efficiency and the development of new methods;
2. Minimum emission power production from fossil sources (20-30 percent): energy production from fossil sources using advanced technologies; reduction of emissions;
3. Renewable energy sources (30-40 percent): the solar house; renewable power plants; renewable energies for rural electricity, local fuel and water; geothermal energy;
4. Energy utilisation and conservation (30-40 percent): new options in energy conversion; technologies for energy saving; energy efficiency in transport, including suitable substitutes for conventional fuels.

Similar topics are currently covered in the JOULE programme (1989-92) (see page 229).

Nuclear Fission Safety Programme

The proposed programme in the field of Nuclear Fission Safety will cover two aspects of nuclear fission safety: radiation protection and reactor safety. The programme will have a budget allocation of 199 MECU and be carried out by means of shared-cost research projects, direct research undertaken by the Joint Research Centre, concerted actions and accompanying measures (eg result dissemination, training).

The programme will cover similar areas of research to the Radiation

Protection Research programme (1990-91) (see page 203), and SCA-RS (1988-91) (see page 167).

Telematic Systems of General Interest Programme

The proposed programme in the field of Telematic Systems of General Interest will cover the following six areas (percentage of the 380 MECU budget allocation in brackets):

1. Support for the establishment of trans-European networks between national administrations (priority areas will be customs, social security, frontier police, indirect taxation, statistics) (29-33 percent);
2. Transport services (road and air) (30-34 percent);
3. Health care services (15-17 percent);
4. Distance learning services (10-12 percent);
5. Libraries (6-7 percent);
6. Linguistic research and engineering (5-6 percent).

The new programme will continue and build on work commenced under DRIVE (1988-91) (see page 228), AIM (1988-90) (see page 227), DELTA (1988-90) (see page 227), and EUROTRA (1990-92) (see page 155).

INDEX